Yes, the doves
made women in
central to the emerging economy
upon mass production and
mass consumption. But how
much agency was there for
women? The vision is neatly
made, as were the planners,
and sermons + later leaders.
Women contributed somewhat to
shaping the direction of goods
production — but not as much
as male leaders did. Her thesis
is over-stated, though, within
proper limits, insightful and
persuasive.

Also she situates the transformation
too early — it does really explode
until after 1962 — stuff goes much
in 1954-61.

Unsophisticated is its use of the term
"standard of living".

Women and Mass Consumer Society in Postwar France

Women and Mass Consumer Society in Postwar France examines the emergence of a citizen consumer role for women during postwar modernization and reconstruction in France, integrating the history of economic modernization with that of women and the family. This role both celebrated the power of the woman consumer and created a gendered form of citizenship that did not disrupt the sexual hierarchy of home, polity, and marketplace. Redefining needs and renegotiating concepts of taste, value, and thrift, women and their families drove mass consumer society through their demands and purchases at the same time that their very need to consume came to define them.

Rebecca J. Pulju is an assistant professor of history at Kent State University in Ohio. Her work has been published in the *Journal of Women's History* and the *Proceedings of the Western Society for French History*.

Women and Mass Consumer Society in Postwar France

REBECCA J. PULJU
Kent State University

CAMBRIDGE UNIVERSITY PRESS
Cambridge, New York, Melbourne, Madrid, Cape Town,
Singapore, São Paulo, Delhi, Tokyo, Mexico City

Cambridge University Press
32 Avenue of the Americas, New York, NY 10013-2473, USA

www.cambridge.org
Information on this title: www.cambridge.org/9781107001350

First published 2011

Printed in the United States of America

A catalog record for this publication is available from the British Library.

Library of Congress Cataloging in Publication data
Pulju, Rebecca, 1974–
Women and mass consumer society in postwar France / Rebecca Pulju.
p.   cm.
Includes bibliographical references and index.
ISBN 978-1-107-00135-0
1. Women consumers – France – History.   2. Consumption
(Economics) – France – History.   3. France – Economic
conditions – 1945–   I. Title.
HC280.C6.P85   2011
306.30944'09045–dc22   2010033341

ISBN 978-1-107-00135-0 Hardback

For my parents, Holly and Edward Pulju

Contents

Figures and Tables

Figures

Tables

Acknowledgments

I have many people and institutions to thank as I conclude this project. This book began as a dissertation at the University of Iowa, and I am grateful to the history department and the graduate college at Iowa for providing funding for my initial research. The Society for French Historical Studies, the Western Society for French History, and the department of Research and Sponsored Programs at Kent State University provided the financial support for subsequent trips to Paris so that I could revise my dissertation. At Iowa, I found a wonderfully supportive community of faculty and graduate students. I wish to thank my advisors, Sarah Farmer and Sarah Hanley, for the support, advice, and help they gave me at Iowa, and have continued giving me long after we have all moved away from Iowa City. I also thank Jeff Cox and Lisa Heineman, who did so much to help me with the dissertation and have continued to advise and support me since. Patricia Howe first introduced me to European history and suggested I consider graduate study, and I thank her for both.

The friends that helped me at Iowa are too numerous to list, but I would like to thank, especially, my colleagues who read and commented on my work both then and later, including Nat Godley, Jennifer Harbour, Mike Innis-Jimenez, Junko Kobayashi, Joelle Neulander, Yvonne Pitts, and Jesse Spohnholz. A special thank-you to Shannon Fogg, who not only read my work, but introduced me to the *Archives Nationales* and the *Bibliothèque Nationale*. In Paris, friends helped me with proposals, edited my awkward French letters, gave me research advice and helped with the logistics of the AN and BN. Thanks especially to Greg Brown, Paul Cohen, Amy Freund, Simon Kitson, Jennifer Sessions, and Edna Yahil.

In Paris, Dominique Veillon at the *Institut d'histoire du temps présent* helped me refine my topic, identify sources, and figure out exactly what I was researching. I thank both her and Michèle Ruffat for the help and advice that they gave me. I am grateful to Sarah Fishman, Vanessa Schwartz, and Steve Zdatny, who each read the entire dissertation and gave me invaluable suggestions about where to go next. Thank you to Curtis Bertschi, Ellen Furlough, Steve Harp, and Paula Michaels for reading chapters and offering insights that have shaped the final product. At Kent State University, I found a new community of scholars and friends, and I thank the entire faculty of the history department, but especially those who read either part or all of the manuscript, including Kevin Adams, Ken Bindas, Dan Boomhower, Patti Kameya, Tim Scarnecchia, Richard Steigmann-Gall, and Sue Wamsley. Thank you to Françoise Massardier-Kenney for helping me with some of my more difficult translations. I also thank the colleagues and friends in my writing group at the University of Hawaii – Njoroge Njorge, Susanna Reiss, and Matthew Romaniello – for their fantastic comments and advice. I greatly appreciate the comments of the anonymous readers of my manuscript, whose suggestions improved the book tremendously. Thank you to Eric Crahan for supporting this project, and to Jason Przybylski for patiently answering my harried e-mails.

A special thank-you to Ned Bertz for always believing in me. Most of all, I thank my parents, Holly and Ed, who have supported me in each and every way from the time I started graduate school through the completion of this book. My dad, a beautiful writer and fantastic editor, read every draft of the manuscript, and his influence is on every page. Tess, Neil, Joe, Peter, and Melissa have provided fun, love, and companionship throughout the journey. More recently, Cass, whose obsession with *The Red Balloon* just might be a budding interest in postwar France, and Ana have made the time I've spent completing this book much more fun.

Material in this book was previously published in Beth Tobin and Maureen Goggin, eds., *Material Women: Consuming Desires and Collecting Objects, 1770–1950* (Aldershot: Ashgate Publishing, 2009), the *Journal of Women's History* 18 (2006), and the *Proceedings of the Western Society for French History* 31 (2003).

Abbreviations

AC	Action Catholique
AFAP	Association française pour l'accroissement de la productivité
CAF	Caisses d'allocations familiales
CETELEM	Crédit à l'électroménager (became Crédit à l'équipement des ménages)
CGT	Confédération générale du travail
CNC	Comité national de la consommation
CNP	Comité national de la productivité
CNRS	Centre national de la recherche scientifique
CREDOC	Centre de recherches et de documentation sur la consommation
IFOP	Institut français d'opinion publique
INC	Institut national de la consommation
INED	Institut national d'études démographiques
INSEE	Institut national de la statistique et des études économiques
JAC	Jeunesse agricole chrétienne
JOC	Jeunesse ouvrière chrétienne
JOCF	Jeunesse ouvrière chrétienne féminine
LOC	Ligue ouvrière chrétienne
MLF	Mouvement de libération des femmes
MLO	Mouvement de libération ouvrière
MLP	Mouvement de libération du peuple
MPF	Mouvement populaire des familles

MRP	Mouvement républicain populaire
MRU	Minstère de la reconstruction et de l'urbanisme
PSU	Parti socialiste unifié
RPF	Rassemblement du peuple français
SEEF	Service des études économiques et financières
SNCF	Société nationale des chemins de fer français
UFC	Union fédérale de la consommation
UFCS	Union féminine civique et sociale
UFF	Union des femmes françaises
UNAF	Union nationale des associations familiales
UNCAF	Union nationale des caisses d'allocations familiales

Introduction

In 1953, the *Salon des arts ménagers*, the immensely popular annual exhibition of home appliances, décor, and housing plans sponsored by the French ministry of education, hosted a "Day of the Consumer" organized by the *Union fédérale de la consommation* (Federal Union of Consumption, UFC). The government's minister of economic affairs, Robert Buron, spoke to the attendees, informing them, "I am, in effect, the minister of consumers; I would even prefer to say the minister of housewives." Buron noted that since the war, shortages and inflation had made the French economy a "seller's market," but with the return of stability and market competition, it could become a "buyer's market" in which the role of consumers would be determinant. To be a good consumer, "which is to say, a good housewife," was complicated, however, and many consumers had neither the time to make good choices, nor the awareness that wise purchasing decisions were good both for themselves and the national economy. Buron had come to urge his audience to be intelligent and well-informed consumers. "Consumption is not a passive act, but a decisively important economic act," he explained, "I count on consumers as much as on producers. It is with a balanced effort from each that we can expect economic expansion and a higher standard of living."[1]

The women in Buron's audience – members of women's, family, and consumer organizations, as well as members of the general public attracted by the commodities and lifestyles on display at the *Salon* – were as eager as Buron for economic expansion and a better standard

[1] "La 'Journée du Consommateur' au Salon des arts ménagers," *Union fédérale de la consommation: Bulletin mensuel d'information* 10 (1953), 15–16.

of living in France. In hindsight, economic recovery and the arrival of
a mass consumer economy following the Second World War appear to
have been breathtakingly fast, but this was likely not the perception of
women and families who had survived war, occupation, and Liberation
followed by food shortages and high inflation. When Buron spoke in
1953, the economy was just beginning to make the turn from poverty to
plenty. Over the next decade, average consumption in France would grow
rapidly and the French populace would come to accept that all families
deserved a standard of living that very few had enjoyed only ten years
earlier. The demands of women and families coincided with a state-driven
modernization effort whose planners, like Buron, were often suspicious
of the rationality of ordinary women consumers, even as they recognized
women's influence on the national economy. The agendas of planners and
these advocates for women, families, and consumers coalesced in a common goal – creating a modern mass consumer economy – and in the conviction that it was necessary to educate and support citizen consumers
who would inform planners and industrialists of their needs, and make
wise purchasing decisions that would help the French economy expand
in a healthy way. They conspired in creating the figure of the citizen consumer, a role that recognized the rationality and influence of recently
 enfranchised women, but, conveniently, did not conflict with the desire to
find comfort in "normalcy" after years of upheaval, and which implied a
particular gendered hierarchy in family, workplace, and polity.

 This book examines how France became a mass consumer society in
the decades following the Second World War, and in doing so, places
the citizen consumer, her home, her family, and her purchases at the
center of its analysis of postwar change. It explores the ways in which
consumption became intertwined with definitions of women's citizenship and why the role of the citizen consumer – the consumer who
benefits society through his or her purchases – was the preferred route
to women's national influence at this moment in French history.[2] The

---

[2] I borrow the term "citizen consumer" from Lizabeth Cohen's work on the United States.
See Cohen, *A Consumer's Republic: The Politics of Mass Consumption in Postwar
America* (New York: Alfred A. Knopf, 2003). Cohen argues for the importance of the
citizen consumer during the Depression, when consumers sought the government as an
ally and consumed for the good of the nation. After the war, the figure of the "purchaser consumer" won out in part because of resistance to government interference in
the economy. Although primarily concerned with his or her own individual needs, the
purchaser consumer could also be seen to serve the public good by driving the economy through his or her purchases. Historians of Europe have also increasingly begun
to ask why, at certain moments, the category of consumer becomes a useful means of

home and the domestic consumer who managed it were central to the changes that occurred in this period. Becoming a mass consumer society required changes in notions of taste and value, luxury and necessity, new patterns of household spending, and new understandings of class and consumption. These adjustments were made in the realm of domestic consumption, and reflected in purchases for the home, which became a premier venue for the introduction of mass-produced consumer durables and the site where "modernization" was experienced through the arrival of conveniences such as hot running water, home appliances, and central heating. Although much has been written about the state modernization drive and the decisions of planners, politicians, and technocrats, relatively little has been said about how these postwar changes shaped the home, family, and gender roles. The ways in which women and their families embraced new methods of spending and ideas about consumption, helping drive economic expansion through their demands and purchases, is another subject we know little about. This book addresses this lacuna in scholarship by exploring the social, cultural, and economic changes of the postwar years through the lens of home, family, and gender, revealing how the push to create a mass consumer society in France helped to define women's role in polity and home, at the same time as women's consumer demands and the new consumer needs of the modern French family drove the creation of the mass consumer economy.

THE CONSENSUS FOR MODERNIZATION: STATE PLANNING

The desire for "normalcy" was common across much of Western Europe in the postwar years, as was the eventual creation of mass consumer economies. Until the 1940s, much of Europe was subject to what Victoria de Grazia has labeled the "bourgeois regime of consumption" in which consumption served to differentiate social classes. After the Second World War, European governments and populations came to accept for the first time that all people deserved a decent standard of living. The ability to provide that standard became necessary for government legitimacy and the consumer was granted new influence as Europeans accepted American notions of service and consumer

organization. See, for example, the introduction and essays in Frank Trentmann, ed., *The Making of the Consumer* (Oxford: Berg, 2006). Trentmann calls historians to examine "the construction of the consumer as an identity and category" rather than assuming this identity was a natural outgrowth of affluence in the 1950s and 1960s. Trentmann ed., *The Making of the Consumer*, 4.

sovereignty. Whereas differences in income and lifestyle obviously remained, these were based on income rather than notions of class privilege, and domestic consumption became less important for defining class status. Wide swathes of European populations started to live more like one another than they had in the past. More people had the option of buying beyond the basic necessities, allowing them to construct their identities through commodities. A variety of mass-produced goods became available to a large portion of the population, both because mass production made them cheaper and because more people were willing and able to supplement their cash purchases with consumer credit.[3] The ability to realize an improved level of home comfort meant that in many places, it seemed a more "home-centered" lifestyle was emerging.[4] Prosperity arrived at different rates across nations as well as across societies, appearing in Britain and West Germany slightly ahead of France and Italy, and achieved in all places by the urban middle class before the working class or rural dwellers. Nonetheless, the economies of all Western European countries expanded in the twenty years following the war. European nations lowered trade barriers, invested significant resources in infrastructure and state welfare systems, increased productivity, and experienced high birth rates, which spurred mass consumption and created millions of new consumers.[5]

Prewar conditions and the experience of the war itself, of course, affected the rate and character of change across Western Europe. For France, an important outcome of defeat and occupation was that whereas many continuities existed between the prewar, Vichy, and postwar periods, in the wake of the war French leaders and many citizens viewed the Third Republic as completely discredited, a system that had not withstood the Nazi challenge and had crumbled, resulting in the Vichy

---

[3] For changes to European consumption habits over the course of the twentieth century, see Victoria de Grazia, *Irresistible Empire: America's Advance through 20th Century Europe* (Cambridge: Belknap Press of Harvard University Press, 2005). For definitions of mass consumer society, see Peter N. Stearns, "Stages of Consumerism: Recent Work on the Issues of Periodization," *Journal of Modern History* 69 (1997): 102–117. For a collection of essays that shows change in European and American regimes of consumption over the twentieth century, see Susan Strasser, Charles McGovern, and Matthias Judt, eds., *Getting and Spending: European and American Consumer Societies in the Twentieth Century* (Cambridge: Cambridge University Press, 1998).

[4] Claire Langhamer complicates this picture in her work on Britain, showing that the aspirations to this lifestyle existed before the war. See Langhamer, "The Meanings of Home in Postwar Britain," *Journal of Contemporary History* 40 (2005): 341–362.

[5] See Tony Judt, *Postwar: A History of Europe since 1945* (New York: The Penguin Press, 2005), 325–326, 331.

government.[6] This national consensus on the need to change has caused both commentators at the time and historians since to describe the impetus behind postwar transformation as being in part, if not primarily, one of attitude. Contemporary critics of the Third Republic often used the term "Malthusian" – by which they meant inclined to decisions that ultimately limited productivity rather than taking risks that might lead to expansion – both when describing the prewar French economy and its declining and aging population.[7] Despite the rapid return of partisan politics after the war, there was widespread agreement that France could not revert to former habits and policies. The man initially responsible

[6] Philip Nord has emphasized how, despite their rhetoric of renewal, many of the postwar technocrats and modernizers were active in the 1930s, and even under the Vichy regime. See Philip Nord, *France's New Deal: From the Thirties to the Postwar Era* (Princeton: Princeton University Press, 2010). See Herrick Chapman, "France's Liberation Era, 1944–47: A Social and Economic Settlement?" in *The Uncertain Foundation: France at the Liberation, 1944–47*, ed. Andrew Knapp (Palgrave Macmillan: New York, 2007), 103–120, for discussion of the roots of planning under the Third Republic and the Vichy regime. Chapman notes that one source of anger among Resisters was that the need for experts for postwar reconstruction meant turning to men who had also worked under the Vichy regime. See W. Brian Newsome, "The Struggle for a Voice in the City: The Development of Participatory Architectural and Urban Planning in France, 1940–1960," (PhD diss., University of South Carolina, 2002), for discussion of urbanization and urban planning first under the Vichy Regime and then under the Fourth and Fifth Republics. See Stanley Hoffmann for discussion of continuities in terms of organizations and individuals involved in economic planning under Vichy and the postwar regime. He points to 1934 as the end of the Republican Consensus upholding the prewar "stalemate society" that valued stability over expansion. Hoffmann, "The Effects of World War II on French Society and Politics," *French Historical Studies* 2 (1961): 28–63. For continuity in French notions of social democracy see Paul V. Dutton, *Origins of the French Welfare State: The Struggle for Social Reform in France, 1914–1947* (Cambridge: Cambridge University Press, 2002). Richard Ivan Jobs points out that despite continuity, there was a postwar obsession with "the new" as France pinned its hopes on youth as a means of recovery and renovation. Jobs, *Riding the New Wave: Youth and the Rejuvenation of France after the Second World War* (Stanford: Stanford University Press, 2007).
[7] For the importance of new attitudes in French economic planning, see Stephen S. Cohen, *Modern Capitalist Planning: The French Model* (Berkeley: University of California Press, 1977). Analysts often pointed to the French family firm, more oriented to family financial stability than expansion, as a hindrance to the French economy. See David Landes, "French Business and the Businessman: A Social and Cultural Analysis," in *Modern France*, ed. Edward Meade Earl (Princeton: Princeton University Press, 1951), 334–353. Historians have since both complicated this understanding and shown how some businesses were able to combine paternalism and economic expansion. See Marjorie Beale, *The Modernist Enterprise: French Elites and the Threat of Modernity, 1900–1940* (Stanford: Stanford University Press, 1999); Stephen L. Harp, *Marketing Michelin: Advertising and Cultural Identity in Twentieth-Century France* (Baltimore: Johns Hopkins University Press, 2001); Michael Miller, *The Bon Marché: Bourgeois Culture and the Department Store, 1869–1920* (Princeton: Princeton University Press, 1981).

for the direction of postwar economic planning, Jean Monnet, famously asserted that France must choose either "modernization" or "decadence," insisting that France needed to embrace change or continue to decline. Modernization meant abandoning the conservative economic practices of the past, eliminating inefficient and outdated producers, expanding productivity, and creating a mass consumer economy. All of this would happen in the context of an economic and social democracy.[8]

To foment this change rapidly, Monnet led the first *Plan de modernisation et d'équipement* of France after the war.[9] The commissariat of the Plan was a body that coordinated between ministries, was autonomous, and answered directly to the prime minister in an attempt to steer clear of parliamentary politics. The atmosphere at the time was one of national imperative and the choice was clear: expansion or decline – and it seemed there was little room for negotiation. Historian Michael Bess uses the term "technological Darwinism" to describe the widespread sense that France needed to change, and quickly, if it was to maintain its autonomy and independence.[10] Though the subsequent economic recovery in France was similar to that in other Western European nations, what made France unique, as historian Richard Kuisel has pointed out, was the "collective sense of national decline and disenchantment" that drove the abrupt changes of the period and inspired the creation of an interventionist state committed to national planning.[11] These methods, too, distinguished France from some of its neighbors, as both Britain and West Germany chose to forego intensive, long-term state planning.[12] The French state's postwar planners and modernizers embraced cooperation and collaboration among government, industry, workers, and consumers out of this imperative for change. The Plan's full-time secretariat set targets for expansion in specific industries,

---

[8] For analysis of economic modernization, see Richard Kuisel, *Capitalism and the State in Modern France: Renovation and Economic Management in the Twentieth Century* (Cambridge: Cambridge University Press, 1981).

[9] Hereafter, "the Plan" refers to the *Plan de modernisation et d'équipement*.

[10] Michael Bess, *The Light Green Society: Ecology and Technological Modernity in France, 1960–2000* (Chicago: University of Chicago Press, 2003). For more on the consensus behind modernization see Robert Frost, "The Flood of 'Progress': Technocrats and Peasants at Tignes (Savoy), 1946–1952," *French Historical Studies* 14 (1985): 117–140. For modernization and urbanization, see Rosemary Wakeman, *Modernizing the Provincial City: Toulouse, 1945–1975* (Cambridge: Harvard University Press, 1997).

[11] Kuisel, *Capitalism and the State*, 280.

[12] Judt, *Postwar*, 329–330. Judt points out that the German government intervened to mitigate tensions between social groups, but it did not attempt to direct economic behavior. Britain nationalized some parts of the economy between the end of the war and 1951, but did not embark on long-term planning.

and then convened eighteen "modernization commissions" from each sector of the economy.[13] These included planners, heads of firms, union leaders, civil servants, and consumers.

The spirit infusing the Plan was that all participants would work together to create a strong, dynamic economy. Cooperation was voluntary, as the Plan was "indicative" rather than dictatorial, but a system of rewards and incentives for firms that cooperated with the state, including lucrative contracts and tax relief, ensured that it was also attractive.[14] Central to the indicative planning model was the sharing of information. The availability of extensive market information would reduce uncertainties for producers of goods and make the plan self-reinforcing. As economist Stephen S. Cohen explained, "the more industry follows the plan, the more accurate the plan's information will be, the more accurate the plan's information, the more reason industry will have to follow the plan."[15] Consumer, family, and women's organizations, with their special knowledge of family needs, could be valuable in this respect. For state planners and the heads of many French firms, a common background and education, in particular in France's elite *grandes écoles*, among them the new *École nationale de l'administration* (ENA), was a spur to cooperation. The growing importance of "technocrats" – the new elite comprised of disinterested, seemingly apolitical, technologically informed experts – was another hallmark of the postwar transformation.[16] The result was what planners called the *économie concertée* – an economy in "concertation," or orchestration, which balanced liberalism with state direction, or *dirigisme*. State direction was also intensified by the creation of an *économie mixte*. The postwar government, looking forward to establishing an essentially free and liberal market but realizing that only the state could produce the capital necessary for reparations and renovations, and in some cases using nationalization to punish collaborators, nationalized deposit banks, coal, gas, electricity, civil aviation, insurance companies, and the Renault car company.[17]

[13] See Kuisel, *Capitalism and the State* for information on the institution of the Plan. The number of modernization commissions started at eighteen, but would increase in subsequent Plans. Stephen S. Cohen notes that by the early 1970s, almost 3,000 people took part in the preparation of the plan. Cohen, *Modern Capitalist Planning*, 274.

[14] John Ardagh, *The New French Revolution* (New York: Harper and Row, 1969), 22–23.

[15] Cohen, *Modern Capitalist Planning*, 10.

[16] Ardagh, *The New French Revolution*, 18–19; Kuisel points out that this meant a change in the attitude and orientation of the administrative elite, but no change in its social or class background. Kuisel, *Capitalism and the State*, 255.

[17] For general information on French economic goals, see Robert Gildea, *France Since 1945* (Oxford: Oxford University Press, 1996). For information on the decision to nationalize

Among the first objectives of planners and modernizers was increasing productivity – producing more material rapidly and at lower cost. As Charles de Gaulle explained in 1945, "Yesterday there was no national duty that had precedence over the duty to fight. But today there is none that can take precedence over that to produce."[18] This goal was initially embraced by parties across the political spectrum, including the Communist party, which launched the "battle of production" and urged workers to agree to extended work hours during this period of national reconstruction. Increasing productivity in France was also a goal of the American government, which played an important role in reconstruction, at least through the early 1950s. American films, American GIs in France, and American images in women's magazines testified to the abundance and prosperity of the model consumer society.[19] Jean Monnet himself spent the war years in Washington and left impressed by the American government's direction of the wartime economy.

When the first Plan was launched in 1947, France lacked the funds to pay for it. The announcement of the Marshall Plan that same year would be instrumental in the success of the Plan. France would eventually receive over two billion dollars in Marshall Plan aid, making it second only to Great Britain among Western European recipients.[20] Despite American resistance to peacetime economic planning at home, France's Plan appeared to be a good model for European reconstruction, and helped convince the Americans that France was determined to

in a key sector of the economy, see Robert L. Frost, *Alternating Currents: Nationalized Power in France, 1946–1970* (Ithaca: Cornell University Press, 1991). For analysis of French economic planning, including nationalizations, see Kuisel, *Capitalism and the State*, especially 202–203 and Chapman, "France's Liberation Era."

[18] Quoted in Stewart Patrick, "Embedded Liberalism in France? American Hegemony, the Monnet Plan, and Postwar Multilateralism," in *The Marshall Plan: Fifty Years After*, ed. Martin A. Schain (New York: Palgrave Macmillan, 2001), 221.

[19] Mary Louise Roberts has recently shown how the influx of American GIs, and their wealth, led to changes in the system of prostitution in Paris. See Roberts, "The Silver Foxhole: The GIs and Prostitution in Paris, 1944–1945," *French Historical Studies* 33 (2010): 99–128. For more on the associations of American GIs with consumer society, see Rebecca J. Pulju, "The Woman's Paradise: The American Fantasy, Home Appliances, and Consumer Demand in Liberation France, 1944–1947," in *Material Women: Consuming Desires and Collecting Objects, 1770–1950*, eds. Beth Tobin and Maureen Goggin (Aldershot: Ashgate, 2009), 111–124.

[20] In millions of dollars, France would receive $2,296; Britain would receive $3,297; and West Germany would receive $1,448. From Roy Gardner, "The Marshall Plan Fifty Years Later: Three What-Ifs and a When," in *The Marshall Plan: Fifty Years After*, 120.

address its economic problems.[21] American influence in the form of aid as well as political pressure through both the American embassy and the Marshall Plan Mission, or Economic Cooperation Administration (ECA), was weighty, but French economic development took shape within the contours of the Plan, which had public consensus behind it. The goals of the Marshall Plan for France were financial stabilization and the creation of a mass consumer economy – goals that coincided with those of French planners. Increasing productivity was a cornerstone of the Marshall Plan and aid would be directed to programs emphasizing this objective. Thousands of French representatives of industry, commerce, and consumption would travel to the United States on missions initially organized by Jean Fourastié, head of the working group on productivity at the Plan and one of France's most prolific modernizers, who would later coin the phrase the *"trente glorieuses"* to describe the postwar transformation. On mission, participants learned how cooperation among these various economic forces had resulted in the creation of the world's pre-eminent mass consumer society.[22] Within France itself, the populace would become targets of Marshall Plan propaganda explaining how "the American way of life" could be achieved in France and why it was desirable.[23]

THE ROLE OF THE CITIZEN CONSUMER

This state-directed drive for modernization was instrumental in creating a mass consumer society in France, but it was not the only force behind

---

[21] See Irwin Wall, *The United States and the Making of Postwar France, 1945–1954* (Cambridge: Cambridge University Press, 1991), 75 and Kuisel, *Capitalism and the State*, 230–232.

[22] Wall, *The United States*, 158–160, 183–4. See also Régis Boulat, "Jean Fourastié et la naissance de la société de la consommation en France," in *Au nom du consommateur: Consommation et politique en Europe et aux États-Unis au XXe siècle*, eds. Alain Chatriot, Marie-Emmanuelle Chessel, and Matthew Hilton (Paris: La Découverte, 2004), 98–114.

[23] For analysis of Marshall Plan propaganda, see Brian Angus McKenzie, *Remaking France: Americanization, Public Diplomacy, and the Marshall Plan* (New York: Berghahn Books, 2005). For a comparative look at propaganda in France, Britain, and Germany, see Sheryl Kroen, "Negotiations with the American Way: The Consumer and the Social Contract in Post-war Europe," in *Consuming Cultures, Global Perspectives: Historical Trajectories, Transnational Exchanges*, eds. John Brewer and Frank Trentmann (Oxford: Berg, 2006), 251–277. For the place of the American kitchen, in particular, in Cold War politics, see Ruth Oldenziel and Karin Zachmann, eds., *Cold War Kitchen: Americanization, Technology, and European Users* (Boston: MIT Press, 2009).

change, nor was the economy the only realm subject to reconfiguration
in the postwar years. Coupled with national planners and modernizers determined to create a modern economy was a population that had
lived through economic depression, war, occupation, and Liberation and
which desperately yearned for better living conditions. More than half
of the adult population of France was made up of women, and these
women became full citizens for the first time in the wake of Liberation.
The concerted drive to create a mass consumer society coincided with
the renegotiation of women's place in the polity and civil society. In the
following pages, I demonstrate how, under these conditions, a multitude
of voices in French society seized on women's power as the consumers
for the nation, vaunting the responsibility inherent in this role and creating a gendered form of citizenship which was essential to the national
economy, but did not upset the gendered structure of home, workplace,
and polity.

   Women's consumer demands and purchases had long had political,
social, and economic importance in France. Scholars have examined the
mixed subsistence and political demands voiced by women during the
French Revolution, and subsistence demands expressed through food
riots and demonstrations had been effective for centuries.[24] These kinds of
actions, though often associated with a period before national food markets and working-class political organization, continued to occur into the
twentieth century when national food distribution circuits faltered. Food
demonstrations occurred under the Vichy government, whose inability to
provision its population, Shannon Fogg has argued, weakened it legitimacy. Demonstrations continued after the Liberation, a period Megan
Koreman has compared to the early modern era because of the ineffectiveness of the national government.[25] Ellen Furlough and Helen Chenut

---

[24] On the French Revolution, see Joan Landes, *Women and the Public Sphere in the Age
   of the French Revolution* (Ithaca: Cornell University Press, 1988) and Olwen Hufton,
   Women and the Limits of Citizenship in the French Revolution (Toronto: University of
   Toronto Press, 1999). For analysis of the political power of subsistence demands, see
   also Belinda Davis' work on Imperial Germany in *Home Fires Burning: Food, Politics,
   and Everyday Life in World War I Berlin* (Chapel Hill: University of North Carolina
   Press, 2000).

[25] On food riots and their continuation into the twentieth century, see Lynne Taylor, "Food
   Riots Revisited," *Journal of Social History* 30 (1996): 483–496. For demonstrations
   under Vichy, see Yvan Avakoumovitch, "Les manifestations des femmes 1940–1944,"
   Cahiers d'histoire de l'Institut de recherches marxistes 45 (1991): 5–53; Donna F. Ryan,
   "Ordinary Acts and Resistance: Women in Street Demonstrations and Food Riots in
   Vichy France," in *Proceedings of the Annual Meeting of the Western Society for French
   History* 16 (1989): 400–407; Paula Schwartz, "The Politics of Food and Gender in

have described how women took part in the working-class consumer cooperative movement that expanded in the late nineteenth century and was closely linked to socialist politics.[26] Marie-Emmanuelle Chessel has shown how bourgeois women motivated by social Catholicism used their consumer power to improve working-class laboring conditions at the turn of the century.[27] And Leora Auslander, Whitney Walton, and Lisa Tierston have demonstrated how bourgeois women's consumer acts were important for defining and representing the nineteenth and early twentieth-century bourgeoisie, for shaping the direction of French industrial development, and for defining understandings of taste and notions of "Frenchness."[28]

Women continued a tradition of activism based on subsistence needs when they made their consumer demands known immediately after the Liberation, taking to the streets to demand food and clothing for their families. These demands were politically salient during this period of upheaval. When food became readily available, but inflation soared, women again acted, monitoring prices and demanding that production be turned toward family need. By taking such actions, women performed citizenship and claimed, often overtly, that they were aiding not only

Occupied Paris," *Modern and Contemporary France* 7 (1999): 35–45; Lynne Taylor, *Between Resistance and Collaboration: Popular Protest in Northern France, 1940–1945* (New York: St. Martin's Press, 2000). For analysis of how difficulties provisioning the population weakened the legitimacy of the Vichy government, see Shannon L. Fogg, *The Politics of Everyday Life in Vichy France: Foreigners, Undesirables, and Strangers* (Cambridge: Cambridge University Press, 2009). For food demonstrations both under Vichy and in the immediate postwar years, see Danielle Tartakowsky, "Manifester pour le pain, novembre 1940-octobre 1947," in *Le temps des restrictions en France (1939–1949)*, eds. Dominique Veillon and Jean-Marie Flonneau (Paris: Institut d'histoire du temps présent, 1996), 465–478. Megan Koreman explores local anger with the ineffectiveness of the national government's meting out of postwar justice in *The Expectation of Justice: France, 1944–1946* (Durham: Duke University Press, 1999).

[26] See Ellen Furlough, *Consumer Cooperation in France: The Politics of Consumption, 1834–1930* (Ithaca: Cornell University Press, 1991) and Helen Chenut, *The Fabric of Gender: Working-Class Culture in Third Republic France* (University Park: Pennsylvania State University Press, 2005).

[27] See Marie-Emmanuelle Chessel, "Consommation, action sociale et engagement publique fin de siècle des États-Unis à la France," in *Au nom du consommateur*, 295–311 and Marie-Emmanuelle Chessel, "Women and the Ethics of Consumption in France at the Turn of the Century," in *The Making of the Consumer*, 81–98.

[28] See Leora Auslander, *Taste and Power: Furnishing Modern France* (Berkeley: University of California Press, 1996); Lisa Tierston, *Marianne in the Market: Envisioning Consumer Society in Fin-de-siècle France* (Berkeley: University of California Press, 2001); Whitney Walton, *France at the Crystal Palace: Bourgeois Taste and Artisan Manufacture in the Nineteenth Century* (Berkeley: University of California Press, 1992).

their own families, but the national economy as well.[29] They were acting as citizen consumers, making purchasing decisions that strengthened France's economy. Women's, family, and consumer organizations stressed the influence inherent in the role of the citizen consumer, creating a specifically feminine variant of citizenship while promoting their own influence by claiming that consuming skills did not come naturally, but through education and training, which they could provide.

At the same time that these women's, family, and consumer organizations heralded the power of consumers to influence the national economy, planners and modernizers were recognizing the importance of understanding consumer demand for raising productivity, and attempting to harness nascent consumer efforts for the good of the economy. Often these forces worked in concert with one another, but there was also tension among them as government planners and modernizers attempted to shape and direct consumers to act in the ways they felt would best serve the national economy. Before the war, French government and industry had shown scant interest in determining consumer taste or rationalizing consumer decisions.[30] Lacking a sophisticated statistical apparatus from the prewar period, in the second half of the 1940s and the 1950s the French government created the *Institut national d'études démographiques* (INED), the *Institut national de la statistique et des études économiques* (INSEE), the *Service des études économiques et financières* (SEEF), and the *Centre de recherches et de documentation sur la consommation* (CREDOC).[31] The electric industry and other manufacturers created their own marketing research organizations to segment and survey the population, tabulate marketing results, and expound on consumer demand in France. In 1955, the *Commissariat du Plan* collaborated with industry in surveying prospective consumer demand, asking families what they would purchase with 20 percent more income.[32] Understanding consumer need, while at the same time helping consumers make the right purchasing

---

[29] Kathleen Canning and Sonya O. Rose discuss citizenship as not merely a legal category, but a "set of social practices" in the introduction to Kathleen Canning and Sonya Rose, *Gender, Citizenships, and Subjectivities* (Oxford: Blackwell Publishing, 2002), 15.

[30] See De Grazia, *Irresistible Empire* and Judith Coffin, "A 'Standard' of Living? European Perspectives on Class and Consumption in the Early Twentieth Century," *International Labor and Working-Class History* 55 (1999): 6–26.

[31] In his examination of continuities with the prewar and Vichy periods, Philip Nord points out that INSEE in fact had its roots in the Vichy era *Service national de la statistique* (SNS). Nord, *France's New Deal*, 150.

[32] *Enquête sur les tendances de la consommation des salariés urbains. Vous gagnez 20% de plus qu'en faites vous?* (Paris: Commission des Industries de Transformation, 1955).

decisions, would help the economy develop rationally. Planners wanted what productivity enthusiast and president of the UFC André Romieu called the "market community," in which consumers informed planners and industrialists of their needs, who then responded in kind, resulting in a rational and profitable economic expansion that benefitted all parties.[33] Government planners and women consumers thus coalesced in trumpeting the importance of consumer citizenship in the new French economy. The citizen consumer could direct the economy toward family need and also increase productivity, strengthening both the family and national economies.

The imperatives of women's and family groups and modernizers concerned with productivity also coalesced in the assertion that the home must become a more productive workspace, since it absorbed more labor power than any other "industry" in France. Those who spoke for women and the family seized on the argument that the home should be modernized both to valorize women's work and to improve family living conditions. As they asserted, the citizen consumer and housewife influenced the economy not just at the point of purchase, but by making items last longer and avoiding the waste of both food and time in the home. With buying power still limited, they advocated consumer credit as a way of investing in home modernization that would also create more consumers, drive mass production, and make goods cheaper. This entailed both empowering and constraining the consumer, as irrational use of credit could increase inflation and lead the economy to expand in the wrong direction. Both state economic planners and these voices purporting to speak for women and the family were working to create a mass consumer society – one that would provide for the needs of the family, raise the standard of living, and be directed by the citizen consumer.

The role of the consumer in driving the French economy had been recognized, and, as women's, family, and consumer organizations would frequently point out, it was women who made the bulk of consumer decisions. Despite the importance of these consumer decisions, and despite the importance of the home as a privileged site for the introduction of modernity and consumer culture, we know much more about the

---

[33] Conférence de presse du 4 février 1955 donnée par M. André Romieu, président de l'Union fédérale de la consommation – "L'Organisation de la consommation facteur de progrès économique: ses premiers résultats en France – ses perspectives prochaines." Paris, February 4, 1955. Dossiers de presse, Bibliothèque de Sciences Po, La consommation en France, code France 582.

state modernization drive and American influence than we know about demand for the products of mass consumer society, how commodities affected women's work and shaped perceptions of the family, and how rational consuming skills became essential to the modern housewife and interwoven with women's citizenship.[34] All of these will be addressed in the following pages. Becoming a mass consumer society required many changes. Accepting that consumer credit was rational, rather than wasteful, entailed modifying deeply held notions of respectability and frugality. Determining that mass-produced goods could also be quality goods undermined notions of class-defined taste and status, while at the same time the need for rational discernment in choosing those commodities created a new kind of status for the domestic consumer.

This book investigates the ways in which women's, family, and consumer groups, as well as state planners and modernizers, adopted and advocated consumer citizenship, how French families became mass consumers, and how consumer society shaped normative views of family, home, and society. It emphasizes the fact that creating mass consumer society was a process, and that the drive to do so came not only from above, but from below, as individual women and women's, family, and consumer organizations demanded the products that would create family comfort and ease the burdens of household labor. In making these demands, they were also exercising citizenship, as they stressed the importance of their

how important was the "self" part in this era?

---

[34] An historian who has integrated gender into the narrative of modernization across Europe and across the twentieth century is Victoria de Grazia. See, especially, *Irresistible Empire*. Scholars in French cultural studies have done more to call attention to gender roles and the home in the postwar period. See Kristin Ross, *Fast Cars, Clean Bodies: Decolonization and the Reordering of French Culture* (Boston: MIT Press, 1996) and Susan Weiner, *Enfants Terribles: Youth and Femininity in the Mass Media in France, 1945–1968* (Baltimore: Johns Hopkins University Press, 2001). For analysis of American influence on postwar French policy, see Wall, *The United States*. For French perceptions of American influence, see Richard Kuisel, *Seducing the French: The Dilemma of Americanization* (Berkeley: University of California Press, 1993) and for modernization and planning, see Kuisel, *Capitalism and the State*. Recently, scholars in French and American history have begun looking at connections and interactions between France and America in this period, including those involving individual citizens. For transatlantic cooperation in postwar cultural change, see Vanessa Schwartz, *It's so French! Hollywood, Paris, and the Making of Cosmopolitan Film Culture* (Chicago: University of Chicago Press, 2007). For efforts of both French and American governments to use private citizens as "ambassadors" to the other, see Christopher Endy, *Cold War Holidays: American Tourism in France* (Chapel Hill: University of North Carolina Press, 2004). For the ways that students participated in French-American cultural exchange and diplomacy in the twentieth century, see Whitney Walton, *Internationalism, National Identities, and Study Abroad: France and the United States, 1890–1970* (Stanford: Stanford University Press, 2010).

own decisions for the health of the economy – something planners and modernizers stressed as well.

This combination of state planners' and citizens' desires for change would lead to a transformation in the postwar years. At the end of the war, almost one-fifth of France's buildings were either damaged or destroyed. Ports, train stations, railroad tracks, and roads all were in disrepair. Housing was a national emergency as decades of insufficient construction had been compounded by the war. In 1946, the average age of buildings in Paris was eighty-three years, and in rural areas it was one hundred and twenty. Old buildings could have been renovated, of course, but 63 percent of buildings still lacked running water, a number that rose to 82 percent in rural areas. Only 5 percent of French homes had a private, indoor bathroom, including 17 percent in France's capital city.[35] The first Plan targeted the economy's base industries, and despite American fears that without more attention to housing and consumer goods the French population would be ripe for Communist influence, planners stuck to their investment strategy, forcing a measure of austerity. As a result, living conditions for the population remained bleak into the early 1950s.

Although living conditions varied by class and income, as well as between urban and rural areas, France as a whole experienced a remarkable rise in living standards after about 1953.[36] The second Plan began to focus on raising the standard of living, and higher wages and the spread of consumer credit spurred an increase in spending on the home, as French families modernized and equipped their domestic spaces. In 1950, the INED conducted a survey that found that 69 percent of workers believed that their standard of living had declined since 1939.[37] The economy was already turning the corner, however, and between 1950 and 1960, consumption per person in France increased by 57 percent, then rose by another 61 percent between 1959 and 1968.[38] In 1956, the level of domestic production was 25 to 30 percent higher than its prewar

[35] Danièle Voldman, *La reconstruction des villes françaises de 1940 à 1954: Histoire d'une politique* (Paris: Éditions l'Harmattan, 1997), 25, 176.

[36] In addition to variety between regions, the continued housing shortage makes it difficult to date a turning point. The year 1953, however, was the beginning of a period that Jean-Pierre Rioux calls 'expansion in stability.' See Jean-Pierre Rioux, *The Fourth Republic: 1944–1958* (Cambridge: Cambridge University Press, 1987), 338.

[37] Alain Girard, "Une enquête sur les besoins des familles," *Population* 5 (1950), 715.

[38] Jacqueline Niaudet, "L'évolution de la consommation des ménages de 1959 à 1968," *Consommation: Annales du Centre de recherches et de documentation sur la consommation* 16 (1970), 28.

peak in 1929.[39] Food declined as a percentage of family budgets, and the products of family comfort, including those associated with health and hygiene, and the products of the mechanical and electrical industries, increased from between 80 and 150 percent from 1950 to 1957.[40] In December of 1954, 7.5 percent of French households had a refrigerator and 8.4 percent a washing machine.[41] By 1968, 72.4 percent had a refrigerator, and 50.1 percent had a washing machine.[42] More than twenty years after the war, not all families, especially those in rural areas, had access to the main elements associated with home comfort. Still, France was a mass consumer society in which a broad spectrum of the population had access to a range of mass-produced goods and the means to buy them. Granted these changes, it is hard to imagine a site in which modernization and the coming of mass consumer society was more dramatic and more intimate than the home.

WOMEN'S CITIZENSHIP, "NORMALCY," AND THE BABY BOOM

The coalescence around this particular notion of consumer citizenship could only have occurred during the postwar period of inflation, productivity drives, and national enthusiasm about reconstruction and modernization. As this book reveals, it was also particular to a specific moment in the history of women's citizenship. The end of the war incited not only discussion of women's role in the economy, but in politics and society, as French women voted for the first time and their right to work was inscribed in the constitution of the Fourth Republic. New political and legal rights were, however, accompanied by concern about the future of the French population and family, and a widespread desire for the return of "normalcy." Along with the sentiment that France must choose modernization or decadence in economic and technological planning existed the belief that without population growth France could not regain a powerful world position. "Normalcy" did not mean a return to the traditions of the past, but a change of course, since the "Malthusian" label for the Third Republic referred both to its economic stagnation and its decreasing and aging population. The same sentiment of national peril

---

[39] Kuisel, *Capitalism and the State*, 264.

[40] "La consommation dans l'économie française," *Consommation: Annales du Centre de recherches et de documentation sur la consommation* 2 (1958), 23.

[41] INSEE, *Annuaire statistique de la France. Résumé rétrospectif.* 72nd Volume. New Series 14 (INSEE: Paris, 1966), 480.

[42] Niaudet, "L'évolution de la consommation," 60.

that drove modernization in the economy justified maintaining the gendered structure of the family, as it was assumed that women would have more children if they devoted themselves to the home. In addition, the promise of a more just society born of the Resistance created hope for prosperity and equality for all, and tied to that promise was the conviction that one's living standards should not decrease with the decision to start a family. There was a long-standing belief in French society that having children was not merely a private decision, but beneficial to the nation as a whole.[43] The constitution of the Fourth Republic stated that "The Nation guarantees to the individual and the family the conditions necessary for their development."[44] Despite women's enfranchisement at the end of the Second World War, most historians have argued that France remained a socially and culturally conservative society.[45] The

---

[43] Joshua Cole, *The Power of Large Numbers: Population, Politics, and Gender in Nineteenth Century France* (Ithaca: Cornell University Press, 2000); Angus McLaren, *Sexuality and the Social Order: The Debate over the Fertility of Women and Workers in France, 1770–1920* (New York: Holmes and Meier Publishers, Inc., 1983); and Karen Offen, "Depopulation, Nationalism, and Feminism in Fin-de-Siècle France," *The American Historical Review* 89 (1984): 648–676 discuss the perception of population crisis beginning in the nineteenth century. Susan Pedersen, *Family, Dependence, and the Origins of the Welfare State: Britain and France, 1914–1945* (Cambridge: Cambridge University Press, 1993) examines the development of the welfare state in both England and France. She shows that the belief that France needed population growth meant that family benefits in France were focused on children, rather than the fathers of families. Rachel Fuchs also argues that the population crisis prompted a uniquely woman- and child-centered focus from the inception of the welfare state in "France in a Comparative Perspective," in *Gender and the Politics of Social Reform in France 1870–1914*, eds. Elinor A. Accampo, Rachel G. Fuchs, and Mary Lynn Stewart (Baltimore: Johns Hopkins University Press, 1995), 157–187. Laura Levine Frader has argued that this perceived crisis strengthened the notion of the male breadwinner ideal and prevented women from becoming full economic citizens during the Third Republic. Laura Levine Frader, *Breadwinners and Citizens: Gender in the Making of the French Social Model* (Durham: Duke University Press, 2008). Miranda Pollard's *Reign of Virtue: Mobilizing Gender in Vichy France* (Chicago: University of Chicago Press, 1998) shows how the imposition of traditional gender roles was central to the Vichy regime's policies, both because of the desire to exert social control and because of the belief that France's population decline was responsible for military defeat. Sarah Fishman, *We Will Wait: Wives of French Prisoners of War, 1940–1945* (New Haven: Yale University Press, 1991) shows some of the difficulties the Vichy government faced in imposing these roles as a defeated and occupied power.

[44] Claire Duchen, *Women's Rights and Women's Lives in France, 1944–1968* (London: Routledge, 1994), 30.

[45] See Hanna Diamond, *Women and the Second World War in France, 1939–1948: Choices and Constraints* (London: Longman, 1999); Éric Alary and Dominique Veillon, "L'après-guerre des femmes: 1947, un tournant?" in *L'année 1947*, eds. Pierre Milza and Serge Berstein (Paris: Presses de la Fondation nationale des sciences politiques, 2000), 487–511; William Guéraiche, "Les femmes politiques de 1944 à 1947: Quelle libération?" *Clio*,

factors that had kept women from voting and had helped determine gender roles for decades did not disappear with the founding of the Fourth
Republic. In fact, French citizens, like their European neighbors, resound-
ingly answered the call for population growth with the baby boom of
the 1950s and exhibited a desire to find security in the family through
the postwar decades. Images of domestic tranquility and fulfillment permeated popular culture even as families struggled to find comfortable
housing in which to raise children in a nation slowly recovering from war
and economic upheaval. The baby boom itself drove the growth of mass
consumer society by first creating demand for commodities associated
with babies and children, and then, by the end of the 1950s, a generation
of young people who were consumers in their own right.[46] It also drove
housing construction, as these young families desperately needed homes,
but the importance of new attitudes is apparent in the fact that couples
were having children before housing was available, expressing optimism
in an expanding economy even in the midst of hardship.

In what follows, I explain how the desire for "normalcy," the recognition that women had become full citizens, the drive for reconstruction and
productivity, and the belief that consumer decisions drove the postwar
economy, all made consumer citizenship an attractive construct at this
moment. Emphasizing the new skills necessary for managing a home with
appliances and making rational purchases when faced with a plethora of
choices was a way of ensuring that women's lives remained focused on
the home. As citizen consumers, women could direct the national and
family economies, provide children for the nation, and create family
comfort. These were ways of recognizing women's new authority in the
polity without upsetting the gendered balance of home, workplace, and
electorate.

In these pages, I will also demonstrate how the home and family were
central to the economic, social, and cultural transformation of the postwar years. The home became the premier site for the arrival of consumer
durables, and the woman consumer who managed the home economy
also helped to change family and class structure as she redefined the

Histoire, Femmes et Sociétés 1 (1995): 165–186; and Jane Jenson, "The Liberation and
New Rights for French Women," in *Behind the Lines: Gender and the Two World Wars*,
eds. Margaret Randolph Higonnet, Jane Jenson, Sonya Michel, and Margaret Collins
Weitz (New Haven: Yale University Press, 1987), 272–284 for discussion of women's
participation in politics and society following the war. For a broader account of politics
in the early Fourth Republic, see Richard Vinen, *Bourgeois Politics in France, 1945–1951*
(Cambridge: Cambridge University Press, 1995).
[46] Judt, *Postwar*, 347–348.

conditions and products that were "necessary" in postwar France. As domestic consumers, women, and their families changed understandings of what constituted luxury and necessity, and affluence and comfort. They also made the ability to consume a right for all French families, and changed associations between consumption and class. Income, of course, as well as access to education and cultural capital, as Pierre Bourdieu has shown, continued to divide the French public.[47] But the "right" to a washing machine, a vacuum cleaner, and a modern home became imperatives for all families, undermining the prewar notion that bourgeois families and working-class families had different needs. The United States had prospered in part due to its deep, wide markets and advocacy of cross-class consumption, in contrast to European notions of class-based consumption.[48] Creating a broad-based middle-class lifestyle that, even while still unavailable to many families, was considered a necessity for all, provided the millions of French consumers necessary for sustaining a modern mass consumer economy.

ORGANIZATION OF THE BOOK

Creating a mass consumer society involved efforts by the state and organizations to create and educate consumers, as well as the negotiation of cultural norms and definitions of need by the French population. Therefore, this book alternates between examining the structural framework created to encourage informed consumption, and the negotiations that the populace made in embracing mass consumer society as appropriate for France. The first chapter explores how women's, family, and consumer organizations, on the one hand, and state modernizers on the other hand, defined the role of the citizen consumer, or consumer for the nation, promoting a sphere for public influence based on women's special knowledge of the home and family. This new consumer identity was closely tied to the problems of the immediate postwar period of rationing, inflation, and reconstruction, and to the desire for modern housing and consumer durables. Women's groups protested in the streets following the Liberation and challenged the provisional government to provide basic necessities for their families. They monitored prices during rationing and years of high inflation, instructing women that the consumer for the

---

[47] See, especially, Pierre Bourdieu, *Distinction: A Social Critique of the Judgment of Taste* (Cambridge: Harvard University Press, 1984).
[48] Victoria de Grazia, *Irresistible Empire*.

nation had an indispensable role in strengthening the economy. Public figures, journalists, and modernizers also stressed this citizenship responsibility as inflation continually plagued the economy. Planners and modernizers recognized the importance of understanding consumer demand if the economy were to expand in a rational and healthy manner, and called on consumer organizations and women's and family groups to advise government planners on the need for consumer goods and home comfort, and to educate their members about their duties as citizen consumers.

The need to both recognize the power of, and to discipline, the consumer is a theme that runs through this book. All of these parties acknowledged that women were the consumers for the nation, and therefore held the power to influence the national economy, but state planners and modernizers, as well as organizations that valorized women's consumer role, also consistently argued that women needed to be educated to make consumer decisions, implying that they would act irrationally without the training available from women's and consumer organizations.[49] They also asserted that the experiences of rationing, shortages, and inflation had made it more difficult to develop consuming skills, and made women willing to buy inferior products at high prices for fear that the goods would disappear. This led to inflation and made consumer education even more important than in a stable economy. As concern about subsistence level consumption faded, many of the same organizations that advocated women's consumer influence following the war, as well as semipublic groups concerned with family welfare, turned to modernizing women's work in the home, again emphasizing housewives' responsibilities as domestic consumers and homemakers whose decisions influenced the national economy.

Chapter 2 examines how these organizations worked to create a mass consumer society in which families, and women in particular, had access to home appliances and conveniences. As citizen consumers and homemakers, women influenced the national economy, and if they and their families had access to consumer credit, they could increase demand for consumer durables that would spur production and create low prices and high standards of living. Advocates of credit latched on to the national

---

[49] The irrational consumer was immortalized by Émile Zola in the late nineteenth century in his *Au bonheur des dames* (1883). Patricia O'Brien ties women's potential for irrationality to a critique of consumer society and the department store, in particular. See Patricia O'Brien, "The Kleptomania Diagnosis: Bourgeois Women and Theft in Late Nineteenth-Century France," *Journal of Social History* 17 (1983): 65–77.

discourse on modernization and productivity to apply the same principles to home modernization. They emphasized the place of the home and the domestic consumer in the modern economy, valorizing household labor while arguing that this work, like any other, required training.

Chapter 3 explores how the demand for a high standard of living, which was possible only through mass consumer society, helped to define marriage and the family of the postwar years. State imperatives for population growth, which were funded by an expansive social security system, combined with what sociologists viewed as a new psychological readiness to have children and to find security in home and family, spurred on the baby boom of the 1950s. This boom began even while living conditions were difficult, apparently inspired by hope for better conditions in the future. Thus, commentators saw home modernization and consumer durables as necessities for newly formed families and also looked to the role of domestic consumer in a new kind of home as a way to balance women's emancipation with the desire to maintain the gendered structure of home and workplace. Thus, the modern family evolved with mass consumer society as families drove economic change through their consumer demands, and the ability to consume came to be considered a right and necessity for families.

The creation of new needs was also essential for challenging conceptions of class and consumption. Consumption had traditionally served to define class, and the notion that bourgeois and working-class families had the same needs and desires frightened both cultural conservatives and socialists concerned about the end of working-class radicalism.[50] Chapter 4 examines how working-class women's organizations incorporated their demands for consumer durables into their working-class political agenda, viewing them not as the products of individual acquisitiveness, but as items that could be collectively owned and which offered a well-earned relief from hard labor. To create consumer society, however, not only the working class had to be convinced of the appeal of mass-produced goods. This chapter also explores how women's magazines made consumer durables seem appropriate to bourgeois and middle-class women, so they were considered neither luxurious nor cheap, but simply necessities for

---

[50] For analysis of how bourgeois women consumed to define their class position, see Auslander, *Taste and Power*; Walton, *France at the Crystal Palace*; Rosalind Williams, *Dream Worlds: Mass Consumption in Late Nineteenth-Century France* (Berkeley: University of California Press, 1982). For debate about the standard of living, see De Grazia, *Irresistible Empire*, and Coffin, "A 'Standard' of Living?"

the modern family and housewife.⁵¹ Women's journals were an immensely popular segment of the postwar mass media, which Susan Weiner has shown was essential for creating and presenting images of women and girls to French society and which Kristin Ross has argued was important for creating the new middle class. These journals, like novels that focused on changes to home, family, and consumption, provide a qualitative understanding of notions of comfort and emancipation through consumption.⁵² The first purchasers of mass-produced consumer durables were wealthy families, primarily from this new middle class. These families spurred on mass consumer society through their purchases. At the same time the new middle class was, in a sense, created by mass consumer society, as it was their spending habits and lifestyle that helped define them as a social group.

The book concludes with an examination of the *Salon des arts ménagers*, the government-sponsored exposition on home modernization, consumer goods, reconstruction, and, in general, mass consumer society. This chapter once again emphasizes the cooperative spirit behind modernization and the role this created for the citizen consumer, as the *Salon* exemplified the coordinated action of the state with industry and women's, family, and consumer groups. The popularity of the *Salon* also highlights the attraction consumer durables and their attendant lifestyle held for the wider populace. The *Salon* was, in fact, a festival of consumption, and its attendance exploded in the postwar period, attracting nearly one and a half million visitors annually at its height in the 1950s.⁵³ Although it drew its biggest crowds from the Paris region, the

---

⁵¹ Robert Frost argues that in the interwar period, domestic appliances did not succeed in France in part because bourgeois consumers were unwilling to buy mass-produced goods. Ellen Furlough has also argued that some American-style methods of merchandizing, the five-and-dime store, in particular, did not succeed in interwar France because they were not in tune with French notions of class and gender boundaries. Robert Frost, "Machine Liberation: Inventing Housewives and Home Appliances in Interwar France," *French Historical Studies* 18 (1993): 109–130. Ellen Furlough, "Selling the American Way in Interwar France: *Prix Uniques* and the *Salon des arts ménagers*," *Journal of Social History* 26 (1993): 491–519.

⁵² This is in part why scholars in French Cultural Studies and literature have been important for our understanding of the historical period. See Susan Weiner, *Enfants Terribles* and Kristin Ross, *Fast Cars, Clean Bodies*.

⁵³ See Claire Leymonerie, "Le Salon des arts ménagers dans les années 1950: Théâtre d'une conversion à la consommation de masse," *Vingtième Siècle* 91 (2006): 43–56; W. Brian Newsome, "The Struggle for a Voice in the City"; Nicole Rudolph, "At Home In Postwar France, the Design and Construction of Domestic Space, 1945–1975," (PhD. diss., New York University, 2005); Jacques Rouaud, *60 ans d'arts ménagers. Tome 2: La*

Salon's influence, including its drive for productivity in the home, spread throughout France, inspiring local events, drawing visitors from provincial youth groups who arrived on special trains provided by the national railroad company, and celebrating the young women that, having won at the local and regional levels, were invited to Paris to compete in the annual Fairy Homemaker contest. The *Salon* celebrated and advocated all of the changes explored in the first four chapters of the book. It was a means of popularizing mass-produced goods; it advocated new methods of buying, such as credit; it taught women to make their household labor more productive; it recognized women as the consumers for the nation; and it sought to educate and guide them in making their consumer decisions more rationally. Most of the family, women's, and consumer organizations mentioned throughout the book participated in the annual event, and many assisted in the year-round planning it required. For its part, the French government sponsored the *Salon* through the ministry of education and used it as a venue to promote its home reconstruction projects, the sale of consumer goods, and the expansion of the French economy.

This book is a story of the postwar years, and, in many ways, of a postwar generation. Even as late as the early 1960s, the products that French society associated with comfort and modern living (e.g. indoor bathrooms, electricity, hot running water, and home appliances) were less widespread than in the United States, and even other European countries, but modernization had already had an undeniable impact on French society.[54] Between 1949 and 1957 the stock of home appliances in France grew by 400 percent.[55] The period between 1944 and 1968 is singular not just for being the first phase in the creation of mass consumer society, a phase which developed slowly, but for being the period in which French society confronted the changes mass consumption would entail in lifestyles, taste, and values. It is also unique for its sentiment that France needed to modernize or would inevitably decline, for its productivity drives in both industry and home, and for the vaunted spirit of

---

consommation (Paris: Syros Alternatives, 1993); Martine Segalen, "The Salon des Arts Ménagers, 1923–1983: A French Effort to Instill the Virtues of Home and the Norms of Good Taste," *Journal of Design History* 7 (1994): 267–275.

[54] Victoria de Grazia points out that by 1960s, French families still did not have the same access to consumer durables that American families and British families had. Victoria de Grazia with Ellen Furlough, *The Sex of Things: Gender and Consumption in Historical Perspective* (Berkeley: University of California Press, 1996), 156.

[55] Cited in Kuisel, *Seducing the French*, 105.

cooperation among state, industry, and consumers inspired by the Plan and expressed in events like the *Salon des arts ménagers*. The confluence of top-down planning and bottom-up demand derived from a rejection of prewar society and conditions, as well as wartime hardship, and a desire for change. These imperatives would lose their appeal as society moved beyond the war and the most active population group became one that had grown up along with affluence and had not experienced war on metropolitan French soil.

By the mid-1960s, the belief that producers, distributers, and consumers needed to cooperate to create productivity and rebuild France was waning as the economy reached its full potential, and consumer organizers moved toward confrontational strategies rather than consumer citizenship. The Plan itself also lost some of its mystique as France entered the Common Market and domestic planning competed with European-wide decision making. The Plan had served as an element of continuity through the years of the Fourth Republic, in which governments changed rapidly but continued to agree on the importance of the Plan. The institution of the Fifth Republic in 1958 also initiated the eleven-year presidency of Charles de Gaulle, which provided political stability, making the Plan less necessary for consistency, and also politicizing the Plan and gradually eroding the multiparty consensus behind it so that the importance of planning itself became a matter of contention.[56]

This is also the story of a kind of liberation through material comfort which for many women, once comfort was widely available, did not seem so liberating after all. By the mid-1960s, consumer citizenship and the power inherent in domestic consumption and management seemed increasingly limiting to a generation of women who had not lived through the war, occupation, postwar shortages, and economic dislocation. By 1965, the French economy had recovered from war and economic crisis.[57] In 1965, the birthrate declined for the first time since the war and the University of Paris campus at Nanterre opened its doors to educate the children of the baby boom.[58] The declining

---

[56] See Ardagh, *The New French Revolution*, 41 and Stephen S. Cohen, *Modern Capitalist Planning*.

[57] Henri Mendras states that by 1965, the French economy had finally caught up to where it would have been had life continued smoothly, peacefully, and prosperously after 1914. Henri Mendras with Alistair Cole, *Social Change in Modern France: Towards a Cultural Anthropology of the Fifth Republic* (Cambridge: Cambridge University Press, 1991), 5.

[58] Ibid., 7.

sense that bearing children was a social and national responsibility
was confirmed by the 1967 legalization of birth control. In 1970, the
Mouvement de libération des femmes (MLF) was formed, and realizing the importance of the *Salon des arts ménagers* for propagating the
notion of liberation through consumer society, held a sit-in at the 1975
Salon.[59] Attendance at the *Salon* itself had been waning since the mid-
1960s. The MLF grew out of the events of 1968, in part because women
participants had been frustrated that its events were male-dominated.
This generation of women demanded a new place in the polity and a
new kind of citizenship. They, and their male counterparts, also held
a very different view of mass consumer society. Now that France had
achieved the standard of living that their parents had hoped for in the
aftermath of war and occupation, they began to question the tenets of
mass consumer society and once again redefined "need" in light of their
own political, economic, and social contexts. These contexts included a
new international situation as well, with renewed confidence in France's
position as a world power and views of America less as an exceptional
land of plenty than as an imperialist nation. This generation voiced
worries and concerns about technological society that were similar to
those of previous generations, but they did not conflate modernization
and Americanization as earlier critics had done. Americans were now
"fellow-victims" of a global problem rather than missionaries of productivity to France and the rest of the world.[60] Thus would begin a new
conversation about women's emancipation and consumer society, one
unthinkable when the need to recover from a Malthusian past and a
destructive war was predominant.

   In 1944, prosperity was years away and the French state and population confronted the need for reconstruction after a humiliating war
and occupation. The atmosphere was one of national emergency and it
seemed that a particular kind of modernization was the only alternative
to a loss of international status and independence. This inspired the cooperative spirit of the Plan and the creation of the citizen consumer. For
women exercising full citizenship for the first time, this was both empowering and constraining, as it implied a new kind of national influence but
meant the gendering of citizenship at the moment of enfranchisement.

[59] Jacques Rouaud, *60 ans d'arts ménagers*, 162.
[60] Paul A. Gagnon, "La Vie Future: Some French Responses to the Technological Society,"
   Journal of European Studies 6 (1976): 174.

This gendered structure was undergirded by the belief that combating Malthusianism meant both economic change and a renewed population drive. These factors, plus the widespread desire for "normalcy," all reinforced notions of liberation through consumption and empowerment in the role of citizen consumer and domestic manager as the home was modernized along with the rest of French society in the years between 1944 and 1968.

I

Consumers for the Nation

Women, Politics, and Citizenship

"Consumers, defend yourselves!" admonished *Le Monde* in November 1946. "Think before buying. Control the prices offered you.... Your wallet will benefit, and so will the franc!"[1] The war was over and France was liberated, but hard times prevailed. In this short announcement, *Le Monde* revealed the tensions inherent in the important role of the consumer in the French economy. At the same time that the newspaper chastised consumers, it urged them to empower themselves and remedy their economic situation. It called on them to be citizen consumers – buyers making purchasing decisions both for their own good and for the good of the nation. The French transition from poverty to plenty was characterized by periods of rationing, shortages, prolonged and intense inflation, and the slow results of the productivity drives of the early postwar economy. Throughout the phases of this social and economic reconstruction, consumers both organized themselves to exercise economic citizenship and were disciplined, cajoled, and called on to assume their appropriate responsibilities in the national economy.

Whereas the postwar turmoil involved numerous international and national political problems, it was the economy that preoccupied much of the population immediately following the war.[2] Under strained economic

---

[1] "Consommateurs, défendez-vous!" *Le Monde* (November 17–18, 1946), 7.
[2] Historians have emphasized the continuities in problems in daily life over the period of the war and into the late 1940s, chiefly because of the continued economic hardship, despite political change. See Dominique Veillon, *Vivre et survivre en France, 1939–1947* (Paris: Éditions Payot et Rivages, 1995); Dominique Veillon and Jean-Marie Flonneau, eds., *Le temps des restrictions en France*; Hanna Diamond, *Women and the Second World War*.

conditions, French women exercised full citizenship for the first time, and couples and families sought to create normalcy, hoping eventually to find prosperity. It was under these conditions that postwar economic planners looked abroad, chiefly to the United States, to determine the best means of creating a stable, just, and modern mass consumer society. For these modernizers, increasing French productivity seemed the only way to achieve economic prosperity and provide cheap, mass-produced goods to the population. Hoping to rationalize and streamline this process, they asserted that increased productivity would not bear fruit if it did not fulfill the needs of the French public, and therefore knowledge of consumer demand was important to the functioning of the economy. This chapter argues that all of these circumstances and goals combined to create a new kind of consumer citizenship in postwar France – one in which the domestic consumer exercised new authority and power, and in which modernizers sought to educate consumers to make rational choices while they measured their desires and predicted their needs.

Thus consumers occupied a new position in the French economy and society, and it was at once empowering and infantilizing. It was a position well suited to this stage of France's economic development, and because it was widely recognized that women were the nation's most important consumers, it was appropriate for a society grappling with women's political enfranchisement and presence in the workforce while at the same time seeking normalcy and tranquility in the wake of war and occupation. Women's, family, and consumer organizations harnessed this new economic authority, advocating women's influence as consumers for the nation, citizen consumers who bettered their families, nation, and class through their demands and purchases.[3] These groups moved from protesting in the street to monitoring prices in periods of inflation and working with government and industries to attempt to direct production toward family needs. They claimed power and influence for domestic consumers, even while the capability of individual women consumers to make rational choices was not always accepted by modernizers and

---

[3] I use the term "consumers for the nation" to explain the role consumer and women's organizations such as the *Union féminine civique et sociale* (Women's Civic and Social Union, UFCS), allotted to women consumers in the postwar years. The UFCS, for example, constantly stressed that women were the chief consumers in the nation and that three-quarters of national revenue passed through their hands. Women could, therefore, orient production toward family needs and strengthen the national economy through their wise purchases. A statement of this belief is in "Les acheteuses et les problèmes de la consommation," *La femme dans la vie sociale* 264 (1954/1955): 1–4.

economic planners, or even female journalists and consumer organizers themselves. Whether seeking to empower or discipline the domestic consumer, the identification of women as consumers and the recognition of the power inherent in that role fostered both the creation of a new type of citizenship appropriate for a modern, consumer-driven economy, and a gendering of political and economic roles as women exercised full citizenship for the first time in the wake of the Liberation.

CREATING A VOICE FOR THE CONSUMER

The conditions of the French postwar economy were such that mobilization around consumer issues was particularly fruitful and necessary. First shortages, then inflation plagued French families, and women's postwar consumer demands began in the streets, often under the direction of the Communist *Union des femmes françaises* (Union of French Women, UFF). Catholic groups such as the *Mouvement populaire des familles* (Working Family Movement, MPF) joined with the UFF and the Communist party in demonstrations and cooperatives, and provided a bridge to new forms of consumer advocacy when subsistence issues had been resolved. When food became more readily available, but rampant inflation infected the economy, the women of the MPF, the UFF, and the Catholic *Union féminine civique et sociale* (Women's Civic and Social Union, UFCS) monitored prices, counseled other women to be thrifty, and told them where to shop. Along with new consumer education and advocacy groups such as the government-supported *Union fédérale de la consommation* (Federal Union of Consumption, UFC), these groups argued that as the consumers of the nation, women could help raise the standard of living, increase productivity, and control inflation. Thus the needs of reconstruction and the transition to mass consumer society inspired consumer organization.

At the same time, the French government recognized the important place of consumers in the economy, tapping women's, family, and consumer groups for information about markets while also supporting their efforts to educate consumers about their role in the French economy. Often, these groups emphasized the importance of intelligent consumption by asserting that women were not born good consumers, but needed to be educated to fill this role. Rational consumption did not come naturally, but was acquired through proper training eagerly provided by these organizations and the national government. This training was particularly important because the experience of war, shortages, and rationing had impeded the development of the skills necessary for consuming in a modern, peacetime economy. When the economy reached its full potential, these groups claimed that education remained a necessity because the range of products and new technologies baffled consumers unaccustomed to such a plethora of choices. Thus, the same rhetoric that vaunted the power of the citizen consumer tended to infantilize her by consistently stressing her need for education. That said, the consumer actions undertaken by women's, family, and consumer organizations in this period are evidence of a vigorous social, political, and economic engagement that is often overlooked in histories of postwar France.

Although Communist and working-class groups remained important consumer advocates, especially during the immediate postwar years, part of the transition to mass consumer society entailed a shift from class-based consumer organizations that proposed an alternative to consumer capitalism to the growth of new consumer advocacy groups that accepted and even promoted liberal capitalism. These groups wished to extend the benefits of capitalism to a larger proportion of French society and hoped that individual consumers could help the markets run more efficiently by keeping government and industry aware of their needs. Productivity advocate and consumer organizer André Romieu called this goal the "market community": a collaborative effort among producers, distributers, and consumers to create a strong, expansive French economy.[4]

As Ellen Furlough has illustrated, France had a strong tradition of consumer cooperation that stretched back to the formation of the *Union coopérative* (Cooperative Union) in 1885 and the *Bourse des coopératives socialistes* (Organization of Socialist Cooperatives) in 1895. These two organizations had competing ideas about the role of cooperatives in the French economy and society. Reformists controlled the Cooperative Union and sought a third way between capitalism and socialism that was not revolutionary but would provide a corrective to abuses in the capitalist system. The Organization of Socialist Cooperatives, on the other hand, sought to create an alternative economic system and used its resources to support strikes, the labor press, and other explicitly political activities. The reformist strain of the cooperative movement grew in strength in the twentieth century, especially after the two groups combined in 1912 to form the *Fédération nationale des coopératives de consommation* (National Federation of Consumer Cooperatives, FNCC) and worked with the government during the First World War.

---

[4] André Romieu, *Conférence de presse du 4 février 1955.*

As the working class became the target of mass-advertising in the 1920s and 1930s, the limited range of goods that cooperatives sold made it increasingly difficult for the stores to compete with capitalist retailers offering a wider variety of products. Furlough has shown that by the 1930s, capitalist consumer culture had triumphed in France. Cooperatives no longer provided a viable alternative to capitalism, but instead attempted to compete with capitalist retailers by appealing to consumers as acquisitive individuals, adopting the techniques of modern advertizing they had once opposed.[5] In the postwar period, cooperatives continued to provide for working-class families, but the FNCC worked with capitalists in efforts such as Romieu's "market community."

While consumer cooperatives struggled in the decade preceding the Second World War, consumer-based advocacy groups began to take shape across Europe. Although the earlier cooperative movement had been weaker in the United States than in Western European countries, America provided a model for this new type of consumer cooperation. Instead of establishing nonprofit stores for working-class customers, as the cooperative movement did, advocacy groups focused on lobbying governments, publicizing information about retail goods and services, and pressuring firms by influencing public opinion and sponsoring boycotts. They saw consumers as an autonomous group not associated with a particular social class.[6]

After the war, as France began to rebuild and modernize, new consumer advocacy groups formed, and existing family and women's organizations focused new attention on consumption. The French government-supported consumer organization, recognizing that this type of cooperation was a strength of the American system, and that understanding and predicting consumer demand was necessary for reaching the levels of productivity and efficiency that would raise the standard of living for all. The United States was the world's pre-eminent service society, in which commerce always sought to satisfy the consumer – a feature frequently cited in the French press. As the women's journal *La femme* reported in 1945, commerce in

[5] Ellen Furlough, "French Consumer Cooperation, 1885–1930: From the 'Third Pillar' of Socialism to 'A Movement for all Consumers'," in *Consumers Against Capitalism? Consumer Cooperation in Europe, North America, and Japan, 1840–1990*, ed. Ellen Furlough and Carl Strikwerda (Oxford: Rowman and Littlefield Publishers, Inc., 1999), 173–190, and Ellen Furlough, *Consumer Cooperation in France*. On advertising techniques see especially *Consumer Cooperation*, 270–75. Efforts to compete were not very successful and Furlough states that by 1928, consumer cooperatives provisioned only 5.5 percent of the population. "French Consumer Cooperation," 183.

[6] See Strikwerda and Furlough, *Consumers Against Capitalism*.

the United States was "in service of the client" and built "true courtesy
which creates a climate of confidence and general cordiality" in American
society.[7] Modernizers and consumer organizers asserted that an economy
at the service of the consumer was the remedy for France's low productivity. Directing production to consumer need and helping consumers
inform planners and producers of their needs could only strengthen the
French economy. Cooperation among consumers, government, and producers was suited to the postwar period, when national concentration was
focused on reconstruction and boosting productivity. By the mid-1960s,
the economy had recovered and many of the features of French postwar
society were changing. As the national imperative for productivity faded,
consumer groups grew impatient with the role accorded them by national
planners and sought more autonomy, at the same time becoming more
militant and more confrontational.

Social and economic reconstruction was years away in the mid-1940s,
however, and the French government and its citizens turned first to recovering from the massive destruction wrought by the Second World War.
Although the goal of the French "*économie mixte*" was to achieve free
markets and prices eventually, the harsh economic conditions in France
and the decision to concentrate on heavy industry necessitated the use
of ration cards until 1949.[8] Relief from rationing occurred in haphaz-
ard fashion across France, and with maddening twists and turns. The
bread ration card, for instance, was suppressed in November 1945, just
before national elections, but then resurrected in January 1946, with even
lower rations.[9] The shortage of food was cause for great frustration in a
population that had been told consistently throughout the war that the
Germans were the reason for harsh conditions. When circumstances did
not immediately improve, and even worsened, many people were angry
at the government's seeming inattention to the needs of its population.[10]

[7] "La courtoisie en affaires: en Amérique, vendeurs et acheteurs savent sourire," *La femme* 24 (1945): 6.

[8] Veillon and Flonneau, *Le temps des restrictions*, 19. For discussion of the liberalization of the economy, see Michel Margairaz, "Le reconstruction matérielle: crise, infléchisse-ment, ou ajustement," in *L'année 1947*, 17–44.

[9] On rationing, see Dominique Veillon, *Vivre et survivre*, 290–300. For the change to the bread card, see 298.

[10] The reports of the Commissaires de la république, regional officials of the provisional government after the war, repeatedly state that the people were satisfied with the govern-ment's actions in matters of foreign policy, but unsatisfied with the government's attention to internal concerns, namely its attention to food supply and heating problems. Ministère de l'Intérieur, Services des Commissaires de la République. Bulletin sur la situation dans les régions et les départements. Archives Nationales (hereafter, AN) F1a 4027–F1a 4029. For unrest among the population, see also Megan Koreman, The Expectation of Justice.

Eventually, when adequate food supplies became available, the problem of shortages was succeeded by inflation.[11] Inflation was particularly rampant during the second half of the 1940s, peaking in 1946 when prices rose by 64 percent. The Marshall Plan, in operation from 1947 to 1953, helped increase productivity and stabilize prices that continued to rise, nevertheless, by about 6 percent annually between 1950 and 1961. In response, and despite its goal of liberalizing the economy, the governments of the Fourth Republic tried blocking prices, setting price ceilings, instituting mandatory price reductions on certain products, and other means of lowering prices.[12] Rationing, price controls, and price liberalization all provided incentives for consumer organization, and many of the same groups that demonstrated in the streets during the occupation and in the early years of the Fourth Republic turned to consumer advocacy in the late 1940s and early 1950s. Their efforts often had government support, as planners and productivity enthusiasts hoped to smooth distribution networks and raise productivity by channeling purchasers toward cheaper prices, and consumer groups constantly asserted the importance of their work for the health of the French economy.[13]

[11] See Christian Bachelier, "De la pénurie à la vie chère, l'opinion publique à travers les premiers sondages 1944–1949," in *Le temps des restrictions*, 479–500. Bachelier cites opinion polls showing that in January 1945 three-quarters of the French population thought the government was not doing all it could in the domain of food provisioning. Bachelier also notes that although opinion polls showed that provisioning was most of the population's first concern from the winter of 1944–1945, the beginning of 1946, and the winter of 1947–1948, by June of 1948 provisioning had decreased in importance and inflation became a major concern.

[12] Catherine Gilles and François Fauvin, "Du blocage des prix vers la déréglementation: 50 ans de prix à la consommation," *INSEE Première* 483 (1996): 2.

[13] There are many similarities among the French, West German, and British contexts in the postwar period, but the existence of the *économie mixte* and the Plan made French women's experience with consumer influence and cooperation somewhat unique. Matthew Hilton and Ina Zweiniger-Bargielowska have explored the influence of British women in this period and Erica Carter and Katherine Pence have done the same for Germany. Whereas there were similarities in the role of women in the marketplace and the importance of consumer education and safety, the French emphasis on state planning meant that women had the opportunity to be drawn into economic planning organizations in a way that would not have happened absent the controls in the French economy. In West Germany, Carter argues, the consumer citizen identity was explicitly tied to the importance of liberal economics. Pence's work shows that women's consumer actions in the period of upheaval immediately following the war were similar to those of women in France, as were the West German government's attempts to both discipline and empower women consumers. However, the Cold War context meant that instituting a free market economy was imperative for distinguishing West Germany from East Germany. See Erica Carter, *How German Is She? Postwar West German Reconstruction and the Consuming Woman* (Ann Arbor: University of Michigan Press, 1991) and Katherine Pence, "Shopping for an 'Economic Miracle': Gendered Politics of Consumer Citizenship

Thus, women's, family, and consumer organizations created a voice for consumers in the postwar period, and at the same time created a new identity for women as rational, educated consumers. The rhetoric used by various groups to assert the citizen consumer role could serve class, family, and national interests. In turn, the French government and French businesses recognized the role of consumers in the French economy and the need to listen to consumers, and women in particular, in this period of great change, reconstruction, and modernization.

DEFINING WOMEN'S CITIZENSHIP

French women attained full citizenship in an atmosphere in which the desire to return to normalcy, ideally in a more prosperous and comfortable France, and the continued push for population growth were salient. That normalcy entailed a particular gender structure in home and workplace, that there was pent-up demand from a population aware of living standards in prosperous consumer societies like the United States, and that there were challenges facing the French economy after the war were all factors making the identity of citizen consumer an effective tool for mobilizing women in the postwar period. Political parties across the spectrum concurred with Charles de Gaulle's assertion that "twelve million beautiful babies" were necessary for the nation's future, and the French public responded with a baby boom: nine million births by 1955, eleven million by 1958.[14] The attempt to reconcile pronatalism with women's new rights pervaded the rhetoric of women's political organizations like the Communist UFF in the immediate postwar years. At their first national congress following the Liberation, the women of the UFF laid out their political platform and goals. They celebrated the fact that women had been finally recognized as the equals of men, and were proud that women had taken a stand against fascism and for the republic, but linked these political achievements to calamities suffered in the household. The experience of the war had helped

in a Divided Germany," in *The Expert Consumer: Associations and Professionals in Consumer Society*, eds. Alain Chatriot, Marie-Emmanuelle Chessel, and Matthew Hilton (Aldershot: Ashgate, 2006): 105–120. Ina Zweiniger-Bargielowska's work demonstrates how housewives were also instrumental in enforcing rationing and price controls in Britain before the postwar economy was liberalized in the mid-1950s. See Ina Zweiniger-Bargielowska, *Austerity in Britain: Rationing, Controls, and Consumption, 1939–1955* (Oxford: Oxford University Press, 2000). And for consumer organization and women in Britain across the twentieth century, see Matthew Hilton, *Consumerism in Twentieth-Century Britain* (Cambridge: Cambridge University Press, 2003).

[14] Quoted in Rioux, *The Fourth Republic*, 351.

women understand that the "daily life of their home, and its future, is tied to the life and future of France."[15] The UFF also recognized that "a condition for the grandeur of a nation is the number of infants," and that since the family was the normal space for raising children, a "politics of the family" was necessary. Women could not have children, and those children could not grow healthy and strong, without state mitigation of the burdens of maternity and the construction of comfortable and healthy homes in the city and the countryside, among other things.[16] Women's citizenship was mediated through the household as the UFF integrated traditional ideas of women's responsibilities in family and society with the new privileges and responsibilities of citizenship.

Government representatives emphasized this same connection between women's new rights and women's special knowledge of the family in government efforts to bring women to the polls. In 1945, Maurice Bourgès-Maunoury, the *commissaire de la république* in Bordeaux, one of the provisional authorities sent to maintain order by the Gaullist government, called on women to exercise their new rights, emphasizing the important influence politics had on their daily lives and drawing particular attention to women's consumer demands. "All of you," he asked, "who want well-being for yourselves and your family, workers, bosses, peasants, functionaries, you, women, who for five years have shuffled through long waiting lines, have you nothing to say, to hope?" Calling on women to make their grievances known, he pointed out, "When you demand more bread, more meat, more clothing, more shoes, more notebooks and schoolbooks, when you fight for the abolition of privilege, real equality before the law, you are being political, and for good reason."[17] He demonstrated that consumer demands were women's demands and could be addressed through political solutions.

Women's journals and women's organizations also encouraged women to vote, both arguing that voting was a national responsibility and hoping that women would influence government policy through their special knowledge of home and family, a knowledge particularly important during this period of reconstruction. In 1945, a journalist from *Le Petit*

---

[15] Union des femmes françaises, *Programme d'action de l'Union des femmes françaises adopté au 1ᵉʳ Congrès National* (Paris, 1945).

[16] Ibid. The UFF also wanted improvements in education that would offer equal access to all children, regardless of their economic status, and the eradication of tuberculosis.

[17] M. Bourgès-Maunoury, Discours prononcé à la radio par M. Bourgès-Maunoury, Commissariat de la république au sujet des élections (Communiqué à la presse le 19 octobre 1945). AN F1a 4020.

Echo de la Mode told her readers, "You vote as 'women.' That is to say, you vote for the candidates who, based on their platforms, appear to you to have an essential concern for the family, which is your own concern." Women were to pay attention to the views of candidates on family allocations, housing, loans for married couples, and the protection of children. "… you will vote with enthusiasm for your candidate," the journalist concluded, "if you know that he, as father of a family, and a good father of his family, knows better than in theory, through imagination, or good will, the problems posed to the material, moral, and spiritual life of a home."[18] The author encouraged women to vote but assumed that the candidates for office would be exclusively male, and told women to make their decisions based on knowledge of the household.[19] Thus, women were assumed to be rational, capable beings, but their new right to vote was justified by their traditional knowledge of, and responsibility to, the household.

In 1945, a journalist for *La femme nouvelle* echoed the widespread belief that France would not retake its place as a world power without an increase in population, but also that the problem of population was not only quantitative, but qualitative. In contemporary France, the family with many children could not survive without what the author called "the heroism of the mother."[20] The author called for a "politics of the family" that called attention to the housing conditions in France, the need for gas and electricity in homes, the need to "quickly modernize our homes in equipping them with electric appliances" and "transforming our kitchens."[21] Also in 1945, a journalist for *Marie-France* wrote of a friend who visited a mountain village where the inhabitants had to walk five hundred meters to reach a source of water that was often polluted by animal waste. The friend asked a resident how this was possible

---

[18] "Vôtre premier vote," *Le Petit Echo de la Mode* 9–12 (1945): 4.
[19] Janine Mossuz-Lavau has explored women's voting in "Les électrices françaises de 1945 à 1993," *Vingtième Siècle* 42 (1994): 67–75. She identifies three distinct periods within the era of women's suffrage, and states that between 1945 and 1969 women's abstention was consistently higher than men's. Claire Duchen has pointed out that it was not until 1968 that there would be a woman prefect, a woman in the Inspectorate of Finances, the ministerial cabinets, or a woman ambassador. See Claire Duchen, "Une femme nouvelle pour une France nouvelle," *CLIO, Histoire, Femmes et Sociétés* 1 (1995): 151–164. Hanna Diamond has argued that despite the vote, material constraints left women uninterested in taking part in "politics as usual." See Hanna Diamond, *Women and the Second World War* and "Gaining the Vote: A Liberating Experience?" *Modern and Contemporary France* 3 (1995): 129–139.
[20] C.D., "Une politique de la famille est nécessaire," *La femme nouvelle* 10 (1945): 4.
[21] Ibid., 4.

and was told that many municipal governments had broached projects for improvement, but political wrangling had always kept them from taking action. "Well! Exclaimed the friend, if there had been women on the municipal council of X ... the problem would have been resolved long ago...." The journalist proclaimed, "When peace returns and our prisoners come home, and we are called to send deputies into positions of power, we will demand from them the guarantee that they will safeguard the essential interests of the family."[22] This will be "our politics," she concluded.[23]

Women answered the calls to vote. According to a survey conducted by the *Institut français d'opinion publique* (French Institute of Public Opinion, IFOP) in 1945, 80 percent of women planned to vote in the coming elections.[24] Government officials in Paris reported to the Ministry of the Interior that there were more women registering to vote than men in almost every *arrondissement*. Although the numbers of women voters were not as impressive in the suburbs, female voters still exceeded male voters in thirty of eighty communes.[25] In Marseille, the prefect noted a clear contrast between the numbers of men and women planning to vote in the municipal elections in early 1945; in February, more than twenty-five thousand more women than men had registered to vote.[26] Granted, many POWs had not yet returned home, but the fact that large numbers of women were planning to vote is nevertheless clear.

Despite the number of women registered, uncertainty about whether women would, or should, enter the political arena is implied in the many calls from journalists for women to perform their "duty" and "responsibility" to vote. One journalist chided women who were embarrassed to be seen voting, fearing that they would look too "suffragette" and would be laughed at. "It's incredible," she wrote, "that women, who were so brave, so decisive, so chic during the war, capitulate before the mocking smile of an imbecile! You know, I know someone who's more ridiculous than the woman who votes... It's the one who doesn't vote, because between us, she doesn't have blood in her veins."[27]

Along with articles chiding women for not voting were many stressing the practical implications of voting and the important role that national

[22] Marthe Doutreuve, "Politique féminine," *Marie-France* 19 (1945): 5.
[23] Ibid., 5.
[24] *Bulletin d'information de l'Institut français d'opinion publique* 6 (1944): 3.
[25] Bulletin sur la situation. January 3, 1945. AN F1a 4028.
[26] Rapport du préfet des Bouches-du-Rhône. January 10, 1945. AN F1cIII 1210.
[27] Marthe Doutreuve, "Nous allons voter," *Marie-France* 7 (1944): 11.

politics played in women's everyday lives. Above all, journalists stressed the domestic concerns of women and the fact that these were not only private, but also public and political. In 1946, *La femme* printed an article titled "The perfect housekeeper: Electricity." The article included descriptions of electric home appliances that were popular in the United States, and contrasted the role of appliances in American homes with that in French homes. France compared poorly. In discussing the automatic washing machine, the journalist noted that while several models existed before the war, and 1,031,000 had been sold in the United States in 1938, only 4,200 had been sold in France.[28] Similar comparisons were made involving the dishwasher, the electric iron, the electric stove, and the refrigerator. For each appliance, the Americans were well advanced both in terms of construction and popular usage. The French industries that built such machines, though, were handicapped by a lack of resources. Additionally, electricity was not uniformly available, and too expensive when it was. The author concluded:

Conclusion: Our domestic comfort will be, in the years to come, a direct result of our economic policy. Ah! Yes, these great problems of importation and exportation, these electrification plans, these new service plans, all of these questions that seem to be above your head, Madame, have an important direct influence on the ease or difficulty of your daily life, and no small influence on the happiness of the home that is so important for your own happiness. So? Do not be disinterested in politics. France is you, because we are a democracy, the French polity is you. And you see how important that is...[29]

The author's attempt to connect daily conditions with national politics reveals the common tendency to associate women with the home and family despite their political enfranchisement. This connection did not imply that women were supposed to be disinterested in public and political issues, but did suggest a gendering of citizenship at the moment of enfranchisement. Women were to use their special knowledge of the home and family to influence national politics in a way that would better their own situation, which in large part meant modernizing their homes and improving their living conditions. The power of the domestic manager and consumer could be wielded to achieve both political and economic ends.

[28] "Cette parfaite domestique: l'électricité. À quand, en France, les machines ménagères?" *La femme* 64 (1946): 4.
[29] Ibid., 19.

THE POLITICS OF EVERYDAY LIFE

In February 1945, a local government representative in the region of
Toulouse reported to the minister of the interior that at seven o'clock in
the evening on the thirteenth of January, a meeting of the *Front National*
and the Communist party spawned a march that ended at the *Place de
la Préfecture*. The official described a cortege of fifteen hundred women
crying, "We are hungry. We are cold." The *commissaire de la république*
agreed to receive a delegation of the women, who claimed that the rationing services had been negligent, depriving the population of coffee, soap,
and sugar. The departmental director of provisioning denied the claims of
the women, but, wrote the *commissaire*, they [the allegations], "have not
failed to unfavorably influence public opinion, the press doing nothing
to put things in order and facilitate the tasks of the government.[30] The
spectacle of these "so-called housewives" frightened public authorities
in Toulouse, as did similar incidents across France.[31] Charles de Gaulle's
provisional government was desperately trying to establish authority and
stability in the wake of occupation and liberation, and the accusation
that the new government was not fulfilling the subsistence needs of families was potent – strengthening the appeal of the Communist opposition.
In this fragile context, women's demands for justice and aid in feeding
their families were potentially explosive.

In the period immediately following the Liberation, authorities frequently lamented the fact that while the public generally approved of
the provisional government's foreign policy, dissatisfaction with internal
policy was a source of national instability. This dissatisfaction was often
expressed publicly by women unable to feed their families.[32] Women's
demonstrations were, for the most part, peaceful, but at times turned vio-
lent. In Aix, women demonstrators left a march and attempted to invade
the *sous-préfecture*.[33] In Nantes and Mans, protestors seized food and sold
it at a price they considered just. Such incidents frightened shopkeepers
and made them hesitant to remain open for business.[34] The *commissaire*
in the region of Laon and Saint-Quentin stated that demonstrations in his

[30] Bulletin sur la situation. February 3, 1945. AN F1a 4028.
[31] "So-called housewives" was the phrase used by the government representative.
[32] This was a frequent theme in the Bulletins sur la situation. AN F1a 4028 and 4029.
[33] Rapport du préfet des Bouches-du-Rhône. August 15–September 15, 1945. AN F1cIII
1210.
[34] Bulletin sur la situation. January 29, 1945. AN F1a 4029.

area had remained calm, "but it is reasonable to wonder if it will always be like this, and if the population will continue to be satisfied with pretty words."[35] The *commissaires*, regional authorities sent to maintain order and represent the provisional government until the establishment of the Fourth Republic, constantly stressed the loss of legitimacy the government faced in not being able to control the food situation before it worsened, and pressured the central government for a national solution to the problem.

Food demonstrations were not an invention of the postwar period, of course, and had been politically potent at least as far back as the Old Regime and as recently as the occupation.[36] In this specific context, demonstrations, many of which were organized by the Communist UFF, were seen as frightening evidence of the strength of the Communist party and the precarious position of the Gaullist provisional government. In April 1945, the *commissaire de la république* at Nancy noted that on the fourteenth of March, fifteen hundred women participated in a demonstration headed by the UFF. The *commissaire* wrote, "I take all measures possible to calm spirits, but it is almost impossible in current circumstances to remedy the current food deficiency and to convince a population suffering from five years of occupation and deprivation that today's difficulties result from the war." Despite his efforts, the representative expressed frustration that, "the extremist parties, in particular the Communist party, which is very active and well organized, do not miss the opportunity to exploit, for propaganda reasons, the difficulties of every sort that the Government encounters in the realm of food provisioning."[37] The prefect of the Bouches-du-Rhône also recognized the influence of the UFF and claimed that their agitation was an effort to demonstrate to women the political influence they could have in the next elections.[38] The Communists, as well as the other parties, attempted to attract women's votes by appealing to their desire for an alleviation of the food situation and poor living conditions.

Food demonstrations continued because they were effective – a fact lamented by local authorities. In Bordeaux, after a large demonstration

---

[35] Bulletin sur la situation. July 13, 1945. AN F1a 4029.
[36] For food demonstrations during the occupation, see Avakoumovitch, "Les manifestations des femmes"; Ryan, "Ordinary Acts and Resistance"; Schwartz, "The Politics of Food and Gender"; Taylor, *Between Resistance and Compromise*. For the occupation and immediate postwar period, see Danielle Tartakowsky, "Manifester pour le pain."
[37] Bulletin sur la situation. April 18, 1945. AN F1a 4028.
[38] Rapport du préfet des Bouches-du-Rhône. March 15– April 16, 1945. AN F1cIII 1210.

against food prices, the price of cherries, one of the contested items, dropped from between eighty and ninety francs per kilo to forty.[39] In November 1945, the *commissaire* at Nancy stated that demonstrations were becoming more and more frequent, a sign that they were a useful tool. He wrote to the minister of the interior, "the population is becoming more and more sensitive," and noted that conditions had escalated to the point "that for the one late distribution of chocolate to one of a branch of stores ... the housewives demonstrated."[40] By September of 1945 the prefect of Charente-Maritime regretted that it seemed that the government paid attention only to the demands from the streets. When shopkeepers were not authorized to sell the goods in their stores, the logical solution for women consumers was to protest in the street.[41] The politics of everyday life took center stage and diverted attention from other national issues and the formal political process. The prefect of Marseille lamented the lack of enthusiasm for the municipal elections of 1945, stating that, "People believe, in effect, that whatever the result, it will have no significant impact on the course of events." Furthermore, he indicated that the population believed the eventual return of the POWs would put any election results in question.[42] Both French women and men felt electoral politics were ineffectual, and in this time of material crisis, women put pressure on the government to fulfill their needs through a series of incidents with definite political ramifications.

The particular conditions of France's postwar economic situation made the time ripe for consumer advocacy movements. The government set prices for goods during the war and the immediate postwar period of rebuilding, but it intermittently freed prices on certain goods during the late 1940s, and many restrictions gave way to the liberalization of the market in the early 1950s. Despite the ultimate goal of full liberalization, the rampant inflation in France prompted the government to consistently call for a lowering of prices and to institute mandatory price controls at times. Faced with the difficult prospect of enforcing price controls alongside a thriving black market, and then of dampening inflation, in the late 1940s and the 1950s government officials and journalists stressed the role of individual consumers in keeping prices down.

[39] Bulletin sur la situation. June 27, 1945. AN F1a 4029.
[40] Bulletin sur la situation. November 10, 1945. AN F1a 4029.
[41] Bulletin sur la situation. September 28, 1945. AN F1a 4029.
[42] Rapport du préfet des Bouches-du-Rhône. March 15– April 16, 1945. AN F1cIII 1210.

Under these difficult economic conditions, family and women's organizations such as the MPF and the UFCS stressed the importance of
women consumers in improving the lot of their nation, family, and class.
The MPF was a family organization that grew out of the Social Catholic
movement of the interwar years. Originally called the *Ligue Ouvrière
Chrétienne* (Christian Worker's League, LOC) the group was created to
provide a home for former members of the *Jeunesse Ouvrière Chrétienne*
(Young Catholic Workers, JOC) once they had reached adulthood. The
LOC and JOC were part of the international *Action Catholique* (Catholic
Action, AC) movement and were created explicitly to re-Christianize the
French working class and combat the appeal of Communism. They did
so through organization by and within the working class itself, and a
major part of their efforts was to provide social services and ameliorate
the conditions of working-class life. The belief that changing the environment and living conditions of the working class was essential to the
greater goal of re-Christianization made the incorporation of subsistence
demands and other consumer needs a natural fit. Given the living conditions of the working class, these were potent issues around which to organize working families, and ultimately draw them back to the Church.

Renamed the MPF in 1941, the movement grew during the war in
part because, as a family organization sponsored by the Church, it was
allowed to operate under the Vichy government. Labor organizations
were banned, prompting activists from other class-based groups to find
a wartime home in the MPF. The MPF expanded its range of social services, supporting an organization for POW wives, helping to provide
better food to working families, operating cooperatives, and sending
packages to prisoners.[43] In the immediate postwar period, the circulation of the MPF's journal, *Monde Ouvrier*, was more than 100,000.[44]
Although the organization became officially nondenominational in 1949,
came into conflict with the Church due to its increasing radicalization,
and had portions of its membership express sympathy with and even

[43] The entry of non-Catholics into the MPF during the war has been cited as a factor leading to deconfessionalization after the war. See Gerd-Rainer Horn, *Western European
Liberation Theology: The First Wave (1924–1959)* (Oxford: Oxford University Press,
2008), 204–206. On activities during the war, see Ibid, 180–182. On the involvement
of the MPF with the *Service des femmes de prisonniers*, see Fishman, *We Will Wait*,
113–122.

[44] Bruno Duriez, "Left-Wing Catholicism in France: From Catholic Action to the Political
Left; The *Mouvement populaire des familles*," in *Left Catholicism, 1943–1955. Catholics
and Society in Western Europe at the Point of Liberation*, ed. Gerd-Rainer Horn and
Emmanuel Gerard (Leuven: Leuven University Press, 2001), 76.

join the Communist party or the Communist trade union, it retained much of its original ideology pertaining to the family, society, and human dignity.[45] After changing its name to the *Mouvement de libération du peuple* (People's Liberation Movement, MLP) in 1949, the organization split into the *Mouvement de libération ouvrière* (Worker's Liberation Movement, MLO) and the MLP in the early 1950s. Both groups continued to oversee a range of mutual aid and service organizations that carried on the activities of the LOC and MPF, and confessing Catholics remained active in both groups, though the goal of improving the conditions of the working class had displaced the goal of re-Christianization, and nonbelievers numbered among the activists.[46]

The UFCS, founded in 1925, also grew out of the Social Catholic traditions of the interwar years and also eventually deconfessionalized, but was not wedded to a particular social class. While it actively attempted to encourage the participation of working-class women in its endeavors, evidence suggests that its appeal was strongest among urban, middle-class women.[47] The UFCS had a membership of 70,000 after the war and was officially recognized as an organization of public utility in 1947.[48] Through its membership, the UFCS had a voice in a variety of family, religious, and political organizations and had strong links to the *Mouvement républicain populaire* (Popular Republican Movement, MRP) a party of

---

[45] See Geneviève Dermenjian, *Femmes, famille, et action ouvrière: Pratiques et responsabilités féminines dans les mouvements familiaux populaire (1935–1958)* (Villeneuve d'Ascq: Groupement pour la recherche sur les mouvements familiaux, 1991).

[46] Many militants in the MLP were also CGT members and in 1951, three leaders of the MLP even traveled to the USSR. See Duriez, "Left-Wing Catholicism," 86.

[47] See Mathilde Dubesset, "Les figures du féminine à travers deux revues féminines, l'une catholique, l'autre protestante, *La femme dans la vie sociale* et *Jeunes femmes*, dans les années 1950–1960," *Le Mouvement Sociale* 198 (2002): 9–34. Naomi Black points out that all voluntary women's organizations had this issue, since active members were most often women without employment outside the home. Naomi Black, *Social Feminism* (Ithaca: Cornell, 1989), 187. Many Social Catholics felt that engagement with social issues and programs was an expression of faith. The UFCS class base and incorporation of consumer interests shows continuity with the activism of the bourgeois women of the *Ligue sociale d'acheteurs* (Social Buyer's League, LSA) that operated at the beginning of the twentieth century. The LSA differed from both the cooperative movement and the organizations discussed here in that it was not principally concerned with consumer power, or orienting production to consumer needs, but in improving working conditions in factories and stores. Marie-Emmanuelle Chessel, "Consommation, action sociale et engagement public fin de siècle, des États-Unis à la France," in *Au nom du consommateur*, 247–261.

[48] Dubesset, "Les figures," 11. The UFCS had sought this recognition since 1938. Thérèse Doneaud and Christian Guérin, *Les femmes agissent, le monde change. Histoire inédite de l'Union féminine civique et sociale* (Paris: Éditions du Cerf, 2005), 115.

the Resistance associated, at least initially, with left-wing Catholics and which competed with the Communists for political dominance in the immediate postwar years.[49] The different constituencies of the MPF and the UFCS meant that the MPF often acknowledged that working-class women needed to work professionally, and was attendant to the practical needs of these women, whereas the UFCS consistently stressed the need for women to dedicate themselves to the home. Despite this difference, the Social Catholic background of both groups meant that they saw the ideal family situation as one in which women should not have employment outside of the home, but should be active in social movements and be informed and active voters.[50]

Amid rampant inflation, in 1947 the governments of Premier Léon Blum and his successor, Paul Ramadier, issued price cuts to retail prices of 5 percent each.[51] Family and women's groups and unions, including the MPF and the Communist CGT, had already created committees to monitor prices, and with the new measures the government regularized these committees, mobilizing consumers, and housewives in particular, to monitor prices. The groups, called "Committees for Market Stabilization" were declared mandatory in towns of over 10,000 people, and prefects were instructed to create them if they did not already exist. The groups were to ensure that the fixed prices of goods were respected, and to investigate the

---

[49] The MRP was initially embraced by left-wing Catholics, including those associated with the MPF. Over time, many of these leftists grew disillusioned with what they saw as the MRP's willingness to compromise and its drift to the right. See Duriez, "Left-Wing Catholicism," 76–77. Eight out of nine of the MRP's women representatives in the first legislative assembly were members of the UFCS. Though the MRP enjoyed great strength in the immediate postwar period, it waned in popularity with the growth of Gaullism. De Gaulle at first professed to be above party politics, and therefore did not join or endorse a party at the beginning of the Fourth Republic. His return to politics and endorsement of the RPF (*Rassemblement du peuple français*) decreased the popularity of the MRP, which declined rapidly in the fifties, and no longer existed by the late sixties. Naomi Black sees the decline of the MRP as an inhibitor for the politically active women of the UFCS. Because of its close ties to the MRP, the party's decline eliminated a channel for political advancement just as more women were becoming politically active. See Black, 197, 214–223.

[50] On the MPF's view of women, see Geneviève Dermenjian and Dominique Loiseau, "La maternité sociale et le Mouvement Populaire des Familles durant les Trente Glorieuses," *CLIO, Histoire, Femmes, et Sociétés* 21 (2005): 91–106.

[51] Frank Giles, *The Locust Years: The Story of the Fourth French Republic, 1946–1958* (London: Secker and Warburg, 1991), 41, 89. For discussion of the many crises of 1947, a year of economic, social, and political problems, including the exiting of the Communists from the government and the onset of the Cold War, see Berstein and Milza, *L'année 1947*.

just prices of items that were not controlled.[52] In their capacity as family consumers, the Housewives Committees of the MPF took on the practical responsibility for monitoring prices. In Marseille, for example, women informers would research prices in their neighborhoods and report back to the committees.[53] The MPF journal printed a story about a milk seller in the Nord who had been selling at above the fixed price. He had been unwilling to tell his milk producers that they must lower their prices until being confronted by the local Committee for Market Stabilization. The committee warned him, and then informed the MPF's women's committees, as well as the women of the UFF, to make sure the seller respected the set prices.[54] By such actions, the consumer groups gave women the chance to be involved in public and political action based on their everyday concerns.

The same decree making the commissions mandatory also allowed for the creation of pilot stores that received priority in provision of certain products in exchange for advertising and honoring fixed prices.[55] In February 1947, the prefect of the Allier informed the national government that the commissions in his region had begun to function, and that he had already instituted two closures of two months duration to stores that had violated the *baisse de 5 pour cent* or other price regulations.[56] The prefect in the Ariège reported the creation of nine commissions in his region; the prefect in the Aude reported ten new commissions in one week; and the prefect in Belfort reported thirteen in his department.[57] The commissions appeared to receive an enthusiastic response from the public and from stores applying for the designation "pilot store," though several prefects reported anger from sellers afraid to buy stocks at one price in fear that another *baisse* would follow, and from peasants forced to sell their produce after a *baisse* had been instituted.[58] Indeed, *Le Monde* reported that in December 1946, peasants near Clermont-Ferrand had attacked a Committee for Market Stabilization with sticks, seriously injuring one

[52] "Les Commissions d'assainissement du marché," *Monde Ouvrier* 34 (1947): 2.
[53] "À la Commission municipale de l'assainissement," *Le Provençal*, February 17–18, 1947.
[54] "Le Comité d'assainissement les fait appliquer les 5%," *Monde Ouvrier* 37 (1947): 1.
[55] "Création de Commissions d'assainissement des marches et de 'magasin-témoins'," *Marseillaise*, January 2, 1947. Although the direct translation of "magasin-témoins" would be "witnessing store," I have used "pilot store" because it more accurately reflects the designation.
[56] Secrétariat générale du gouvernement et Services du Première Ministre, letters from Préfets to Monsieur le Président du gouvernement, 1947. AN F 60 674.
[57] Ibid.
[58] Ibid.

man, who only escaped the village under police escort.[59] Not everyone approved of efforts to enforce low produce prices. UFF members who participated in the committees reported recriminations even from other housewives, who resented being told not to buy meat at above the official price when there was none available at that price.[60]

Nevertheless, mobilizing consumers, and housewives in particular, to monitor prices and restrain inflation remained an objective of the government, press, and women's and family groups throughout the years of inflation at the end of the 1940s and early 1950s. Those who asked consumers to use their influence were calling on them to exercise a kind of economic citizenship rather than remaining passive victims of inflation. An Angers newspaper told women "Don't buy just anything!" but to join in "UNITY, DISCIPLINE. Only patronize the stores that sell quality goods at the lowest prices."[61] "Take care of your money!" instructed *Le Monde*, adding, "don't lessen the value of your work by buying anything at any price."[62] Presumably, buying quality goods as cheaply as possible would help keep inflation in check whether prices were controlled or not.

Administrations changed rapidly, as did policies on price, but the call for consumers to control prices could be used both for monitoring fixed prices and for directing consumers to the cheapest sellers of liberalized products as well.[63] When free-market conservative Antoine Pinay became premier and minister of finance in 1952, he launched the battle for the "Defense of the Franc," stating that ending inflation was necessary to build confidence in the government both inside and outside of France.[64] Pinay summoned retailers, butchers, hairdressers, and other business

---

[59] "Des paysans du Puy-de-Dôme attaquent à coups de bâton les membres de la Commission d'assainissement des prix," *Le Monde*, December 6, 1946.

[60] Sandra Fayolle, "L'Union des femmes françaises: Une organisation féminine de masse du parti communiste français, 1945–1965" (Thèse de doctorat, Université Paris I, 2005), 236. Fayolle notes that anger from other housewives and small shopkeepers led the UFF to step back from the commissions; in their efforts to build a mass movement they did not want to risk alienating segments of the population.

[61] "Halte à la hausse: Consommateurs! Commerçants ! Unissez-vous contre la vie chère," *Courrier de l'Ouest*, March 13–14, 1948.

[62] "Prenez soin de votre argent! ..." *Le Monde*, October 6–7, 1946.

[63] From 1944 to 1958, France had twenty-five different governments, each lasting an average of seven months. Jobs, *Riding the New Wave*, 40.

[64] The president of the council, or premier, was the prime minister in the governmental structure of the Fourth Republic. Le discours du président du conseil au banquet des indépendants, March 20, 1952. Le Centre des archives économiques et financières (CAEF) record B 17663.

people to the Hotel Matignon to ask them to reduce their prices. Tags labeled "Defense of the Franc" marked products whose prices had been reduced, directing consumers to cheaper goods. Pinay called himself "Mr. Consumer" and asserted that good sense and the spirit of saving could rescue the French economy. His commonsense approach to ending inflation, which he publicized with modern marketing tools, won him surprising popularity compared to other politicians of the Fourth Republic, particularly among women.[65] *Paris-Match* magazine reported in 1952 that "the new President of the Council has given the impression that he governs not for deputies, but for housewives." As *Paris-Match* explained, the public was inspired by the belief that it was "engaging directly in action, taking part, basically, in its own history."[66] A counterinterpretation was offered by the UFF, which asserted that Pinay was basically saying, "If prices are too high it's your own fault. You don't know how to shop."[67] Calling on consumers to monitor prices and halt inflation was a means of empowering women, but it also implied that if prices did not come down, it was due to poor decision-making by those same rational consumers. Commentators commonly argued that the experience of war and scarcity had robbed women of their consumer skills, and that they had to be retrained to shop wisely.

As Pinay was directing his battle against inflation, women's and family organizations were asserting that while government, industry, unions, and shopkeepers all claimed to want to lower prices, and while productivity had risen to levels that made a drop in prices possible, it was chiefly the role of women consumers to lower prices by monitoring them and shopping wisely.[68] Asking whether women truly understood their national responsibilities as consumers, the UFCS noted, "The war perturbed the economic market. The weakening of the franc, on the one hand, the scarcity of products, on the other hand, have raised prices and created the arbitrary power of the seller. The consumer has lost all of her critical sense; she has gotten into the habit of buying anything at any price, and the result is an apparently incurable apathy."[69] The UFCS called on

[65] See Giles, *The Locust Years*, 162–163 and Rioux, *The Fourth Republic*, 196–201 for information on Pinay's economic policies.

[66] "Le Président Pinay part en guerre contre la vie chère," *Paris-Match* 158 (1952): 11. In CAEF record B 17663.

[67] "Pour une véritable baisse des prix pour une vie meilleure. Notre action contre le gouvernement de misère et de guerre de M. Pinay," *La vie de l'Union des femmes françaises* 24 (1952): 10.

[68] "Femmes: Faisons baisser le coût de la vie," *Notre journal* 243 (1952): 1.

[69] "Dans l'économie nationale: la femme consommatrice," *Notre journal* 236 (1951): 2.

mothers to unite through their organizations to stabilize the national economy, helping strengthen their family economies at the same time.

As inflation continued through the early 1950s, the UFCS enthusiastically embraced the important task of directing the economy through domestic consumption, dedicating itself to forming "good buyers" who would provide for their families and the nation through wise purchases. A good buyer was competent in judging quality and price and creating a hierarchy of human needs.[70] The UFCS argued that if all the French were good buyers there would be less money spent on alcohol and more for reconstruction, less money spent on the production of automobiles and more on the modernization of rural homes.[71] The UFCS launched consumer campaigns, created Buyer's Commissions in cities across France, and held annual informational congresses called the "Days of the Good Buyer."[72] Along with participating on these committees, individual women and mothers were responsible for controlling prices through wise purchases. The UFCS maintained that three-quarters of national revenue flowed through women's hands. Therefore, women could control prices by buying cheaper products, and they could help orient production toward family needs through their demand for consumer goods.[73]

The UFCS encouraged local committees to take action, and publicized their efforts. In 1954, they reported on the success of a group of consumers in Marseille. After the decree of August 8, 1953 eliminating price impositions, the women had dedicated themselves to monitoring prices. The group began by identifying certain products to follow closely. They found differences in prices according to which part of the city the products were sold in; Nescafe, for example, ranged from 238 to 285 francs. The commission then publicized the prices for the benefit of other shoppers.[74] In Dinan, the UFCS was congratulated by the subprefect for studying the evolution of the market across France and indicating the just price for basic necessities. In Lyon, the prefect organized a "Committee for the Defense of the Franc" that, using information provided in part by the UFCS, created a family budget and a list of just prices for goods

[70] "Les acheteuses et les problèmes de la consommation," *La femme dans la vie sociale* 264 (1954): 1.

[71] Ibid., 1.

[72] In 1956, *La femme dans la vie sociale* reported that *Journées de la Bonne Acheteuse* had been held in Marseille, Versailles, Lille, Toulon, Toulouse, Grenoble, Nancy, Nantes, Dole, Clichy, Melun, and Annecy, among other locations. From "La Bonne Acheteuse à Toulouse: Les secrets d'une résulte," *La femme dans la vie sociale* 274 (1956): 4.

[73] "Les acheteuses…" *La femme dans la vie sociale* 264 (1954): 1–4.

[74] "Avec les commissions des acheteuses," *La femme dans la vie sociale* 261 (1954): 2.

that were then monitored by the women. At Vitry-le-François, the UFCS set up a permanent base near the market indicating the lowest prices available for certain goods. In Paris, they published a tract with the same information, and the prefect of the Mulhouse joined the effort by hiring a man to circulate through the market wearing a sandwich sign indicating just prices. The UFCS spoke to shoppers over Radio France, and the *secrétariat national* reported that several industrial sectors indicated a drop in prices in response to the women's efforts.[75]

The UFCS and the MPF, both of which pre-existed the postwar consumer turn, began to orient themselves more toward consumer needs because of the hardship of the immediate postwar period, the inflation of the late 1940s and early 1950s, the new attention to consumer demand by industries and planners, and the example of consumer societies abroad. They were not organizations created explicitly for consumers or consumer issues, but rather saw these issues as natural extensions of their larger projects. The first explicitly consumerist group was formed in 1951, when government officials concerned with productivity attempted to harness grassroots efforts to organize consumers by creating the *Union fédérale de la consommation* (Federal Union of Consumption, UFC). This was a new kind of consumer organization. The UFC wanted to strengthen price-control efforts and support family, women's, and labor groups in empowering their members through consumption, but it was primarily concerned with increasing productivity and helping the French economy expand. The UFC was meant to aid consumer organizations, but also to educate consumers about their responsibilities in the national economy. For state planners, organizations like the UFC were valuable because they could both provide information about and direct consumer demand, which would result in increased productivity and decreased waste. This kind of organization perfectly suited the goals of the *Plan de modernisation et d'équipement*, whose "modernization commissions" included representatives from all sectors of the economy in an attempt to be representative, consensual, and efficient.[76]

The UFC wanted to create connections between groups and persons intent on helping consumers "take their position in economic life and

---

[75] Dhellemmes, Marg, "Acheteuses: Notre Action," *Notre journal: La femme dans la vie sociale* 244 (1952): 1. The cooperation between the prefect and the UFCS in Lyon was part of a "pilot project" and was publicized in many venues, leading to the claim that Lyon was the "cheapest city in France." On Lyon, see Doneaud and Guérin, *Les femmes agissent*, 120.

[76] For information on this kind of economic planning, see Kuisel, *Capitalism and the State*.

participate, through their actions, in increasing productivity as a means of raising the standard of living."[77] The basic philosophy underlying the UFC was that consumers needed to take an active role in the economy, and that production would grow if industry and government adapted their goals to meet consumer demand. The president of the UFC, André Romieu, was head of the Group for Distribution and Consumption at the *Commissariat à la productivité*, and was motivated by what sociologist Louis Pinto has called "a technocratic variant of economic humanism."[78] The organization grouped together representatives of women's and family groups, unions, and government representatives to share information and teach the French public how to consume wisely.[79] The goal of this kind of consumer organization was not as much to defend consumers in their adversarial relations with producers or sellers, as to help all of these forces cooperate in the joint goal of raising productivity. As Romieu said in 1955, "With the same 1,000 F bill a consumer could buy 1,500 or 500 F worth of services, depending on whether he buys well or buys poorly. Researching in his own best interest, in that circumstance, serves the general interest because his net gain benefits the entire economy."[80] UFC publications contained information on consumer issues like safety labeling, the use of credit, and new household technologies, and consistently stressed the important role of the housewife in orienting national production. The organization began by publishing a bulletin for cooperating groups, but soon turned to publishing pamphlets with advice on buying complicated products (such as home appliances) and issues of interest (such as credit) to the general public.[81] The UFC received funding from the *Fonds national de productivité* and consulted with government-supported research groups as well as receiving consultation

---

[77] Union fédérale de la consommation, *Constitution* ... March 1955. Dossiers de presse, Bibliothèque de Sciences Po, La consommation en France, code 582.

[78] Louis Pinto, "Le consommateur: Agent économique et acteur politique," *Revue française de sociologie* 31 (1990): 191. Pinto also explains this sentiment as being a reconciliation of the "capitalist marketplace and humanism." Ibid., 192.

[79] See Paul Maquenne, "Un fait économique nouveau: Les consommateurs s'organisent," *L'Actualité Fiduciaire* 261 (1954), 114–119, Comité national de la consommation, "1945, Une prise de conscience," *Un monde en mouvement: Les organisations de consommateurs* (Paris: Ministère de l'économie et des finances et le Comité national de la consommation, 1975), François Daujam, "Information et pouvoir des consommateurs : Le rôle de l'Union fédérale des consommateurs" (Thèse, Université des Sciences Sociales de Toulouse, 1980), and Régis Boulat, 98–114.

[80] André Romieu, Conférence de presse du 4 février 1955.

[81] See Maquenne for more information.

from professional associations and organizations that created quality standards for consumer products.[82]

This cooperation among consumers, government, and producers was suited to the productivity drives and attempts to expand the economy of the postwar period. It was a step in the creation of the "market community" that benefited consumers, but was not aimed primarily at defending their particular interests. It intended, rather, to enrich them individually by providing them with cheap, high-quality goods in a highly productive economy. Unlike the consumer cooperatives that thrived in the early part of the twentieth century, the UFC and its member movements, at least at this stage of their development, worked within the capitalist marketplace, hoping to create more efficient systems of distribution and orient production toward consumer need, thereby decreasing waste. Although the goal was answering consumer need, this was obtained by disciplining consumers, helping them learn to purchase more efficiently, and encouraging them to inform producers of their needs. As a representative of the secretary of state for economic affairs noted at a UFC "Day of the Consumer" at the *Salon des arts ménagers*, consumers had the tendency, through an "ignorance" that was a natural aftermath of a period of scarcity, to buy the most expensive products, believing they were of the highest quality. The consumer needed to learn "to appreciate the quality of the products he was buying."[83] Buying the cheapest article, considering that it was of the requisite quality, was the way to strengthen the economy. A good example of the desire to smooth out circuits of distribution through consumer-commerce cooperation was the *Conseils de clienteles* that involved major department stores and women's organizations, including the UFCS, and whose activities were celebrated by the UFC. Made up of women consumers, the *conseils* would advise store management on the selection of products, advertising, and the organization of the stores themselves. Some stores had women take products home, use them, and report on their quality. Along with receiving this

[82] In 1955, the UFC reported that seventy percent of its costs were funded by the *Fonds national de productivité*. For this and information on the activities of that year, see Union fédérale de la consommation, Rapport du Conseil à l'Assemblée Générale du 26 AVRIL 1955, April 12, 1955. Dossiers de presse, Bibliothèque de Sciences Po, La consommation en France, code France 582.

[83] "Le troisième Journée du consommateur au Salon des arts ménagers," *Union fédérale de la consommation: Bulletin de l'information* 21 (1954), 3. In many of these texts, I use the "neutral" pronoun "he" in keeping with the original text, even though speakers also almost always asserted that the most important consumers were housewives.

marketing information from women, the stores benefitted by then advertising the products as "Recommended by the *Conseil de clientele*."[84] The
UFC and UFCS also cooperated in a *Commissariat générale à la productivité* visit to a shoe factory in 1954. The women of the UFCS advised the
company on their tastes in shoes in hopes that the company could reduce
the number of styles manufactured, increasing productivity, and, presumably, passing reduced costs on to the consumer.[85]

Thus, the image of the woman as citizen consumer, as well as the
belief that consumers influenced the market and could help raise productivity in the national economy, was shared by women's, family, and
consumer organizations and the French government. Consumer organization was fostered by the confluence of women and families who had
experienced years of poverty with a dearth of consumer durables and a
government-led productivity drive intended to restore national prosperity and prestige. Consumer groups were in their nascent stages, and only
achieved impressive membership numbers in the 1970s and 1980s, but
they were growing over the course of the 1950s and 1960s. During this
period, however, this was not a mass-mobilization of individuals as consumers, but government sponsored attempts to integrate consumers into
the "market community." The UFC focused its efforts primarily on consumer education and information – which meant, in large part, teaching
women to make intelligent and informed purchases.[86] This was especially
important as the governments of the Fourth and Fifth Republics continued to place more emphasis on the economic role of consumer demand.
One of the reforms included in the first Plan was the creation of a new
statistical apparatus for France. The SEEF, INED, and INSEE all helped
to provide sociological, economical, and psychological information on
French consumers. The lack of state information on demand and distribution was identified as one of the weaknesses of the prewar economy,
and measuring, categorizing, and describing the French population was
deemed necessary for raising productivity and expanding the economy.
In 1953, the *Commissariat générale à la productivité* spurred the creation

[84] Ibid., 26–28.
[85] Irène Mançaux, "A propos de chaussures," *La femme dans la vie sociale* 261 (1954), 4.
[86] See Gunnar Trumbull, "Strategies of Consumer-Group Mobilization: France and
Germany in the 1970s," in *The Politics of Consumption: Material Culture and Citizenship
in Europe and America*, eds. Martin Daunton and Matthew Hilton (Oxford: Berg
Publishers, 2001), 261–282, for discussion of the height of consumer group mobilization
in France. In 1974 *Union fédérale des consommateurs* (formerly *Union fédérale de la
consommation*) membership reached 240,000. See François Daujam, "Information et
pouvoir des consommateurs," 21.

of CREDOC to study changes in demand by product and socioprofessional population group, to analyze the comportment of consumers, to make predictions about demand, and to develop methodologies for market research. In 1956, the commissariat commissioned the first national study on household budgets in France.[87]

The analysis of demand was a hallmark of the American consumer economy, and in 1952 representatives of the UFCS, UFC, and domestic science education traveled to the United States on a Marshall Plan Mission for the Study of Consumption.[88] The mission was led by UFC president André Romieu and when it returned, its members reported on the importance of market research in the United States, the need to orient production toward consumer demand, and the imperative of creating liaisons among producers, consumers, and sellers. The belief that cooperation, not opposition, was key to success in the American economy was clear in the suggestion that advertizing was part of an effort to "give the consumer what he wants" by presenting pleasant products easy to choose, hold, and carry.[89] Romieu's conclusions emphasized the attitudes that underlay American commercial success, including "a spirit of initiative among all participants in the market, including the consumer, the care to plan, the constant awakening of inventiveness, faith in competition as a factor in progress." All of these were part of recognizing "the principal that the consumer, in exercising his free and informed preference, shapes economic progress (that which is clear in the popular expression *'to vote with dollar'*), which appears to be the natural complement to a true political democracy."[90] Romieu's comments emphasized both the responsibilities of consumer citizenship and the importance of cooperation as a means of increasing productivity.

In 1957, the French economy reached a critical turning point when Western European governments signed the Treaty of Rome, creating the Common Market. In preparation for the changes the treaty entailed, the government of the new Fifth Republic charged Jacques Rueff and Louis Armand with the task of determining "the obstacles to economic

---

[87] "Avis et rapports du Conseil Économique et Social, Session de 1963. Séance du 7 mai 1963. Etude des statistiques de la consommation. Rapport présenté au nom du Conseil Économique et Social, par. M. Pierre Laguionie," *Journal Officiel de la République Française* année 1963, no. 10 (1963): 383.

[88] See *Union fédérale de la consommation: Bulletin d'information*, supplement concerning the organization of CREDOC, 19 (1954), 1.

[89] Centre d'études du commerce, *Commerce et consommation aux États-Unis* (Paris: Centre d'études du commerce, 1952), 5

[90] Ibid., 16.

expansion" still facing France. Basing their work on the assumption that economic expansion and heightened productivity would bring a better standard of living to all, in 1960 the ministers identified the obstacles that still hindered French economic progress, and outlined recommendations for their removal. According to the report, the economy was handicapped by a series of problems including an inability to adapt industrial supply to demand, a lack of information on consumer demand, fraud, and the failure of the French consumer to understand his or her role in the French economy.[91] Many of these problems fell within the purview of consumer organizations and the report urged the government to "give a moral or material support ... to representative and efficacious [consumer] groups," to encourage consumer information, and to "assure these groups of their participation in all organizations whose work includes issues of interest to consumers."[92]

To remedy the continuing dearth of consumer information, the minister of economy created the *Comité national de la consommation* (National Committee of Consumption, CNC), to study demand and increase consumer power. The decree of December 19, 1960 stated that the CNC's goal was "the permanent confrontation of public representatives and representatives of the collective interests of consumers for all problems concerned with consumption."[93] The secretary of state of interior commerce presided over a council made up of representatives of nine government ministries and nine consumer organizations. The UFCS, a successor to the MPF, and many other women's and family organizations were prominent among these. The minutes of the first meeting of the CNC highlight the belief that the citizen consumer had not yet learned to fill his or her position in the economy. The "'client-king' is less and less able to fill his role, because of the new conditions of the economy. While production and distribution have become collective operations, elaborate and organized, the act of consumption remains an individual act, subject to all sorts of risks, and sometimes even caprice," noted Secretary of State of Interior Commerce Joseph Fontanet. He cited the new complexity of modern

[91] See *Les conclusions du comité Armand-Rueff*, texte de la conférence faite au 21e diner d'information du C.E.P.E.C. le 25 octobre 1960 (Paris: Centre d'études politiques et civiques, 1960) and Rapport sur les obstacles à l'expansion économique, présenté par le comité institué par le décret n. 59–1284 du 13 novembre 1959 (Paris, 1960), 1–36. CAEF record B 55366.
[92] Rapport sur les obstacles, 68.
[93] Décret n. 60–1390 du 19 Décembre 1960 portant création d'un Comité national de la consommation. CAEF record B 55872.

products, and the conditions of modern life that led the consumer, in particular the housewife, to have less time in which to make her purchases.[94]

One of the major roles of the consumer organizations in the CNC was to educate the public, and the council created a subgroup on "information" that produced, among other things, educational material for teachers, and radio and television broadcasts for the general public. This committee advised consumers on issues such as quality and labeling, the informed use of consumer credit, and the threat of door-to-door salesmen.[95] Although helping consumers to rationalize their purchases was one of the tasks of the CNC, the subgroup that perhaps most directly responded to the concerns of the Armand-Rueff report was the one working on the role of consumers in the *Plan de modernisation et d'équipement*. The CNC was created in part to empower consumers by informing and organizing them, but the consumer organizations in the CNC were most useful to national planners through their ability to inform government and industry of consumer demand, and therefore increase productivity and avoid spoilage.[96]

Consumer groups were to provide their expert opinions on what consumers needed in order to help the government set production goals for each sector of the economy. In addition, the groups were to help consumers to play a more efficient role in the economy by "helping them better perform their role as buyers" – which in theory would strengthen both individual consumers and the national economy.[97] Though not contradictory, these various objectives created tension between consumer groups and government planners. Too often, the government set the agenda and consumer organizations had to remind ministerial representatives that consumers wanted to profit from the relationship as well. In his report concerning the creation of the fifth Plan, the reporter for the subgroup on consumption also objected to the fact that consumer groups had been consulted too little and too late in the construction of the fourth Plan, leaving producers too much power in determining consumer "needs." Claude Quin argued, "This procedure is not only illogical nor merely out of line with the goals expressed in the plan. The

[94] Procès-verbal de la réunion inaugural du Comité le 13 Février 1961. February 16, 1961. CAEF record B 55872.
[95] Comite national de la consommation/Secrétariat général, Etat des travaux du comité, June 1965. CAEF record B 55872.
[96] Comité national de la consommation. Exposé des motifs. 19 Décembre 1960, 1. CAEF record B 55872.
[97] Ibid., 2.

preoccupations of consumers – to have their needs better served, to be better protected, to be better informed – should inspire the construction of the plan in its entirety and to orient essential decisions. That is the only way, in our opinion, to respond to the needs of the greatest part of the population." Quin pointed out that the philosophy behind the Plan was to create priorities in line with social need, and that with producers in charge, "there is a real danger of seeing the stimulation of artificial, secondary, needs while fundamental needs are left unsatisfied."[98] Quin's statement reveals both the belief that ordinary consumers were vulnerable to negative influence without the aid of consumer organizations, and the conviction that consumer organizations were not fully benefiting from the formation of the CNC. It also undermined the assertion that all parties benefitted from producer-distributer-consumer cooperation in the "market community."

The "market community" may have increased productivity, but it did so by disciplining consumers and measuring their desires, not necessarily by giving them a strong voice in economic change, as Romieu advocated. Hindered by the subordinate role granted consumer organizations in the Plan, the CNC also lacked the grassroots level influence that individual women could find through demonstrations and price monitoring. In the rhetoric of the organization, "consumers" consisted of a mass of undifferentiated buyers whose individual decisions shaped the national economy, an image that was less militant than that of angry women staring down shopkeepers and public officials. While women representatives of the UFCS and other groups sat on the CNC, they were outnumbered by men and their role came to be one of providing information and educating other women to protect themselves and their families through safe and rational consumer decisions. Furthermore, while the economic importance of consumer demand continued to increase, the explicitly political tone of discussions about women's consumer needs and demands faded as the issue of women's suffrage faded from prominence in national discourse.

In 1967, the CNC created an organization called the *Institut national de la consommation* (National Institute of Consumption, INC), in which consumer groups had a majority influence, to provide more assistance

---

[98] Comité national de la consommation/Secrétariat général, Exposé présenté par M. Claude Quin, rapporteur de la sous-commission "consommation" de la commission du commerce du 5ème Plan à la réunion du groupe du 24 Janvier 1967. CAEF record B 55872.

and information to consumer organizations and the public, in particular through research and product comparisons.[99] Cooperation among consumers, producers, and the state, however, was clearly a feature of the period of productivity drives and reconstruction following the war, and by the mid-1960s consumers were seeking the more confrontational organizations that would result in the boom in consumer organization of the 1970s. The INC was hampered by its association with the state and would not gain a mass following. In 1969, just after the INC's formation, the UFC reported that "despite the promises that have been made to us, it [the INC] has oriented itself more and more toward activities like our own, rather than being the support for us that we expected."[100] The UFC was in the throes of change, as was the consumer movement in general, after 1968. As Louis Pinto has pointed out, the importance of the politics of everyday life expressed in the events of 1968 made consumerism an attractive issue around which to mobilize, but in a different way and for different reasons than the efforts of the late 1940s and 1950s. The UFC went on to greatly expand its membership after 1968, but by breaking its links to the government, dropping the notion of collaboration in the "market community," and becoming more militant and confrontational. In 1970, the UFC changed the formula of its journal *Que choisir?* to appeal to a wider readership and in 1972, it broke with the INC.[101] Some of the goals of the early UFC, the CNC, and the INC appear naïve in their attempts to harness the aspirations of government planners, consumers, and industry in raising productivity. Despite their weaknesses, the organizations were an attempt by the French government to include the voices of consumers in production decisions, and a recognition of the power of

[99] Ministère des finances et des affaires économiques, Direction générale du commerce intérieur et des prix, Travaux préparatoires à la constitution de l'Institut national de la consommation. Réunion du 7 décembre 1965. CAEF record B 55873. The INC was created by the Décret no. 67–1082 du 5 décembre 1967 fixant l'organisation et le fonctionnement de l'Institut national de la consommation. CAEF record B 55873. According to the decree, twelve of the twenty-three seats on the administrative council went to representatives of consumers and five went to representatives of the government.

[100] UFC, "Rapport du conseil d'administration à l'assemblée générale du 28 mai 1969," 1. Centre des archives contemporaines de Fontainebleau (hereafter, CAC) 19850023 article 64.

[101] See Alain Chatriot, "Qui défend le consommateur? Associations, institutions et politiques publiques en France (1972–2003)," in *Au nom du consommateur*, 165–181. For information on the change following 1968, see Pinto, "Le consommateur." Gunnar Trumbull emphasizes the militant nature of consumer organization in France in the 1970s in "Strategies of Consumer-Group Mobilization." This was the height of consumer group mobilization in France.

the consumer in the modern French economy – a power women's and family organizations had been asserting since the end of the war.

Whether interested in their own profit margins, the future of the French economy, the living conditions of the working-class family, or the social and civic duties of women, institutions and individuals across France recognized the power and value of female consumers in the postwar period. The rhetoric linking consumer activities and national, class, and family responsibilities helped to create the identity of the consumer for the nation. This identity balanced traditional roles with new rights at a time when consumers were recognized as having an important role in the economy, but the future of France seemed predicated on the maintenance of the traditional French family. This citizen consumer role was suited to an emerging mass consumer society, as, on the one hand, women's, family, and consumer organizations demanded increased production of the goods that could make families more comfortable, and, on the other hand, state planners and manufacturers sought to increase productivity through determining consumer demand. Women were the consumers of the nation. As a professor of economics informed women at a "Day of the Good Buyer," "Your force is the money that passes through your hands. If you are conscious of this force, it will no longer be the producers who direct this nation's economy; it will be you, Mesdames!"[102]

---

[102] "Les journées de la bonne acheteuse," *Union fédérale de la consommation: Bulletin de l'information* 30 (1955): 14.

2

The Productivity Drive in the Home
and Gaining Comfort on Credit

In October 1957, the journal of the *Union national des caisses d'allocations familiales* (UNCAF), the network of organizations that distributed family welfare funds in France, published an article on the economic value of housework. In order to demonstrate how a housewife's competence and knowledge could influence both family life and national revenue, the author described the *technique ménagère* of Mme L, a housewife with four young children. Mme L, "was aware that her work enriched her home and benefitted society in the same way that it would were she to exercise a professional occupation." She created a relaxing environment with regular meal and sleeping times that kept her loved ones healthy, sparing both her family and the nation the cost of medical care, and ensuring that those old enough to work were not weakening production by depriving the nation of their labor. Mme L's purchases "affected the sector of production" and she disciplined producers by choosing the most essential and highest quality foods, and oriented production toward cheap, modern goods through her furniture purchases.[1]

Mme L was certainly productive, but the author went on to explain how much more productive housework could be with access to a washing machine, a vacuum, an electric floor polisher, and a rationally constructed kitchen. These would allow women to do more work in less time and to achieve better results. With the time that machines saved, "women could dedicate more time to another productive task." Women could increase their own personal productivity, while at the same time the

[1] Mme L. Vimeux, "La valeur économique du travail ménager," *Informations Sociales* 11 (1957): 995–997.

spread of appliances would "further the development of a new industry that could itself enrich the nation," and the competence of consumers in this domain could, "favor the producers of quality machines at the lowest price." The author pointed out how important housework was to the national economy, how important an education in housewifery was for becoming as productive as Mme L, and, further, that it was only just that women be provided with "housing and household equipment appropriate for our century, at an affordable price."[2] The author showed that women influenced productivity and the national economy not just at the point of purchase, but in all of the tasks they performed in the home. To assert that modernizing the home was as important as modernizing industry, she drew on the discourse of productivity so important in postwar France.

Although postwar consumer organization had begun around subsistence issues, by the mid-1950s the French public was increasingly demanding access to consumer durables, modern homes, and a higher standard of living. For consumer and family advocates, home economics experts, modernizers, and planners, the way to raise the standard of living was to create a mass consumer economy in which serialized production made cheap, quality goods available to a wide sector of the population. Unfortunately, consumer goods were not a priority of the first Plan, and while they were incorporated into the second Plan, launched in 1954, they remained prohibitively expensive for much of the French population.[3] The economy thus lacked a broad base of affluent consumers that would drive mass production and lower prices.

This chapter reveals how, in order to change these circumstances, family, women's, and consumer advocates adopted the rhetoric of planners and modernizers intent on raising productivity, employing the language that had heretofore been used to describe the business world to the domestic sphere. They identified consumer credit as an important means of increasing home productivity, posing a challenge to French notions of thrift and responsibility. State modernizers shared the goal of creating a mass consumer society, and understood that the widespread use of credit was necessary for creating this kind of economy. To make credit respectable, however, credit's advocates had to reconcile its use with

[2] Ibid., 998–999.
[3] In 1955, a study conducted by representatives of the Plan and of industries among urban families found that for many, buying a home appliance would require one or two years of saving. It also found that 37 percent of the families included would buy items currently unaffordable if they could use credit. *Enquête sur les tendances*, 67–69.

long-standing French values that dictated that credit was wasteful and destructive.[4] An important issue in this debate was the rational capability of the French consumer: Was the French housewife a citizen consumer like Mme L, who would make wise purchases, increasing productivity in her own home while at the same time strengthening the French economy, spurring production, and lowering prices? Or was the French housewife an irrational spender who would drive her own family into poverty while at the same time contributing to the ever-present inflation in the postwar economy? Planners, modernizers, and women's, family, and consumer representatives colluded in encouraging the "rational" development of credit and educating, shaping, and informing the domestic consumer. This work was done primarily in the mid- and late 1950s, as specialized credit organisms spread, the state created new regulations for credit, and demand for consumer durables grew.

For women's, family, and consumer representatives, encouraging pro-ductivity in the home was not only necessary for expanding the economy, but for valorizing the work that the housewife and mother did in her own home. These advocates defined the home as an important workspace in the French economy and argued that only consumer credit would make it possible to modernize the home and thereby strengthen the national and domestic economies. They touted credit as the "modern form of sav-ing" and argued that home technology was a practical capital investment. Citizen consumers acting in the marketplace had already been pulled into the postwar productivity agenda; now, their work in the home was incorporated into the same agenda. These advocates both celebrated and infantilized housewives, stressing the productive nature of housework, but insisting that many women lacked the education necessary to run a modern household effectively. This continued the gendering of citizen-ship important since the Liberation by at once stressing women's national influence and avoiding a challenge to the gendered structure of home, marketplace, or polity. Furthermore, these advocates helped to create new definitions of necessity by arguing that all French families deserved to live in modern homes with consumer durables – something that could only come about through the creation of a society of mass consumption.

---

[4] Michel Wildt argues that German consumers held to the idea that buying on credit was inadvisable even while they expanded their use of credit in the 1950s. See "Continuities and Discontinuities of Consumer Mentality in West Germany in the 1950s," in *Life after Death: Approaches to a Cultural and Social History of Europe during the 1940s and 1950s*, eds. Richard Bessel and Dirk Schumann (Cambridge: Cambridge University Press, 2003), 211–229.

PRODUCTIVITY IN THE HOME

Rationalizing the home, and women's work in it, was not an entirely new idea in post–Second World War France. Paulette Bernège was the principal French promoter of what was called "Taylorism" in the home in the 1920s and 1930s. Believing that housewives could be a force for modernization and progress, she published her *De la méthode ménagère* in 1928 and created an institute for domestic science in Paris in 1930.[5] Advertisements encouraged women to find fulfillment in the modern home and portrayed technologically assisted housework as acceptable for "respectable" women who were forced to do without domestic servants.[6] At the time, however, the insistence of experts like Bernège that the modern housewife needed a vacuum, washing machine, and other consumer durables was entirely unrealistic for all but the smallest minority of French families.[7] Further, the few families that could afford these items were unenthusiastic consumers of mass-produced goods – a fact that would change in the late 1940s and the 1950s.[8]

A number of factors led to a change in standards following the Second World War, including the commencement of the productivity drives encouraged both by French planners and Marshall Plan officials and the recognition that the same arguments used for industrial modernization could be applied to the home. The awareness of better living conditions in the United States, with its mass consumer economy; the proposed construction of millions of new French homes; and a prominent national discourse on modernization, productivity, and technology created a rapid change in perceptions of "adequate" living conditions in the late 1940s

[5] The French term for housewifery education is "enseignement ménagère" which translates roughly as "homemaker's education." I often use the terms "domestic science" and "home economics" in place of this, since they are current in English language usage. For more on Bernège's philosophy and pedagogy, see Jackie Clarke, "L'organisation ménagère comme pédagogie: Paulette Bernège et la formation d'une nouvelle classe moyenne dans les années 1930 et 1940," *Travail, genre, et sociétés* 13 (2005): 139–156; and Jackie Clarke, "Homecomings: Paulette Bernège, Scientific Management and the Return to the Land in Vichy France," in *Vichy, Resistance, and Liberation: New Perspectives on Wartime France*, eds. Simon Kitson and Hanna Diamond (Oxford: Berg, 2005), 171–182.

[6] Adam C. Stanley, *Modernizing Tradition: Gender and Consumerism in Interwar France and Germany* (Baton Rouge: Louisiana State University Press, 2008). Stanley argues that this discourse was also meant to encourage women to stay out of the workforce, and that these images were similar in both France and Germany.

[7] See Martine Martin, "Ménagère: Une profession? Les dilemmes de l'entre-deux-guerres," *Le Mouvement Social* 140 (1987): 89–106.

[8] See Robert Frost, "Machine Liberation."

and the 1950s. At the same time, the shortage of domestic servants, a weakening of bourgeois fortunes, and the widespread touting of appliances as modern and practical helped to break down elite resistance to mass-produced goods.[9] While the national modernization consensus drove attempts to rationalize industry, measure consumer demand, and increase productivity, women's, family, and consumer organizations insisted that the home could not be excluded from the modernization occurring in the rest of French society. Standards for women's work in the household that may have been regrettable, but normal, before the war, were met with outrage in the 1950s. That these standards were outrageous or unacceptable did not mean that they immediately disappeared, of course. Even in 1973 only 61 percent of French homes had hot running water, an indoor toilet, and a shower.[10] Despite the economic expansion of the postwar years, wages did not keep pace with inflation and the Plan's concentration on base industries left the prices of consumer durables high and delayed construction of new homes. A Fordist, or American-style consumer-driven economy in which workers make enough money to buy the goods they produce, was impossible under these conditions.

With "productivity" holding such an important place in national discourse, proponents of home modernization set about arguing for the importance of home productivity, the means of achieving it, and the place of the home in the national economy. They asserted that the domestic consumer was not only performing citizenship, or orienting the national economy, in the marketplace, but in all of the tasks she completed in the home. In the immediate aftermath of the war, with home appliances and modernization years away, women's and family groups demanded better food, clothing, and housing for families, and argued for the economic value of the housewife and domestic consumer during reconstruction. By the mid-1950s, as subsistence needs were assuaged, several groups

---

[9] When sociologist Marguerite Perrot studied bourgeois account books for the period 1873–1953, she found that the wages of domestic servants had risen so much during the first half of the twentieth century that a family at the beginning of the 1950s spent the same proportion of their budget on a single maid that a family in 1914 would spend on several; usually including a housekeeper, chamber maid, and cook. The housing crisis and food prices also made live-in help prohibitively expensive and the use of home appliances made housework more acceptable for wealthy women. *Le mode de vie des familles bourgeoises, 1873–1953* (Paris: Librairie Armand Colin, 1961), 137–139. See Chapter Four for discussion of class and mass consumer society.

[10] This was still a marked increase from the postwar years, when the percentage was 9. See Antoine Prost, "Public and Private Spheres in France," in *A History of Private Life*, Vol. V., by Antoine Prost and Gérard Vincent (Cambridge: Harvard University Press, 1991), 59.

focused on the importance of home modernization, rationalization, and appliances for the housewife's productivity. These included women's organizations such as the UFCS and domestic science experts, who hoped to valorize and professionalize women's work in the home, as well as other organizations either primarily interested in family living conditions or in national productivity, or both, like the UFC. They found common cause in the drive to modernize the home. Throughout the shifting economic contexts of the postwar decades, they emphasized the importance housework held for the national economy.

For many of the women's organizations who demanded home modernization, asserting the importance of productivity in the home was meant both to improve home conditions and to valorize women's work in the household. This valorization was intended to convince women to dedicate themselves to the home full-time, but also to convince the rest of society to provide the financial support to make that commitment possible. In the interwar period, the UFCS had advocated the family-wage, and in the postwar period they consistently asserted the need for more welfare benefits for women who did not work outside of the home. In the late 1940s and the 1950s, the UFCS both advocated women's social and national responsibilities and held that women best served their own families and society by leaving the workforce. As we have seen, the power that women wielded as consumers for the nation had political, social, and economic ramifications, but it could be exercised most effectively, in the view of the UFCS, by women primarily concerned with their responsibilities as wives and mothers. While the organization's claims for the economic value of women's work in the home were a continuation of interwar efforts, the UFCS now argued that the conditions of reconstruction made this work particularly important and arduous. In 1945, *Notre journal: La femme dans la vie sociale*, asked readers to respond to an inquiry about the economic value of women's household labor. "At a moment where France has called for the hard work of all of its children to increase its agricultural output, its industry, its production in all domains" *Notre journal* argued, it was important to show that this recovery would happen in two realms: in the professional world, and "in the family, in the home through the work of the wife and mother."[11]

The UFCS, like other women's, family, and consumer groups, maintained that women's work in the household economy, especially the important tasks of saving and making goods last longer, benefitted the

[11] "Ma femme vaut son pesant d'or, ou, la valeur économique de la mère au foyer," *Notre journal: La femme dans la vie sociale* 175 (1945): 5.

national economy during this time of austerity. Rational saving, as well as consuming, was a skill necessary for housewives. Responses to an inquiry asking families to calculate the economic value of women's labor arrived from across France, including both urban and rural areas. The budget and schedule of one of the farm women the journal featured demonstrates the heavy burden of housework, particularly in rural areas. The woman estimated that replacing her work would cost the family 2,825 francs a month. This included the fee for doing the laundry, on which she spent forty-five hours each month, caring for a household of twelve, including her immediate family, her parents, and three employees.[12] The UFCS stressed the heavy burden of this labor, but was ultimately most concerned with exhibiting its benefit to the rest of society. After describing the work of several other women, the journal stressed the important role of housewives in conserving precious amounts of food and clothing and in reducing the national cost of medical care through their healthy menus and proper care of family members.[13] The UFCS demanded that women who devoted themselves to the home be given, as soon as economic conditions permitted it, an allocation equal to 100 percent of the male worker's salary used to calculate child allowances for the social security system, and that any woman who had raised three children be given a pension by the organization responsible for her husband's pension.[14]

Productivity meant producing more, in less time, with less labor, and national studies of household labor revealed that in addition to being a heavy burden for women, housework was entirely unproductive because of poor housing conditions and a lack of modern equipment. Sociologists reinforced the claims of groups like the UFCS by quantifying and describing women's labor in the home. In 1947, Jean Stoetzel of the state's INED conducted a sociological study of the work done in the home by 1,795 married women in urban areas. The results were published in the journal *Population* in 1948 and were frequently cited in the late 1940s and the 1950s by those eager to modernize French homes.[15]

---

[12] Marguerite Dhellemmes, "Ma femme vaut son pesant d'or: Réponses à l'enquête," *Notre journal: La femme dans la vie sociale* 178 (1945): 4. For comparison's sake, the journal *Population* used in 1947, for the average monthly salary for a male manual laborer, 8,100 francs, and for his wife, 7,400 francs. Albert Michot, "Les conditions d'existence des familles: Comparaison des revenus et des besoins des familles modestes au 1èr Octobre 1947 suivant le nombre d'enfants," *Population* 4 (1947): 692.

[13] Ibid., 5.

[14] Ibid., 5.

[15] Jean Stoetzel, "Une étude du budget-temps time de la femme dans les agglomérations urbaines," *Population* 3 (1948): 47–62.

While acknowledging the problems in the study, including the fact that the researchers had asked very busy women to add to their daily work by keeping track of the amount of time it took them to do each of the day's tasks, Stoetzel drew some useful conclusions about the amount of time dispensed in running a household and caring for children. He calculated that a married woman with no children averaged just over fifty-seven hours of housework a week – a figure that rose by about five hours for each child, reaching almost seventy-six and a half hours for women with three or more children.[16]

Stoetzel's study included a smaller proportion of working-class families than did the general population, and urban ethnologist Paul-Henry Chombart de Lauwe's studies of working-class families in the Paris suburbs in the early 1950s found even longer work weeks. He found that 63 percent of the working-class women in his studies did housework for more than twelve hours per day, and 19 percent for more than fourteen hours. Some women, usually those with several children and no outside help, worked more than sixteen hours a day and one hundred hours a week.[17] Chombart de Lauwe blamed housing conditions for many of women's problems, noting that doing laundry, in particular, was laborious if one had to continually run up and down stairs to a tap in the courtyard. In 1946, only 37 percent of French homes had running water inside the house, and 18 percent still used a public pump or fountain. By 1954, almost 70 percent had running water in the home, but only about 13 percent had a shower or bathtub and 28 percent had a private, indoor toilet (36 percent had a private toilet near the house).[18] Advocates of home modernization quickly seized on these statistics, as well as those of

---

[16] Ibid., 54.

[17] Paul-Henry Chombart de Lauwe, *La vie quotidienne des familles ouvrières* (Paris: CNRS, 1956), 44. Chombart de Lauwe's scholarly efforts were influenced by his social Catholic beliefs. Chombart de Lauwe taught at the Uriage School early in the Vichy regime, but later joined the Free French in North Africa. After the war, he turned his attention to the urban poor. The aim of most of his scholarship, and public advocacy, was for national planners and architects to listen to the thoughts and desires of those who were eventually to inhabit their apartment complexes and for the poor to be empowered to change their own living situations. Some of Chombart de Lauwe's later work was done in collaboration with his wife Marie-José, who had close ties to the Communist Resistance. See W. Brian Newsome, "Paul-Henry Chombart de Lauwe: Catholicism, Social Science, and Democratic Planning," *French Politics, Culture, and Society* 26 (2008): 61–91. I would like to thank the author for providing me a draft of the article before its publication.

[18] Jean Fourastié and Françoise Fourastié, *Histoire du confort*, second edition (Paris: Presses Universitaires de France, 1962), 109–110.

Stoetzel on the number of hours spent in housework, to argue that home productivity should be a national goal. Neither Stoetzel nor Chombart de Lauwe suggested that a more equitable sexual division of labor was the answer – both assumed that maintaining the home was a feminine responsibility. Therefore, they issued no challenges to the gendered hierarchy of labor in home or marketplace, instead focusing on the need for domestic science education and better housing conditions.

Efforts by women's, family, and consumer groups, as well as scholars and researchers, to improve living conditions in the postwar years often pointed to two solutions as the answer to women's problems: home modernization – including access to appliances – and domestic science education. Unlike the complaints from the women's demonstrations and the price monitoring of the postwar period, demands for home modernization came, for the most part, from official organizations, professors of domestic science and other recognized experts, and the state welfare apparatus. They responded to demands by their women constituents, but also stressed the need for education, which they were often eager to provide. In this way, their belief that experts should guide women meshed with the imperative to educate consumers asserted by the UFC and the CNC. In general, the discourse on productivity in the home both valorized housework, by equating it with any other profession that required vocational training, and demeaned women by implying that they were to blame for their hardships in part because they were not very good housekeepers.

The need to create modern rational homes directed by educated housewives provided regular material for women's journals, publications by domestic science experts, and programs at the annual *Salon des arts ménagers*. Modern domestic appliances demanded training, but even before these were available, perhaps especially when they were not available, these journals and professionals counseled women on the need to reorganize their homes and their own labor in an effort to be more efficient. Women's journals often printed scientific charts explaining where to place household items, at what angle tasks were best performed (sitting, standing, etc.), and when and how to perform tasks. An *Electro Magazine* chart, for example, featured the appropriate heights for kitchen placements so that women could see and grasp them with minimum exertion. Items were to be arranged according to how they were used, how often they were needed, and how much they weighed. (Figure 2.1) A 1956 publication called *Petit guide de la ménagère: Pour tout faire bien ... et vite*

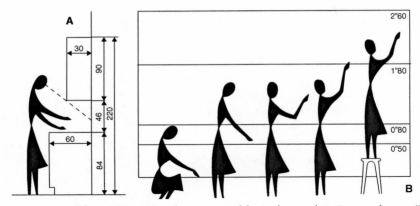

FIGURE 2.1. *Electro Magazine* demonstrated how the need to "see and grasp" should dictate kitchen design.
Source: G. Raffy, "Le fief de la femme: La cuisine," *Electro Magazine* 65 (1957): 36.

exemplifies the type of rationalization of the home popular in the 1950s.[19] The guide declared, "A GOOD HOUSEWIFE HAS NOT ONLY TWO HANDS, BUT A BRAIN!" and noted that "the modern woman must know how to organize herself, equip herself, and economize her money, her time, and her energy."[20] The *Petit guide*, written by three instructors of domestic science, divided women's household tasks into three categories: "major" obligations that needed to be done at the same time each day (shopping, cooking meals, washing dishes), "occasional" obligations (buying clothes, mending, making conserves), and "important" obligations (laundry, ironing, big cleaning projects, watching children on days off from school). The book included tables with a weekly schedule, in thirty to sixty minutes intervals, for a married woman with no children who worked outside the home and a married woman with two children and no employment outside of the home.

The *Petit guide* devoted significant space to women's responsibilities as domestic consumers, including instructions for making a detailed budget, knowing how to shop, where to shop, when to shop (time of day and season of year), and how to read scales, labels, and product guarantees.[21] Domestic science experts consistently emphasized the benefits wise purchases brought not only to the individual and family, but also to

[19] *Petit guide de la ménagère. Pour tout faire bien...et vite* (Paris: Les éditions sociales françaises, 1956).
[20] Ibid., xii-xiii.
[21] Ibid., 13–20.

the nation. Consuming skills were becoming crucial in definitions of the educated, modern French housewife, or *ménagère*, of the postwar years. As Pierre Laroque, first director of the postwar French social security system, explained at a 1957 congress on domestic science education, scarce resources made consuming skills central to women's education. "Experience has shown," he noted, "that with equivalent resources, two families can have extremely different standards of living." Women had to be taught to organize a budget, make wise purchases (including on credit), avoid the pressures of modern advertising, and make materials last as long as possible.[22]

The *Petit guide* also included instructions for rationalizing household tasks through well-designed household equipment and furniture and even the position of the housewife herself. Women were taught to be as efficient as humanly possible. An article in *Elle* instructed women not to work "with an empty head" and to learn to work with their left as well as right hand.[23] Officials from domestic science institutions and the *Salon des arts ménagers* created a center for the study of household rationalization and economy, and stressed that this was a sector of national activity, like industry, that needed to be further studied to become more productive.[24] This broadly perceived need for education, in addition to legislation requiring domestic science education in the schools, prompted the spread of programs in domestic science and even created new careers for women. These included innovations like *"conseillères ménagères"* who were attached to social service organizations and could offer advice on domestic economy, hygiene, and nutrition to struggling housewives without the time or resources for more formal coursework.[25]

Studies of home productivity were not limited to those in women's organizations or domestic science education. They were also conducted by the organisms leading the state's productivity drives. "The most important French industry, in terms of the quantity of work expended, is the

---

[22] "Premier congrès de l'Union nationale des professeurs et monitrices d'enseignement ménager familial," *Cahiers d'enseignement* 11 (1957): 30.

[23] Alice Roche, "4 Femmes sur 5 ne savent pas organiser leur travail. Soit donc le cinquième," *Elle* 20 (1946): 19.

[24] Note concernant le projet de constitution d'un "Centre d'études et de liaison de l'économie ménager." CAC 19850023 article 63.

[25] Legislation requiring domestic science education was passed by the Vichy regime, and continued under the Fourth Republic. See, "Premier congrès," 5–48. See also Jobs, *Riding the New Wave* for discussion of the profession of *travailleuses familiales*, a form of social work open to young women, and how these women became agents of modernization to the families they served.

industry of housework" announced *Productivité française*, the journal of
the *Association française pour l'accroissement de la productivité* (AFAP)
in 1952.[26] The AFAP was a semiofficial agency created after Marshall
Plan officials prompted the founding of a *Comité national de la productivité* (CNP) in France. It executed CNP programs, publicized the benefits of increased productivity, received subsidies from both the American
and French governments, and organized missions to the United States.[27]
The home, they claimed, was an "industry," composed of twelve million
"family workshops" which employed twenty-three million workers and
cost forty-five billion hours of work a year, nearly the same amount of
time as all of the professional work, including that in agriculture and
administration, conducted in France.[28] The AFAP analysis of productivity
in the home was published at the time of the annual opening of the *Salon
des arts ménagers*. The article stressed the place of the household in the
national economy by portraying it as an industry like any other. If France
were to increase its productivity, the author argued, it had to take into
account an activity that expended nearly half of the productive labor of
the nation.

Calling attention to the productive work done in the home pulled the
household into the national economy and valorized the role of housewives at the same time that it cemented a sexual division of labor and
implied that women were to blame, at least in part, for their difficult
situation. Those who spoke for women and the family drew on this productivity discourse to encourage investment in home modernization. The
fact that women who devoted themselves to the home were not considered part of the "active" population incited a sense of inferiority that
caused nervous problems in women, according to a doctor from the
International Association of Women Doctors writing in a special issue
on housework in the journal of the UNCAF.[29] The UNCAF performed a
variety of family services and was a major provider of domestic science

[26] Jean Dayre, "La 1ère industrie française manque de productivité," *Productivité française*
3 (1952): 4.
[27] On creation of the CNP and the AFAP see Richard Kuisel, *Seducing the French*, 73–4. For
creation of a *Comité national de la productivité* see Wall, *The United States*, 184.
[28] Dayre, "La 1ère industrie française," 4.
[29] Dr. G. Montreuil-Straus, "Aspects humains de l'activité ménagère: Le surmenage de la
mère de famille française," *Informations Sociales* 7 (1953): 1012–1022. Though part of
the state social security apparatus, each UNCAF *caisse* had a governing board that was
elected by its constituents. Half of the seats were held by representatives of the beneficia-
ries, half by representatives of their employers. See Chapman, "France's Liberation Era,"
103–115.

courses. Its journal, *Informations Sociales*, advocated for families and
published information of use to social workers and other groups
and individuals interested in the family. Seventy-six of the one-hundred
and twenty-three women in their study agreed that housework had negative repercussions for their health.[30] The mixing of psychological and
physical woes was apparent in one woman's claim that "I have nervous
troubles, not only because the work is never done, but because I'm at
the mercy of everyone."[31] The women doctors who studied these problems advocated both better domestic science education and access to
home appliances. A professional orientation in housewifery similar to
that given women in other fields, rather than the assumption that women
would master these skills "without difficulty and almost through intu-
ition" would both help women complete their work and raise society's
appreciation of household labor.[32]

Along with calling attention to women's needs, the UNCAF journal
devoted ample space to the economic aspects of housework and the connection between the home economy and the national economy; they
reinforced the notion that women were both performing citizenship in
the marketplace and strengthening the nation through their work in the
home. The myriad skills needed to fulfill these responsibilities were now
essential to the modern French housewife.[33] Citing the 1947 Stoetzel
study, the authors pointed out first that freeing women from their
household labor could allow them to enter the productive workforce
in other ways.[34] They placed more stress, however, on the notion that
even without entering the workforce, women influenced the economy

[30] Ibid., 1017.
[31] Ibid., 1018.
[32] Ibid., 1019.
[33] Amelia Lyon's work on Algerian families in the 1950s shows how domestic science
experts evaluated Algerian women's housekeeping skills in order to determine their level
of assimilation. Thus, being a good housewife was also a sign of Frenchness. See Amelia
Lyons, "Invisible Immigrants: Algerian Families and the French Welfare State in the Era
of Decolonization (1947–1974)" (PhD diss., University of California Irvine, 2004).
[34] Historian Ruth Schwartz Cowan has pointed out in her work on the United States that
the introduction of modern household goods did not actually reduce the time women
spent cleaning, as a rise in standards always accompanied new goods. See Cowan, *More
Work for Mother: The Ironies of Household Technology from the Open Hearth to the
Microwave* (New York: Basic Books, 1983). On the other hand, although the time spent
in household labor remained equal, the character of that labor changed significantly
with modernization and appliances. For analysis of how housework changed with economic and technological change, see Susan Strasser, *Never Done: A History of American
Housework* (New York: Pantheon Books, 1982).

through their work in the home. The UNCAF asserted that it was the household economy that inspired "the little miracles of economy that an informed housewife makes in her own home," but that these same decisions influenced the broader economy and could be made in the service of the nation.[35] This meant things like using food before it spoiled in order to avoid wasting resources, as well as getting the most nutritional value out of that food. It meant careful treatment of clothing and linens so that they lasted longer. It also meant influencing production through wise purchases. The authors pointed out that consumer decisions about quality vitally affected the economy, and that decisions women made about what to buy with their limited resources could affect agricultural as well as industrial production. "We wouldn't cultivate so much wheat in France if the French didn't eat so much bread," the authors pointed out.[36] More to the point, "... each time a well-informed housewife refuses to buy a second-rate product and chooses instead a product better fit for the service she needs, she accomplishes, however modest the purchase, a gesture profitable to everyone. Repeated millions of times, a gesture like this leads to the rationalization of production and distribution, and orients the economy toward the optimum use of resources and materials."[37] Thus, women exercised a gendered form of citizenship and shaped the economy through their individual purchases and decisions.

Given the importance of women's consumer decisions, and the onerous nature of household labor, the authors reiterated the call for educating and informing housewives, both about organizing their households and consuming wisely. They also pointed out that orienting the family economy toward the better satisfaction of future needs required both meeting present needs and planning; this entailed both saving money and investing money in better home equipment.[38] Home modernization, in particular through the purchase of home appliances, could immediately increase the housewife's productivity. The problem for many families was that investing in home equipment was entirely impossible when salaries remained low and prices high. It was difficult to rationalize the purchase of a washing machine in 1952 when the price, an author in *Productivité Française* claimed, was the equivalent of 1,200 hours of wages for a domestic servant. The price was 300 to 400 hours of wages in the United

---

[35] "Aspects économiques de l'activité ménagère," *Informations Sociales* 7 (1953): 1031.
[36] Ibid., 1031.
[37] Ibid., 1033.
[38] Ibid., 1034.

States, on the other hand, which had achieved low prices and high standards of living through mass production and mass consumption.[39] Mass production could lower prices and make the products available, but required a mass of affluent consumers to buy the appliances. One was faced with the dilemma of "squaring a circle," according to *Productivité française*: Reducing the price of home appliances depended on mass production, which depended on widespread demand. Demand, however, would not grow without lower prices. Furthermore, housewives could not improve their own productivity, which would in turn strengthen the national economy, without better equipment. [40] It was this dilemma that prompted the advocates of home modernization to redefine an old practice: buying on credit. Credit could create consumers, who would in turn stimulate mass production, which would lower prices for everyone.

THE CONSUMER CREDIT DEBATE

The national modernization and productivity drives, anger about the conditions in which women performed domestic labor, and a general desire for consumer goods shaped the debate on consumer credit in the postwar years. As M. Krafft, director of the credit organization Cetelem explained, "No mass production without a mass of clients; no mass of clients without credit."[41] Cetelem (originally named *Crédit à l'équipement électroménager*) had been created in 1953 through the cooperation of major French banks and appliance manufacturers and with the support of the state's *Conseil national du crédit*.[42] It provided credit specifically for home equipment and was one of the many specialized credit organizations established in the postwar period.

Creating a mass consumer economy required extending new purchase options to consumers. The problem was that buying on credit was not considered respectable by many in France, or indeed in much of Europe,

---

[39] Dayre, "La lère industrie française," 7. He referred to a washing machine with dryer.
[40] Jacqueline Bernard, "La période des inventions se termine, la période de l'organisation commence," *Productivité française* 3 (1952): 10.
[41] "Parce que la promotion sociale offre le confort aux foyers modestes, les crédits à l'équipement ménager: +300% depuis 1958," *Combat*, December 10, 1962.
[42] For creation of Cetelem see Fontenay, "L'expérience du crédit à l'équipement électro ménager," *Union fédérale de la consommation: Bulletin d'information* 29 (1955): 45–48; A. Braive, "Confort à crédit," *La maison française* 8 (1953): 33–34; Rosa-Maria Gelpi and François Julien Labruyère, *Histoire du crédit à la consommation: Doctrines et Pratiques* (Paris: Éditions de la Découverte, 1994), 186; and *De la 4 CV à la vidéo, 1953–1983, ces trente années qui ont changé notre vie* (Paris: Communica International, 1983).

before the war.[43] Elsa Triolet's popular 1959 novel, *Roses à credit*, tells the story of Martine, a beautiful but poor young girl from the provinces, who is enticed by modernity and its cleanliness, beauty, and comfort. Growing up in squalor with a promiscuous mother, Martine finds refuge in the home of a friend's mother, the local beauty parlor operator. At this woman's home, she is "baptized" in the modern bathtub. As Triolet writes, "'modern comfort' arrived with one fell blow, with running water, pipes, electricity..."[44] Martine moves to Paris where she marries and diligently works to earn some creature comforts, but, she eventually discovers the utility of buying on credit and spends uncontrollably to outfit her modern apartment with the latest furnishings and appliances.

While Martine is unable to resist the attraction of modern consumer goods, instead driving herself to ruin through her purchases, her husband represents the rational, scientific side of modernization. A former Resister and the son of a wealthy rural family, he studies diligently at university and then pours his efforts into creating a rose with the color of a modern rose and the smell of an old rose. As Susan Weiner has argued, he values the "authentic" world of nature and science, as evident in his desire to create "the kind of scientific technology that respects the past instead of trying to erase it."[45] Martine is, instead, obsessed with the "inauthentic" and artificial products of mass consumer society. Her husband, unable to deal with her obsessions, finally leaves her for an American and Martine ends up back in the hovel where she was raised. Her story ends in ultimate degradation: She is attacked and killed by rats.[46] The idea that credit was evil, espoused by Triolet, a communist intellectual, had to be overcome to create the kind of society that Cetelem's M. Krafft desired.[47] The debate ensued in the mid-1950s, as the French government considered how best to regulate its use and organisms dedicated specifically

---

[43] See Michel Wildt, "Continuities and Discontinuities," for the debate in West Germany. "Offensive sur les ventes à tempérament?" *Le Monde*, July 22, 1956, discusses worries about credit across "the old Europe" and the low level of debt in France, West Germany, the Netherlands, and Britain compared to the United States. Of all of these, France had the lowest level of debt, which was equivalent to less than one percent of national revenue, compared to 9 percent in the United States.

[44] Elsa Triolet, *Roses à crédit* (Paris: Éditions Gallimard, 1959), 37–38.

[45] Susan Weiner, "The *Consommatrice* of the 1950s in Elsa Triolet's *Roses à crédit*," *French Cultural Studies* 6 (1995): 136.

[46] Ibid.

[47] Triolet was a communist supporter, though she never joined the party. Weiner, "The *Consommatrice*," 131.

to granting credit, like Cetelem, spread rapidly.[48] Concerns about credit lasted into the 1960s, but by this point it was clear that the practice would continue to expand, that credit had increased production of consumer durables, and that it now influenced the way that families budgeted their money.[49]

Advocates of consumer credit usually encountered two different strains of opposition. On the one hand, leftist intellectuals and political activists worried that credit would turn the working class into capitalists and make workers less likely to strike for fear of facing months of payments without a salary. On the other hand, much of the population associated credit with poverty, usury, and profligacy. This belief was commonly associated with the rural population, but often with the bourgeoisie as well; to create a mass consumer society, all of these groups would need to change their attitudes toward consumption. Advocates of credit came from various perspectives on the issues. For state planners and productivity advocates, credit could help the economy expand, but they worried that its unfettered use would worsen inflation. Appliance manufacturers, for their part, saw credit as a means of expanding their operations and financing mass production. These groups, along with family, women's and consumer organizations, domestic science educators, and women's journals, needed to convince the public that the educated and controlled use of credit was not wasteful, but, rather, a practical tool for equipping their homes. By identifying appropriate uses of credit, they at the same time asserted the rationality of domestic consumption and implied that consumers, like Triolet's Martine, were naturally irrational and therefore needed training and education.

By the late eighteenth century, working families rarely paid cash for food and French housewives struggled with their debt to the butcher, wine maker, and, above all, the baker. Credit for nonalimentary goods spread in the late nineteenth-century, principally because of the popularity of the sewing machine.[50] The emergence of department stores in the late

[48] In 1949, there were sixty-six credit organisms in France, by 1956 there were one-hundred and seventy-two. This stabilized at between 130 and 140 by 1961. See "La vente à crédit est encore faible en France," *Combat*, June 23, 1961. Cetelem dominated the credit market for home appliances. On specialized credit organisms, "Le crédit à la consommation en France," *Les problèmes économiques*, 614 (1959): 3–4.

[49] "La vente à crédit s'acclimate en France," *Le Monde*, November 28, 1962.

[50] See Judith Coffin, *The Politics of Women's Work: The Paris Garment Trades, 1750–1915* (Princeton: Princeton University Press, 1996), 81–82. Clare Crowston's work on the eighteenth century examines how, despite being denied legal control of their own property, women were able to spend on credit because of the daily requirements of running

nineteenth-century also increased recourse to credit, as well as the association of credit with the working class, as stores like the Grands Magasins
Dufayel opened in poorer neighborhoods and offered purchases on
credit, while the more bourgeois stores accepted only cash.[51] The image
of credit was altered to appeal to more wealthy consumers with the
beginning of automobile sales after the First World War. The manufacturer Citroën participated in the creation of the *Société pour la vente à
crédit d'automobiles* (SOVAC) in 1919, which was followed by societies
created by Renault and Peugeot. By 1939, one-quarter of the cars sold
in France were financed by credit. The automobile industry continued to
absorb about two-thirds of the credit expended in France into the 1960s,
but even before the war, producers of domestic equipment had begun to
create credit societies as well.[52]

It was not until the early 1950s, however, that a significant proportion
of the French population was wealthy enough to consider the purchase of
a car or a domestic appliance, even on credit. The state took an increasing
interest in consumer credit, both as a potential problem and as a means
of economic expansion, after the Second World War. The government
created a *Conseil national du crédit* in 1945 and tightened its regulation of the industry in the early 1950s.[53] For those wishing to modernize and expand the French economy, it seemed practical to support the
extension of credit to French consumers. Commentators frequently drew
attention to the role of credit in American economic growth, sometimes
appearing stunned at the level of individual American debt, and at other
times pointing to the role of credit in allowing average American families
to buy home appliances and cars.[54] Despite its possibilities for spurring

a household. She argues for the importance of credit to the expansion of the consumer
economy in France and the identification of women with consumption. Clare Crowston,
"Family Affairs: Wives, Credit, Consumption, and the Law in Old Regime France," in
Family, Gender, and Law in Early Modern France, ed. Suzanne Desan and Jeffrey Merrick
(University Park: The Pennsylvania State University Press, 2009), 62–100.

[51] See Coffin, *The Politics of Women's Work*, 82–88; Auslander, *Taste and Power*; and
Miller, *The Bon Marché*, 178.

[52] For origins of the credit organisms, see Gelpi and Julien-Labruyère, *Histoire du crédit*,
185. In 1963, the automobile industry absorbed more than two-thirds of credit. See
"L'automobile absorbe en France plus des deux tiers du crédit à la consommation."
L'Echo, August 7, 1963.

[53] Alain Chatriot, "Protéger le consommateur contre lui-même: La régulation du crédit à la
consommation," *Vingtième Siècle* 91 (2006): 95–109.

[54] A 1954 article pointed out that individual debt in the US totaled 22 billion dollars, something the journalist feared could lead to an industrial slow-down if families could not
meet their financial obligations. "Le développement des ventes à crédit dans la région
du Nord," Informations et Documents section, *Perspectives* 10 (February 6, 1954): 3–6.

economic growth, many in the government worried about the financial and social effects of credit. Although expansion was necessary, irrational purchases on credit would not necessarily help the economy expand in the most rational way, and might lead to inflation, already a major concern. In 1953, the *Conseil économique*, a council that advised legislators and ministers on economic issues and was composed of representatives of different economic "constituencies" – including employers, unions, cooperatives, and family organizations, among others – issued a report detailing the benefits and risks that credit currently posed and recommending changes that were necessary to both take advantage of credit and minimize its potential hazards.[55]

The *Conseil économique* took up the study of credit both because it was becoming more widespread in France, among the wealthy as well as those of modest income, and because offering credit was becoming an advertising tool for sellers. Consumer credit was most commonly used for cars and electric appliances, followed by radios, furniture, bicycles and motorbikes, clothes, and sporting goods.[56] In describing the benefits of credit, the *Conseil économique* reflected the widespread acceptance of new living standards in France and the belief that these new comforts were worth great expense. The council pointed out that while individuals most often needed to buy furniture and other "goods of home comfort" when they were between the ages of twenty and thirty-five, they could best afford them between the ages of forty-five and sixty. Credit could close this gap and be a kind of "future savings" that would allow one to enjoy purchases immediately.[57] The description of credit as a form of saving was characteristic of the discourse of the 1950s. Choosing to buy on credit was

The same journal pointed out later that month that many American families were able to purchase cars and consumer durables and pay them off long before the items were old, due to recourse to consumer credit, and that credit could be a useful economic tool for a government seeking a third way between a planned economy and a laissez-faire economy. "La vente à crédit étranger," Informations et Documents section, *Perspectives* 10 (February 27, 1954): 1–4. In 1955, the amount of credit dispensed represented .7 percent of the French economy and 10 percent of the American economy. Jean Boissonnat, "Sous la signe de l'automobile et de la machine à laver, la vente à crédit révolutionné la France," *La Croix*, May 25, 1955.

[55] Creating a council that included diverse interests was a way to give these groups a voice in governance so that they would not resort to lobbying legislators. See Edward Lewis, "The Operation of the French Economic Council," *The American Political Science Review* 49 (1955): 161–172.

[56] Marius Allègre, "Étude du crédit à la consommation. Rapport présenté au nom du Conseil Économique, par M. Marius Allègre," *Conseil économique* (March 4, 1954): 268.

[57] Ibid., 271.

a decision to limit other spending in order to make payments, something the council called "the educative role of installment buying."[58]

In describing credit as a form of saving, the council was both highlighting its positive, healthy characteristics, and pointing out that using credit did not actually mean an increase in one's buying power, but a decrease. The council spoke out strongly against sellers who declared that buying on credit was a means of augmenting one's buying power. The report stated that, "Immediately and quantitatively, a purchase on credit effectively limits one's buying power in the sense that along with the deferred expense of the purchase, there is the cost of buying on credit itself." It labeled sellers who claimed otherwise dishonest and abusive.[59]

The *Conseil économique* approved of a certain kind of expansion, but expressed a hesitancy about it common among journalists, political figures, and the same organizations that hoped it would improve living conditions. Although many of these parties viewed American levels of prosperity as desirable, they often also worried about the role of credit in the American economy, both on a national and family level. Newspapers consistently pointed out that in the late 1950s, and even the early 1960s, French consumer debt was the equivalent of around 1 percent of national revenue, while American debt was reported to be as high as 9 percent of national revenue.[60] Over two-thirds of American families carried consumer debt.[61] By 1963, average debt per individual in France was 115 francs, compared to 125 francs in West Germany, 235 francs in Great Britain, and 1,210 francs in the United States.[62] Many public figures and journalists in France expressed concerns about the consequences of carrying this level of debt. Along with the fear that demand would grow too quickly, leading to greater inflation, there was a sense that credit could make the economy grow in unnatural ways, and that if there were an economic crisis, credit would make that crisis more acute. A journalist for *Le Monde* asserted that the American economy was "a prisoner to consumer credit" and that the 1929 crash had been exacerbated by the widespread use of credit in the United States.[63]

[58] Ibid., 271.
[59] Ibid., 275.
[60] See, for example, "Offensive sur les ventes."
[61] Ibid. The author also stated the average individual American debt had gone from 475 to 800 dollars between 1948 and 1955.
[62] "5 Millions de français ont eu recours au crédit ménager entre 1953 et 1962," *Combat*, August 6, 1963. These are new francs.
[63] "Offensive sur les ventes."

In speaking out against the notion that credit expanded one's buying power, the *Conseil économique* also voiced one of the objections that the Communist Party had to credit. In 1956, the Communist *L'Humanité* advised its readers on the "underside of consumer credit." The journal acknowledged the benefits that workers enjoyed through credit, describing one worker who had gone "from chicken coop to *pavillon*" – "*pavillon*" being the term for a small single-family home – through the use of credit, and another who had been able to move his family of eight out of a three-room apartment because of credit. This meant, however, "the end of cigarettes!" and "the end of cinema!" for the family, and the journal stressed the reduction in buying power that credit had created.[64] Along with the perils of credit, the journal voiced a second concern of the Communist Party, labor unions, and leftist intellectuals: Employers benefited from the extension of credit because workers with scheduled payments would be more willing to work overtime and less willing to strike. Some industries even offered themselves as guarantors for workers seeking credit – a practice *L'Humanité* clearly found suspicious.[65]

The journal *L'Express* also examined the issues of credit, working-class demands, and new consumer needs in a forum in 1957. In answer to the question of whether the working class would become less combative because of new consumer needs, sociologist Edgar Morin noted that society was experiencing a "sociological and social *embourgeoisement* of the working class" but prophesied that, rather than pacifying workers, this movement would make them more belligerent because they had more needs to fulfill.[66] However, he also noted that it was very difficult to build a worker's movement calling for reduced hours because the great majority of workers were willing to work extra hours in order to consume more.[67] Communist ideology and warnings were not enough to deter workers from using credit or longing for consumer goods, and in 1956, Cetelem, the largest provider of consumer credit for home appliances in

[64] "Rien à payer, ou les dessous du crédit à la consommation," *L'Humanité*, July 3, 1956.
[65] Ibid.
[66] "La machine à laver, tourne-t-elle dans le sens d'histoire?" *L'Express*, March 1, 1957, 14–15.
[67] Ibid, 15. See Gary Cross, *Time and Money: The Making of Consumer Culture* (London: Routledge, 1993) and "Time, Money, and Labor History's Encounter with Consumer Culture," *International Labor and Working-Class History* 43 (1993): 2–17 for analysis of how European workers made this choice in the first half of the twentieth century. See also Victoria de Grazia's critique of this argument, in which she argues that the choice between leisure time and more income is not as stark as Cross asserts. "Beyond Time and Money," *International Labor and Working Class History* 43 (1993): 24–30.

France, reported that during the previous year, 32 percent of the credit it had extended had gone to workers, a group which represented 33 percent of the French population.[68] Workers were clearly willing to buy on credit, and the Communist Party resorted to advocating stronger protective legislation for consumers, as it was clear that the most vulnerable of buyers were subject to the most predatory lending practices.[69]

The predatory lending practices common in the early 1950s were a major focus of the report by the *Conseil économique*. The council noted that "the seller often does not reveal to the buyer the real cost of the credit he is offering," explaining that the interest was often calculated on the total price of the object, not the price after the initial payment of 25 percent of the cost, nor the subsequent payments.[70] The council provided an example of this practice in which a 6 percent interest rate was actually 36 percent, and newspaper articles about credit cited examples of 60 percent and higher interest rates.[71] The social and economic risks of credit, among which inflation was consistently cited, led to strict legislation in the early and mid-1950s. The government monitored institutions that provided credit, imposing punishments for predatory interest rates and requiring that buyers be informed of the exact costs of purchasing on credit. The government also effectively limited credit, and the risk of inflation, by decreeing that installment payments had to be completed within a limited number of months and that consumers must pay a substantial portion of the price of the purchased object up front. These conditions would be modified as national economic conditions warranted. [72]

Perhaps more interesting than the regulation of credit, and more revealing of the suspicions surrounding credit and its users, was the moralistic tone taken by the *Conseil économique* in determining who should use credit and for what. In addition to speaking out strongly against the notion that credit increased one's spending power, and advising that credit should instead be considered "a decision to save," the council advocated credit

[68] "Où en sont les ventes à tempérament en France?" Informations et Documents section, *Perspectives* 12 (July 28, 1956): 5.

[69] See Alain Chatriot, "Protéger le consommateur," for more information on regulation.

[70] Allègre, "Étude du crédit," 270–271.

[71] Ibid., 270–271. See, for example, Boissonnat, "Sous la signe de l'automobile."

[72] Jean Luc, "La réglementation des ventes à tempérament et la protection des acheteurs," *Le Monde*, December 23, 1956. In 1955, for example, buyers had to pay 20 percent of the cost of items up front, and pay off their purchases in eighteen months. See "La réglementation du crédit à la consommation va être complète," *Le Monde*, May 7, 1955. The purchase conditions varied according to item and remained in place until 1979. See Alain Chatriot, "Protéger le consommateur," 99.

only for goods that were "durable and useful."[73] The council, like advocates of credit, believed that consumers should never use credit for goods whose use would be expended before the payments were finished. Credit was acceptable only when it was used for purchasing a durable good, like an automobile or a home appliance, which would be worth a subsequent decline in purchasing power because of the increased productivity or family comfort it provided. Thus, the council wished to constrain and educate consumers, who needed to make rational decisions but often needed prompting from experts to do so. The productive, healthy use of credit was also consistently trumpeted by manufacturers; organizations focused on women, the family, and consumers; and women's journals. These groups all advocated a measured use of credit to expand production in industry and the home, and thereby create a society of mass consumption.

EDUCATING CITIZEN CONSUMERS AND ADVOCATING THE "MODERN FORM OF SAVING"

In 1955, Cetelem's annual report showed that the percentage of credit extended to population groups was fairly similar to each group's numeric predominance in the French population, with one glaring exception: the agricultural population. Although agricultural producers represented 27 percent of the French population, they were only 1 percent of Cetelem's business in 1955.[74] This population group, as well as the bourgeoisie, would have to be convinced of the benefits of buying on credit. In February of 1954, *Elle* magazine reported on the experiences of Bourg-Achard, a village of 1,200 people in Normandy. The national electric company (EDF) had worked with the new credit organization to make Bourg-Achard a "pilot village" in a campaign to spread home technology and the use of credit.[75] In the case of Bourg-Achard, Cetelem offered to finance appliance purchases over the course of twenty-four months with no interest.[76] The generous terms of the agreement are evidence of the company's perception that rural families were adamantly reluctant to buy on credit.[77] According to *Elle*, the program worked, as 267 electric

[73] Allègre, "Étude du crédit," 277.
[74] "Où en sont les ventes," 5.
[75] Claude Fontenay, "Arts ménager appliqués: Grace à 24 mois de crédit, Bourg-Achard est devenu le village pilote de l'équipement ménager," *Elle* 428 (1954): 24–5, 66–7.
[76] Fontenay, "Art ménagers appliqués," 65.
[77] Laurence Wylie also found that the rural families he studied valued saving, hated to go into debt, and looked down on those who were forced to use credit in the local stores. See Wylie, *Village in the Vaucluse*. Second Edition (New York: Colophon Books, 1964).

appliances were installed in the 350 homes of Bourg-Achard, making the village "almost as comfortable as the whole of the United States," and allowing the Verhaegue family in the photo to equip themselves in an "ultra-modern fashion."[78] (Figure 2.2)

Cetelem was created by appliance manufacturers, whose reasons for supporting the expansion of household equipment are obvious. Women's journals, too, had a vested interest in the sale of appliances, or at least in expanding the profits of their manufacturers. The pages of *Vente et Publicité*, a national advertising journal, were lined with ads by women's magazines boasting of the size of their readership and its desire to spend. *Elle*, for example, publicized its vast diffusion and advertised itself as "the magazine of women who buy," and *La maison française* called its clientele "exceptionally receptive to advertising because it *wants to* and it *can* buy."[79] Advertising sometimes claimed half the pages of an issue of *Elle* and between 40 and 45 percent of *Marie-France*, *L'Echo de la Mode*, and *Arts Ménagers*. Despite occupying less space in *Marie-France* than in *Elle*, ads provided about 70 percent of the magazine's profits, making it one of the journals most reliant on advertising.[80] In 1957, *Marie-France* claimed that by seventy years of age, a mother of two would have sewed on twenty-thousand buttons, washed one-hundred thousand cups and saucers, and laundered one-hundred thousand square meters of clothing. "How can one be surprised," the author asked, "to see women dream of the household appliances destined to liberate them from this slavery?"[81] She advocated credit, "the modern form of saving," as a powerful means of helping women. Throughout the postwar years, *Marie-France*, and many other journals, would print informative articles on credit, educating their readers on how the practice worked and which providers were fair and reliable.

Along with women's journals, proponents of credit included women's and family organizations and consumer organizations, including the *Fédération nationale des coopératives de consommation* (National Federation of Consumer Cooperatives, FNCC).[82] These organizations steered consumers toward nonabusive providers of credit. They sharply

---

[78] Fontenay, "Arts ménagers appliqués," 65, 25.

[79] *Vente et Publicité* 8 (1953): 23 and *Vente et Publicité* 11 (1953): 49.

[80] Evelyne Sullerot, *La presse féminine* (Paris: Armand Colin, 1963), 232, 67.

[81] "Le crédit ménager: Formule moderne de l'épargne," *Marie-France* 12 (1957): 126.

[82] The championing of credit by consumer cooperatives was particularly surprising as they had traditionally opposed credit, believing that it led to the servitude and dependence of the working class. See Chenut, *The Fabric of Gender*, 239.

Marcelle Verhaegue qui tient dans ses bras sa petite fille Catherine (3 semaines) accueille sa machine à laver. Avec son mari ils ont aussi acheté un réfrigérateur pour que leur ferme du Bois de la Mare à 4 kilomètres de Bourg-Achard, soit équipée d'une façon ultra-moderne. La cuisinière électrique viendra quand la moisson sera rentrée.

FIGURE 2.2. Marcelle Verhaegue with her new washing machine. The journal noted that the family had also bought a refrigerator and would be getting an electric stove after bringing in the harvest.

Source: Claude Fontenay, "Arts ménagers appliqués: Grâce à 24 mois de crédit, Bourg-Achard est devenu le village pilote de l'équipement ménager," *Elle* 428 (1954): 25. Jean Lattès (1917–1996). Paris, Bibliothèque Forney.

© Jean Lattès / Bibliothèque Forney / Roger-Viollet / ELLE / SCOOP

differentiated the modern, correct, and productive practice of buying
on credit from earlier, more abusive, forms of credit and argued that
the conditions of women's work in the home were deplorable in light of
technological and industrial advances. They also adopted the language
of modernizers and productivity enthusiasts, stressing that home appliances were, in fact, capital investments, and would strengthen the French
economy by spurring mass production of consumer durables.

The 1953 UNCAF issue devoted to housework advocated the growth
of credit as a means of strengthening the economy, equipping households,
and easing women's burdens.[83] Equipment could increase women's productivity in the home, which would benefit the national economy in much
the same way that wise consumption did. Since saving money on food
was helpful, for example, using a refrigerator to prevent spoilage would
increase the real value of current agricultural production. "Bringing
technical progress into the home," claimed the UNCAF, was "profitable."[84]
The authors argued that as a productive realm with national economic
influence, households should use credit in the same way that industries
did – for capital investment. "Do we reproach an artisan for using credit
to buy a tool or machine that will increase the volume of his work, and
consequently, his profits?" asked the UNCAF.[85] In fact, "the situation of
families in view of progress in the home is the same as any enterprise
wanting to produce more and better. That kind of investment cannot
always be covered by the treasury and justifies recourse to credit, whose
expenses will be honored thanks to the economies of all sorts that better
equipment allows."[86]

This characterization of credit fit well with the national discourse
on modernization and productivity and included a moralizing strain
that steered buyers toward rational purchases and away from those
defined as merely excess. For advocates of consumer credit, the home
was a workspace in need of modernization and thus should benefit from
credit and investment in the same way that industry did. Credit, however, should not be used for "*consommation courante*," that is to say, for
goods that would be consumed before the payments were concluded.
The UFC stated that the first rule of credit was that its use "must only
concern those items that are indispensable, or at least necessary, for the

[83] "Aspects humains de l'activité ménager," 1012–1022.
[84] "Le crédit à l'équipement ménager," *Informations Sociales* 7 (1953): 1036.
[85] Ibid., 1036.
[86] Ibid., 1036.

bonne marché of a home. Objects that are simply pleasant should not be bought on credit."[87] The UFC promoted the notion that women were influential, rational consumers, but only when educated (and education was a service it provided). Without education, they asserted, consumer credit could be harmful, but with education it would allow families access to goods that were otherwise unavailable, and would open new markets for manufacturers, allowing them to produce more goods at lower prices.[88] Its overarching goal being to increase productivity, the UFC viewed credit as a tool that could be used to create an economy of mass production and mass consumption, a Fordist economy in which women and their families could orient and stimulate production through their consumer power.

The contrast between rational and irrational use of credit fit into bourgeois understandings of consumption that viewed excess spending as immoral and frugality as moral. The women's journal *La maison française* assured its readers that using credit for "useful and durable equipment" was "highly moral" because it encouraged one to avoid wasteful spending on "superfluous knick-knacks" in order to keep up one's payments. Only the use of credit for unnecessary goods, they argued, in conditions clearly beyond one's means and unprofitable, and for goods of short-term use, was immoral and dangerous, and inevitably led to indebtedness.[89] The journal noted that the French population was realizing this distinction and that even the middle classes were "triumphing over their ancestral repugnance to guessing what the future holds" and realizing that only the well-regulated use of credit would lead to the expansion of the national economy.[90] *La maison française* claimed that the war and instability that followed had made it impossible for families to save enough to equip their homes, making credit their only option.

The fact was that to become a society of mass consumption, French families would have to begin spending beyond their means, and the discourse on credit rationalized this practice, insisting that the home, and women's work in it, were worth the risk. *La maison française* educated its readers about Cetelem, explaining how credit could be used to improve women's productivity and lamenting that "it seems inconceivable that in our era of the scientific organization of work, a *chef de famille* can stand to see his wife waste her time and energy in a poorly equipped

---

[87] *Union fédérale de la consommation: Bulletin d'information* 29 (1955): 4.
[88] Ibid., 1.
[89] A. Braive, "Confort à crédit," *La maison française* 8 (1953): 33.
[90] Ibid., 33.

home."[91] The journal listed the purchases that a family should make, in order of importance. Along with stressing the practicality of using credit, it attempted to integrate home equipment into a definition of Frenchness. One could equip one's household "*à l'américaine*, that is to say, only considering the present without preoccupying oneself with the demands of the future. If the item no longer responds to one's needs, one does not hesitate to replace it. One sells and buys again." Or, in contrast, "*à la française*: the solutions to future problems are already seriously considered in what one chooses from the beginning. One thinks of the future as an extension of the present. One does not replace, one adds."[92] The necessity of making this distinction reveals that although there was great demand for home comfort in the postwar years, it coexisted with anxiety about becoming an American-style consumer society. Criticism of the wasteful habits of Americans was frequently cited in this context, with little evidence that average Americans were unconcerned with saving and constantly replaced old items with new. The journal reassured its readers that far from being wasteful and luxurious, credit and home equipment could be subsumed into "French" notions of practicality and conservative spending.

Despite claims to practicality, buying on credit was still relatively expensive in the early 1950s, and consumers worried about the terms of purchases on credit. Family, women's, and consumer organizations reassured the public that mechanisms were in place to protect them and their families should the buyer die or lose income before paying off an appliance, or should the appliance itself break down before payments were completed. In the interwar period, sellers, left unprotected by laws that stated that possession was the main determinant of ownership, had created private contracts that usually allowed them to seize an object for nonpayment without remitting any previous payments. Consumers, understandably worried by this practice, needed to be reassured and protected, which postwar legislation would ensure.[93] The UFC informed customers of reputable providers of credit, and some organizations supportive of families and consumers, including local *Caisses d'allocations familiales* (CAF), began providing credit themselves, sometimes without interest.[94]

[91] Ibid., 34.
[92] Ibid., 34.
[93] "La réglementation des ventes à tempérament."
[94] A. E., "Crédits et prêts à l'équipement ménager, services collectifs," *Informations Sociales* 11 (1957): 1037. *Union fédérale de la consommation: Bulletin d'information* 29 (1955): 1–78. This volume is a special issue entirely on credit.

Even with protections in place, commentators frequently worried about the practices of door-to-door salesmen, who were accused of badgering housewives until they made purchases they later regretted. The criticism of these practices often contradicted claims about women's skills as rational consumers, because they often described harried women unable to resist their overbearing and uninvited visitors. One remedy for such abuses, proposed by the UFC, on whose board sat representatives of many women's organizations, was that signatures of both husband and wife be required for all large credit purchases.[95] The need for regulation of abusive practices, plus the lengths that sellers went to in obtaining information about buyers is evident in the report to the UFC by an employer in the Nord, who complained of receiving a request for information about the financial situation of one of his employees. The employee's wife had encountered a door-to-door salesman selling a fur coat. She could only, he explained, "extricate herself from the situation by promising to buy the coat, without having had the time to speak with her husband about it." The wife did not need the coat, and the only way out of the situation was for the husband's employer to issue a negative financial report on his own employee.[96]

The wife's purchase went against all the rules of rational credit – it was not for a capital investment in the home, it was unnecessary, and it was not in accord with the family budget. The report in the UFC bulletin underscored the notion that women were not necessarily good consumers, but needed the education available from women's, family, and consumer organizations. The situation the employer described also indicates the lengths that businesses went to in order to determine the solvency of their clientele. Although they sometimes objected to embarrassing inquiries into consumer's lives, family and consumer organizations also advocated the creation of some kind of organization to research prospective buyers in the hopes that making the process cheaper for sellers would also make the prices of appliances cheaper for families.[97]

---

[95] *Union fédérale de la consommation: Bulletin d'information* 29 (1955): 5.
[96] Ibid., 5.
[97] R. Aubourg, "Deux problèmes de la consommation: L'évolution des besoins et crédit," *Coopération* 31 (1961): 21. As of 2007, France still did not have a centralized organization that created a "credit score" for clients, as in the United States. Objections are that this information invades privacy and could be used by lenders to encourage good clients to borrow more. See Damien de Blic and Jeanne Lazarus, *Sociologie de l'argent* (Paris: La Découverte, 2007), 61–63.

THE COST OF CREDIT AND THE EXPANSION OF THE MARKET

Although Elsa Triolet's heroine in *Roses à credit* is constantly acquiring new appliances and furnishings on credit, these kinds of purchases remained quite expensive into the 1960s, even with recourse to credit. The requirement that a fraction of the purchase, initially 25 percent, be made up front, as well as the limited time in which to complete payments meant that this kind of credit was not a tool of the poor. In fact, credit expanded as France grew more prosperous, reflecting the necessity of both extra income to go toward monthly payments and confidence in one's financial future. The families that used credit through specialized financial organs like Cetelem were not wealthy, but were comfortable enough to set aside money. Civil servants, who had a fixed income and could more easily plan ahead than others, were good candidates for buying on credit.[98] When *Marie-France* inquired into who used Cetelem, it found that 36 percent of users were families with one or two children whereas only 16 percent were families with three or four children, and 5 percent were families with five or six children. It concluded that the budgets of families with more than two children were too constrained to use credit.[99] The UNCAF, which was coming to the aid of *familles nombreuses* with loans for appliance purchases, also observed that credit was affordable only for a portion of the working population.[100]

Despite strict terms and its expense, credit did allow for an expansion of the sale of appliances starting in the mid-1950s and all signs pointed toward further expansion. The efforts of credit's advocates to convince the French population of the benefits of credit seem superfluous

[98] See "Le crédit à la consommation," 5, for discussion of the fact that credit's users were wealthier than average, though not rich. In 1955, almost one-quarter of the customers of one credit society were civil servants. "Les français et la vente à crédit," Information et Documents section, *Perspectives* 11 (November 19, 1955), 2.

[99] "Le crédit ménager," 127.

[100] The UNCAF was cited for stating that families needed to have resources of 50,000 francs a month for credit to be affordable. "Le crédit ménager," 127. A study in 1956 found that 74 percent of workers and 63 percent of salaried employees earned less than 40,000 francs a month. Paul Thibaud and Benigno Caceres, *Regard neufs sur les budgets familiaux: Initiation aux mécanismes économiques* (Paris: Éditions du Seuil, 1958), 20. These figures do not include family allocations, which during this period formed a considerable part of family budgets. According to a 1953 law, a family with two children received 22 percent of the salary of a metal worker in the Paris region, and 33 percent of that salary with the third and subsequent children. See M. P. Steck, "L'évolution des prestations familiales de 1945 à 1983," in *La politique familiale en France depuis 1945*, directed by Pierre Laroque (Paris: Documentation française, 1985), 217.

considering that the *Conseil économique* took up the study of credit precisely because the practice was expanding rapidly. One journalist estimated, in 1955, that the volume of sales on credit grew by 60 percent each year.[101] In 1955, the UFC reported that 150,000 French families had used Cetelem to buy one or more appliances, totaling between nine and ten million appliances.[102] *Marie-France* later reported that 600,000 families had used Cetelem in 1956 alone.[103] A market study done by the Plan in 1955 found that 37 percent of its respondents intended to use credit to buy home appliances, furniture, cars, and even clothing and linens.[104] The rural population remained underrepresented as buyers into the 1960s, and the market expanded first in the heavily industrialized Nord, around Paris, Marseilles, Bordeaux, and Grenoble, whereas areas like the Vendée and the Hautes-Alpes saw virtually no use of credit in the mid-1950s.[105] However, resistance to credit was slowly breaking down among the young in rural areas, and in 1955 the electric industry's market research organization, *Union pour l'étude du marché de l'électricité* (UNIMAREL), found that demand for washing machines had opened new markets and that 69 percent of rural families that wanted to buy a washing machine had favorable opinions on credit.[106]

The notion that credit was rational and modern was reinforced by the fact that it was most popular among the young, whether because they were more receptive to it, because they had a greater need to make large purchases, or because credit and family organizations thought them most deserving of credit. The FNCC, for example, gave priority to couples who had been married for less than five years.[107] These couples could be viewed in contradictory ways. Either they were optimistic about the future, or they were intent on "having it all" without waiting for maturity and stability.[108] Either they had grown disillusioned with the efficacy of

---

[101] Boissonnat, "Sous le signe de l'automobile."
[102] L'expérience du crédit à l'équipement électroménager," *Union fédérale de la consommation: Bulletin d'information* 29 (1955): 47.
[103] "Le crédit ménager," 126.
[104] *Enquête sur les tendances*, 69.
[105] "Les français et la vente à crédit," 1.
[106] UNIMAREL, *Le marché de la machine à laver domestique* (Paris: UNIMAREL, 1955), 46.
[107] "Le crédit à la consommation: L'Union coopérative de crédit ménager," *Union fédérale de la consommation: Bulletin d'information*, 37. In its washing machine study, UNIMAREL found that 35 percent of young families had already used credit, versus 9 percent of the elderly. *Le marché de la machine à laver*, 46.
[108] The two sentiments could also be combined. Historian Charles Moraze stated in *L'Express* that the young used credit because they did not fear the future. He also stated that this weakened their sense of personal responsibility. "La machine à laver, 15."

saving after years of high inflation, or they had confidence in a growing French economy that would provide jobs and allow them to make installment payments. In either case, by the early 1960s, just over 50 percent of credit's users were between twenty-five and forty years of age.[109] One journalist noted in the mid-1950s that those between thirty and thirty-five years of age were the most suited category as they were "at that age where the head of the family has reached a level of stability where he can think of equipping himself. No doubt under the counsel of his wife, he buys first a vacuum cleaner, then in the following order and with his own possibilities in mind, a refrigerator, a washing machine, a stove, and finally a television set." It is revealing that the journalist identified the buyer as male, but noted that his wife guided his purchases, and that all but the final item were most likely for her use rather than his own. He also asserted that by age forty-five, workers started thinking about saving for retirement, and so curbed their purchases.[110]

By the late 1950s and early 1960s, journalists observed that the spread of credit was having an effect on the market, both by assisting those of modest (though not too modest) means to buy items, and by helping bring down the prices of durable goods. Into the 1960s, the working class used credit more than any other class, in 1961 making up just under 34 percent of Cetelem's customers, followed closely by "employees" (a category which excluded those in the liberal professions and managerial positions), who represented 33 percent.[111] In that same year, 30 percent of the vacuums and floor polishers, 20 percent of the televisions, 10 percent of the washing machines, and 30 percent of the refrigerators sold in France were sold on credit.[112] Many families clearly found useful a purchasing method that allowed them to use a machine without paying the entire purchase price up front.

The increase in market base had also allowed for a drop in the price of appliances. The high inflation of the postwar years made it hard to compare prices directly, but a journalist from *Le Monde* noted in 1962 that despite a rise in salaries, the value-added-tax (TVA), the cost of aluminum, and the cost of public services, the price of vacuum cleaners had seen no increase in the past five or six years, which he considered a drop

[109] Michel Renault, "La vente à crédit s'acclimate," *Le Monde*, November 28, 1962.
[110] "Les français et la vente à crédit," 2.
[111] Michel Renault, "La vente à crédit s'acclimate," *Le Monde*, November 29, 1962.
[112] Ibid.

in real prices.[113] He also noted that whereas in 1947 France had produced eight-hundred refrigerators and sold them at around 1,000 francs per liter, in 1961 it had produced one million and sold them at around seven-hundred francs per liter.[114] Prices would continue to drop through the 1960s, in part because the commencement of the Common Market and the gradual elimination of customs duties between member nations forced French manufacturers to compete with manufacturers from other European countries. From 1960 to 1968 the prices of refrigerators and washing machines fell dramatically.[115] By 1968, 72 percent of French households had a refrigerator, 50 percent a washing machine, and 50 percent a vacuum cleaner.[116] Credit helped families afford items, but of course the drop in prices, and the fact that average buying power – a measure calculated based on total revenue and price indexes – increased by 50 percent between 1959 and 1968, were major factors as well.[117] Furthermore, the French public had come to fully accept that these items were necessary tools for household laborers.

Between 1954 and 1957 the production of electric appliances for the home increased by at least 30 percent per year. The industry itself was virtually a postwar creation and whereas 88 percent of appliances bought in France before 1939 were imported, that number had shrunk to almost zero by the late 1950s. From the summer of 1957 to the summer of 1958, however, there was a drop in sales in refrigerators and washing machines, which together made up two-thirds of the market of home appliances. One journalist blamed this on the stricter regulation of credit, as the government had recently reduced both the length of time one had to pay off a purchase (from eighteen to twelve months) and increased the minimum cash payment required (from 25 to 35 percent of the cost of the machine).[118] The drop in sales revealed both the

---

[113] Renault, "La vente à crédit," November 28, 1958. The general price of goods and services went up 75 percent between 1950 and 1960, then nearly 38 percent between 1959 and 1968, making direct price comparisons difficult and illustrating why holding steady could be seen as a decrease. Niaudet, "L'évolution de la consommation," 22.

[114] Renault, "La vente à crédit," November 28, 1958. Note that these are *ancien francs*, despite the article dating from after the currency reform of 1958.

[115] From a price indexed at one hundred in 1959, by 1968 the refrigerator had fallen to forty-one and the washing machine to fifty-four. Niaudet, "L'évolution de la consommation," 61.

[116] Ibid., 60.

[117] Ibid., 18.

[118] "Comment on prépare une crise: L'exemple de l'électro-ménager," *La vie française*, August 1, 1958.

effectiveness of the regulation of credit for controlling economic expansion, and the efficacy of credit for the buying population. The journalist noted that France would now manufacture 410,000 refrigerators in 1958, compared to 550,000 the previous year; a worrisome change considering the imminent opening of the Common Market and the need to compete with West Germany, which expected to produce 1,350,000 refrigerators that same year.[119]

Those who advocated credit's expansion often emphasized the increased productivity that home appliances could bring, but there is little evidence to suggest that this motivated individual consumers. The use of credit did stimulate production on a national level, but whether a precise calculation of the hours and money women saved with the purchase of an appliance went into individual family decisions is debatable considering the number of articles scolding women for not considering which appliances, in particular, were most useful for their families. An article in *Informations Sociales*, the UNCAF journal noted, "the idea of seeing one's laundry automatically cleaned is so seductive to housewives that they rarely ask themselves whether, in their own case, the washing machine is profitable." The journal explained that the washing machine was only profitable for families with three or more children, or in areas without public laundromats.[120] The popularity of refrigerators seemed to support this assertion. As *Informations Sociales* noted, many families still used the refrigerator as if it were a luxury item, not an instrument of work, since most women continued to shop for food daily and did not necessarily think about choosing one large enough to "stock" when they made the purchase.[121] In any case, studies have repeatedly shown that the purchase of home appliances does not save women time, as it undoubtedly leads to an increase in standards, so the notion that women might seek other productive work, perhaps even outside the home, after the purchase of appliances was likely specious.[122]

In 1958, sociologist Alain Girard repeated the 1947 INED study of women's household labor, again examining an urban population. By this point, 28 percent of the working-class families, 38 percent of the families of civil servants and employees, and 45 percent of the families of middle managers had washing machines. For refrigerators, the percentages were

[119] Ibid.
[120] Anne-Marie Max, "L'attitude de la femme en face du progrès ménager," *Informations Sociales* 11 (1957): 984.
[121] Ibid., 985.
[122] See Cowan, *More Work for Mother*.

23, 34, and 42, respectively.[123] Despite this, women without professional work and with three or more children at home still averaged 77.5 hours of housework per week – one more hour per week than Stoetzel found in 1947![124] A large proportion of the population was still without appliances, but the fraction that did have them had not significantly reduced the average workweek. Despite this, for those who did have a washing machine, the elimination of a full day of boiling water, scrubbing clothes, then rinsing and wringing them out, most likely changed the character of the week's work even if it did not shorten it. A desire for home comfort, hopes for a reduction of hard labor, and acceptance of new standards of cleanliness and modernity were likely stronger motivating factors for most families than were national or personal productivity.

Martine's tragic fate in *Roses à crédit* suggests the continuing unease about credit that existed in French society in the postwar decades. At the same time, it also reveals the widespread demand for home comfort and the popularity of credit, particularly among young couples (and, as Triolet implied, young women in particular). Whether it was merely a yearning for comfort or the desire to improve personal and national productivity that inspired decisions to buy on credit, evidence suggests that the public's perception of credit changed in the postwar years. The same *Informations Sociales* article questioning the importance of home productivity in purchasing decisions stated that "in three years, the mentality of the consumer has completely changed: that which was dishonorable before has become simply another form of investment."[125] The argument that investing in the home was as rational and necessary as investing in business had borne fruit even if the productivity discourse had not.

Whether or not productivity was a motivating factor, the increase in purchases on credit in the postwar years also reveals a change in notions of what was "necessary" for family comfort and what were acceptable working conditions for women. For women's, family, and consumer associations, not only was creating a society of mass consumption imperative for the national economy, it was the only way of bringing the home, and women's work in it, into the modern world. They saw this modernization as just and necessary not only for the families and women concerned, but also essential to the nation, as the work women performed in the household benefitted the economy as a whole. The discourse on consumer

[123] Alain Girard, "Le budget-temps de la femme mariée dans les agglomérations urbaines," *Population* 13 (1958): 601.

[124] Ibid., 614.

[125] Max, "L'attitude de la femme," 984.

credit thus reveals both the resonance of national goals of modernization and productivity and the skillful harnessing of this rhetoric by groups that wished to see the incorporation of the home, and women's work in it, into the modernization project. The home was a space for personal and national recovery, and a good standard of living would provide comfort to individuals at the same time that women's household labor as producers and consumers for the nation would strengthen the French economy, as did their purchases in the marketplace.

3

For Better and For Worse

Marriage and Family in the Consumer Society

In Christiane Rochefort's 1961 novel, *Les petits enfants du siècle*, Josyane, the young heroine, endures a troubled adolescence as the oldest of eleven children in a working-class family in one of the *grands ensembles*, the huge new housing complexes on the edges of Paris and other French cities. The story begins with Josyane's parents arriving at the hospital two weeks before her birth, hoping to register her arrival early in order to qualify for the *prime de naissance*, a grant for couples who had their first child within a short period after being married. Josyane grows up taking care of her younger brothers and sisters, each of whom arrives with a new government allowance, and usually, a new home appliance. Josyane fantasizes about the neighbor woman who has borne enough children to form at least a firing squad for the nation, and imagines them being killed on the battlefield and buried under tombstones labeled, "Television Mauvin, Car Mauvin, Frigidaire Mauvin, Mixer Mauvin, Washing Machine Mauvin, Carpet Mauvin, Pressure Cooker Mauvin" – and leaving a government pension sizable enough to buy a vacuum cleaner.[1]

Rochefort's satirical meditations on postwar family life were shaped by two phenomena of 1950s France: the baby boom and the beginnings of mass consumer society. Much had changed between the end of the war and the novel's publication in 1961. France was emerging from poverty to plenty, and while living conditions remained difficult for many people, industry was booming, new apartment complexes were multiplying, and mass consumer society was gradually becoming a reality. In

[1] Christiane Rochefort, *Les petits enfants du siècle* (Paris: Éditions Bernard Grasset, 1961), 86.

95

the mid-1940s, the home was still a space in which families provided children for the nation even as they struggled to survive amidst poverty and shortages. By the early 1950s, however, marriage, home, and family were increasingly seen not as national responsibilities, but as sources of personal fulfillment, intimacy, and comfort. Young families elicited interest because of these characteristics, and because of their ubiquity. Critics of the prewar economy had castigated the "Malthusianism" of French business owners and industrialists who refused to take the risks that would lead to expansion. That same charge was leveled at the population as a whole, as it seemed that young people were avoiding possible discomfort and sacrifice by eschewing marriage and parenthood. This perceived crisis was stunningly resolved by the baby boom, and just as new attitudes and outlooks were often cited in explaining the postwar economic transformation, demographic change was often seen as caused both by the need to recover from war, and by a new spirit of optimism accompanied by the desire to create a different, more comfortable, modern, and egalitarian future. Social scientists, journalists, and policy-makers asserted that today's family was a new, very modern, kind of French family, one that was shaped by the unique context of war and occupation followed by prosperity and the introduction of mass consumer society. As was apparent in the discourse on consumer credit of the 1950s, the ability to consume had become vital to the family as new needs emerged and comfort came both through personal relationships, and through hot running water, central heating, personal bathrooms, and home appliances.

Just as the economic conditions of reconstruction and the evolution of mass consumer society fostered the creation of the citizen consumer in both polity and the marketplace, consumption helped to define gender roles within the family, as the French public grappled with the perception that enfranchisement and economic opportunity had made women equal to men. There seemed to be a possibility that these changes could transform the gendered structure of the family, and the role of domestic consumer and manager offered a means of elevating women's social position while maintaining the centrality of women's responsibilities as wives and mothers. Thus consumption defined the modern family at the same time that the family helped create mass consumer society through its new needs and demands for modern housing and consumer durables. In the aftermath of war, and amidst continued economic and political turmoil, the privacy of home and the security of family offered a means of social and cultural renewal. Turning to marriage as a refuge, young couples, though damaged by the past, were hopeful that a future together in a prosperous France would provide the comfort and security they desired.

CHOOSING HOME AND FAMILY

Rochefort suggested one hypothetical explanation for the baby boom – couples were having children to pay for consumer durables – but hers was not the only one offered. In many ways, government goals and private motivations converged to create the baby boom of the late 1940s and 1950s. Public policy encouraged young people to marry and start families, and shaped the form of those families as well. Since the late nineteenth century, the French government had been concerned with a low birthrate that seemed to portend national decline, especially in comparison to Germany. The Third Republic instituted financial support for families, and the Vichy government, though hampered by the German occupation, reinforced the belief that having children was a national duty deserving of state support.[2] After the war, the governments of the Fourth Republic strengthened and expanded the system, both out of a desire for justice, born out of the Resistance, and the perceived need for population growth.[3] The need to support the family was acknowledged in the constitution, and strengthening it was central to plans for renewal and rejuvenation. Although concern for the family crossed party lines, and there was overwhelming support for the welfare system, public policy on the family was not uncontroversial or "neutral," and the kinds of aid offered shaped the structure of families. About 800,000 women had headed families while their husbands were POWs during the war, and France traditionally had a high rate of women's employment even before the war.[4]

---

[2] For demographic fears and family policy, including allocations, see Pedersen, *Family, Dependence* and Fuchs, "France in a Comparative Perspective." On the Third Republic, see also Kristen Stromberg Childers, *Fathers, Families, and the State in France, 1914–1945* (Ithaca: Cornell University Press, 2003) and Laura Levine Frader, *Breadwinners and Citizens.* For Vichy, see Miranda Pollard, *Reign of Virtue.* Antoine Prost traces policy from the end of the Third Republic into the Fourth and Fifth Republics in "L'évolution de la politique familiale en France de 1938 à 1981," *Le Mouvement Sociale* 129 (1984): 7–28.

[3] A 1947 poll by the *Institut français d'opinion publique* reported that 73 percent of the French population shared the belief that a population increase was desirable. Prost, "L'évolution," 11.

[4] On POW wives, see Fishman, *We Will Wait.* Sîan Reynolds states that in the 1950s and 1960s women's participation in the workforce was actually the lowest of the century, as women dropped to 33 percent of workers. Sîan Reynolds, "Who Wanted the Crèches? Working Mothers and the Birth-Rate in France, 1900–1950," *Continuity and Change* 5 (1990): 175.

These factors, along with emancipation through the vote and recognition of women's right to work, could potentially change the normative family structure. Indeed, the two dominant parties of the early Fourth Republic, the *Mouvement républicain populaire* (MRP) and the *Parti communiste français* (PCF), battled over the shape of the family through debates on public policy. The MRP, founded by Catholic members of the Resistance, heralded itself as the party of the family and initially attracted members of social Catholic groups like the MPF and the UFCS, and had the support of the church hierarchy. The more radical MPF members would gradually grow disillusioned with the MRP as it drifted toward the center of the political spectrum, but it would retain its identity as the family party and be a strong factor in making the Fourth Republic what sociologist Rémi Lenoir has called the "golden age of familialism" in France.[5] The MRP won out in establishing the allocation for the *salaire unique*, a subsidy given to families with a single income earner, preferably the father, despite PCF objections that this penalized the neediest families, in which both parents were forced to work.[6] Communist groups also decried the

[5] Rémi Lenoir, "Family Policy in France since 1938," in *The French Welfare State: Surviving Social and Ideological Change*, ed. John S. Ambler (New York: New York University Press, 1991), 159. The church hierarchy saw the MRP as a good choice after the war because it advocated state support for Catholic schools and because the more conservative parties it might have preferred, and members of the Church hierarchy itself, had been compromised by collaboration with Vichy, while the MRP was born in the Resistance. The church would eventually withdraw its support from the MRP because it was not forceful enough on the schools issue and because it opposed amnesty for collaborators. The MRP, in turn, though many of its members were involved in AC, kept the church at arm's length because it was uncomfortable with direct church involvement in politics and was worried about alienating working-class voters. See Carolyn Warner, *Confessions of an Interest Group: The Catholic Church and Political Parties in Europe* (Princeton: Princeton University Press, 2000) and Michael Kelly, "Catholicism and the Left in Twentieth-Century France," in *Catholicism, Politics, and Society in Twentieth-Century France*, ed. Kay Chadwick, (Liverpool: Liverpool University Press, 2000): 142–174. For MPF disillusionment with the MRP, see Duriez, "Left-Wing Catholicism," 76–77.

[6] See Prost, "L'évolution," 11. The policy also had unintended consequences because women often worked illegally in order to keep the *salaire unique*. Looking back on the Fourth Republic, feminist Evelyn Sullerot recalled that "one could not find a cleaning woman, for example, that would stand for being inscribed in the social security system" and noted that in protecting women, the state had subjected them to new dangers. See Evelyn Sullerot, "La démographie en France," in *Société et culture de la France contemporaine*, ed. Georges Santoni (Albany: State University of New York, 1981), 76. Sandra Fayolle describes the difficulty the Communist UFF had with this issue. They objected to it in principal but did not want to eliminate the subsidy entirely, since many of their members depended on it. They instead sought to extend it to all mothers, even those in families with two salaries. Fayolle, "L'Union des femmes françaises," 261–262.

fact that child-care funding was neglected by the state.[7] The MRP lost a battle when the state determined to give allocations to illegitimate children, but the overall thrust of family policy was to favor the formation of nuclear families, with children, in which the father worked outside the home and the mother dedicated herself to the household.[8] The state also recognized the importance of families for national rejuvenation by giving them an official voice through the *Union nationale des associations familiales* (National Union of Family Associations, UNAF). While the UNAF posited itself as apolitical, Communist and other working-class groups consistently criticized the association because it was dominated by conservative and Catholic family groups. The UNAF became the voice of family organizations to the administration, taking action on issues like housing construction and conditions, and family allocations – matters critical to French families. As the official organization representing families, it was funded through the allocations pool and was consulted on legislative issues concerning the family.[9]

In the end, despite the potential for change to the family structure due to the upheaval of war and women's new civic status, the desire for normalcy (another effect of the war), and the need for population growth would trump the factors heralding change. By the late 1940s, welfare funds both provided a significant income boost and encouraged the formation of single income families with at least three children. Along with the *salaire unique*, the state granted allowances to pregnant women, the *prime de naissance* for couples who had a child in the first two years of marriage, and monthly allocations for each child in the family. The *prime*

[7] Daycare facilities were sometimes built on local initiative with social security funds, but there were only 360 of them, nationally, in 1947. Lenoir, "Family Policy," 163. Claire Duchen states that by the end of the 1950s there were 481 crèches in France meaning daytime care available for 17,746 children under the age of three, and 786 *garderies*, or places for 32,800 children between the ages of three and six. By that time, there were almost four million French children under the age of four. Duchen, *Women's Rights*, 112.

[8] Lenoir, "Family Policy," 157.

[9] The UNAF distributed state aid, some of which was granted to families to help pay for children's education. Communists asserted that this was a way to fund Catholic schools with state money. Papers of the Président du Conseil, De la santé publique et la population. May 31, 1948. AN F 60 1424. The UFF also criticized the UNAF for this reason, among others, and accused it of being reactionary and practicing a "paternalistic family politics." J. Saillant, "Rapports sur les journées nationales des associations familiales," *Les cahiers de l'Union des femmes françaises* 33 (July–August 1948): 39–41. For funding and organization, see also Jean Meynaud and Alain Lancelot, "Groupes de pression et politique du logement. Essai d'analyse monographique," *Revue française de science politique* 8 (1958): 831–832.

de naissance encouraged couples to get started quickly, and the allowances, which started with the second child and increased significantly with the third, encouraged them to have large families.[10] In 1947, for a family with two children, family allowances and the *salaire unique* were roughly equal to a working woman's salary. In families with three children, the subsidies were equivalent to one and a half times that salary.[11] In the mid-1950s, the *salaire unique* would be renamed the allocation for the "mother in the home" as it was extended to agricultural families and then independent artisans and shopkeepers.[12] A means-tested rent subsidy was also created in 1948, and in 1949 it was extended to couples without children, in the belief that they would start families if only they had better housing.[13]

Thus, state and private goals converged in creating a baby boom that soothed the demographic fears of the previous decades. In a study of glassworkers in rural France, a sociological team asked whether, as Rochefort accused, families were having children for the allocation payments. They were not, the researchers concluded, but allocations provided a sense of security in that parents knew they could count on the funding if they did conceive a child.[14] Whereas there were just under 616,000 births in 1939, there were over 862,000 in 1950, and the number remained over 800,000 for the next twenty years.[15] The French population increased from 40 million in 1946 to 44.5 million by 1958, then to 49.8 million by 1968.[16] By the end of the 1950s, the mass influx of children into the public education system became a cause for concern, and by the 1960s the family system was called into question as people began to ask whether allocations should be based on need, instead of family size.[17]

[10] The policy of holding off on monthly allocations until the birth of the second child was part of the *code de la famille* created under the Third Republic. Prost, "L'évolution," 9.
[11] Calculations from Christine Bard, *Les femmes dans la société française au 20e siècle* (Paris: Armand Colin, 2003), 185.
[12] It was extended to those in agriculture in 1955 and to independent professions in 1956. Ibid., 185.
[13] There was also an allocation for families changing from one home to another. Steck, "L'évolution des prestations," 209–212. Duchen, *Women's Rights*, 104. At their height in 1949, family payments made up almost 40 percent of social security spending. Lenoir, "Family Policy," 152.
[14] Lucien Bernot and René Blancard, *Nouville: Un village français* (Paris: Institut d'Ethnologie, 1953), 127.
[15] "Naissances depuis 1900," Institut national des études démographiques, www.insee.fr/fr/ffc/figure/NATTEF02218.XLS. See also Duchen, *Women's Rights*, 97.
[16] Rioux, *The Fourth Republic*, 351. Niaudet, "L'évolution de la consommation," 10.
[17] Dominique Veillon states that by 1960, there was a need for 70,000 new classes for children born in the 1950s. *Nous les enfants, 1950–1970* (Paris: Hachette Littératures,

Although allocations provided significant help, living conditions for many French families remained difficult through most of the 1950s, prompting a search for alternative explanations for the baby boom. In the late 1940s and early 1950s, people were not having children simply to buy commodities, because the commodities were not yet widely available and affordable. Creating a mass consumer society was a slow process and people embraced the private home and family long before modern housing and consumer durables were easily available in France. The 1955 study of consumer demand commissioned by the *Commissariat du Plan* reported that of the 3,000 Parisian wage earners in its survey, 30 percent of the total, and half of those under age thirty-five, were searching for new housing.[18] Ten years after the war, most French families still did not have the conveniences generally accepted as *éléments de confort*. Among those in the study, 79 percent of families had running water in the kitchen, but 76 percent did not have hot water, and 84 percent did not have a bathtub or shower.[19] These statistics were for urban families; rural families lowered the averages considerably. The 1950s were a transitional decade between poverty and prosperity. One-fifth of French housing was in shambles after the war, but by the mid-1950s an era of reconstruction had evolved into one of new construction, and by the early 1960s, massive housing projects were widespread.[20]

In 1954, one-third of the French population lived in housing classified as "overcrowded" and the fact that the birthrate was strong despite these conditions surprised and perplexed sociologists, journalists, and policymakers who set out to research the reasons for this phenomenon, as well as to analyze "the family" and "the couple" of the postwar years.[21] In defining this family, they also helped redefine necessity and minimal standards of living in a way that reveals France's position as an emerging mass consumer society. The war, economic uncertainty, and industrial society, they argued, all encouraged young people to find solace and fulfillment

2003), 18. See also Lenoir, "Family Policy," 163. A 1972 law would end the practice of distributing equal allocations regardless of a family's economic situation. Allocations were eliminated for families above a certain income level. Prost, "L'évolution," 20–21.

[18] *Enquête sur les tendances*, 18.
[19] Ibid., 18.
[20] Newsome, "The Struggle for a Voice," 87.
[21] Statistic on overcrowding from Voldman, *La reconstruction des villes*, 342. To be overcrowded, an apartment had to have an average of more than one person per room (i.e., three people in two rooms was "temporarily admissible," but "normal" was two rooms for two people, and four people in two rooms was "critical"). Voldman, *La reconstruction des villes*, 323.

in marriage and family. The baby boom began before the arrival of cheap goods and modern homes, but the new needs of these young families created pressure for consumer durables and new housing. They created a mass consumer society at the same time that their consumer needs came to define them. Despite hardships, these young people and their families had new understandings of "necessity," and consumption and comfort were more important than in the past. Both present insecurity and optimism about the future encouraged them to form families, hoping for the day when they would be able to create and furnish their own homes.

Social commentators created a composite image of the French family of the 1950s and early 1960s that, whether rooted in reality or not, evidences both hope and anxiety about France's future as well as the acknowledgment that becoming a mass consumer society was necessary and inevitable. The typical couple was young, egalitarian, and devoted to each other and their children. Richard Ivan Jobs argues for the importance of "the new" in the postwar years as well as a fascination with youth, in part because it was figured as a means of national regeneration.[22] The young couple commentators described provided regeneration not only through its very youthfulness, but through its willingness to produce children. The demographic characteristics of this couple, as well as the relationship between the spouses, was understood to be new, modern, and a creation of the war, which had caused a profound break with the past.

In April 1953, *Le Monde* published a series of articles titled, "For Better and for Worse," exploring the phenomena of young marriage and the modern French family. The author, Pierre Drouin, began by expressing his surprise at an innovation in French university culture: the university *crèche*, or daycare center. "The 'bohemian life,'" he wrote, "often passes today by the path of the mayor's office, or even the church."[23] Drouin was shocked by the number of students who were married or had children (7 percent of male students had children and 12 percent were married, as were 6 percent of female students), as well as the low age of marriage in France. In 1946, the average age at marriage was twenty-seven to twenty-eight for men and twenty-four to twenty-five for women, but it fell steadily from this point until the 1970s.[24] The age at marriage would not

[22] See Jobs, *Riding the New Wave.* Susan Weiner looks specifically at the fascination with young girls in postwar culture, connecting this to a France both willing and fearful to accept change, in particular that change represented by mass consumer society. See Weiner, *Enfants Terribles.*
[23] Pierre Drouin, "Pour le meilleur et pour le pire," *Le Monde,* April 2, 1953.
[24] Duchen, *Women's Rights,* 97.

have been so surprising to Drouin were it not for the fact that the young students in his study were bourgeois, a social group that had traditionally married later than the working class.[25] Drouin and others saw the fact that bourgeois men and women were marrying at a younger age than preceding generations as a direct result of the war, which had caused a decline in bourgeois fortunes. Although traditionally the bourgeois family had been defined by its ability to pass on family property, parents could no longer "establish" their children, who were instead marrying and trying to "make it" on their own. University students exemplified this trend, as they were clearly establishing families before beginning their careers.[26] However, university students were not the only young people following this path: Drouin also found that more young men were marrying before completing their military service.[27]

The phenomenon of young marriage engendered both hope for the future and worry that young people were making rash decisions and forever altering the nature of the French couple and family. This tension suggests a perceived crisis in the family even while marriage and parenthood seemed more popular than ever.[28] For the pessimists, young marriage was the result of young women's emancipation, the desire to break free from parental control, and other selfish, rather than self-sacrificing, reasons for creating a family. In 1955, Marcelle Auclair, writing for *Marie-Claire*, did an exposé on young marriage. Auclair interviewed a lawyer who pointed to the increasing number of divorces in France and a chaplain who advocated lengthy engagements, saying that, "young boys and girls should be prepared to not confuse friendship and attraction for the true love that alone can guarantee the solidity of a family."[29] The reduced economic stature of bourgeois families aggravated this situation as parents interfered in marital choices less now that family property was no longer an issue.[30]

[25] Drouin, "Pour le meilleur."
[26] "Débats," *Colloques internationaux du CNRS. Sociologie comparée de la famille contemporaine.* (Paris: Éditions du Centre national de la recherche scientifique, 1954), 153.
[27] Drouin, "Pour le meilleur."
[28] This seems analogous to Elaine Tyler May's findings on the 1950s in America. She argues that families turned to the home in part to save themselves from themselves as society seemed liable to internal decay. Elizabeth Heineman notes that assuming there was a "rush to the home" in West Germany in the same period obscures society's real fear that the family was crumbling. Elaine Tyler May, *Homeward Bound: American Families in the Cold War Era* (New York: Basic Books, 1988). Elizabeth Heineman, *What Difference Does a Husband Make? Family and Marital Status in Nazi and Postwar Germany* (Berkeley: University of California Press, 1999).
[29] Marcelle Auclair, "Faut-ils vous marier jeunes?" *Marie-Claire* 11 (1955), 40.
[30] Alain Girard noted the "liberty" and "anarchy" that reigned in marriage choices in, "Situation de la famille française contemporaine," *Economie et Humanisme* 103 (1957), 7.

Marcelle Auclair also interviewed a mother who complained, "Before, you got a position, you married, and then you had your first child. Now, Madame starts by having a baby, then you marry, and then finally you look for a position."[31] A sociologist Auclair interviewed recommended that if the wife was young, the husband should be older in order to be able to teach and support his young spouse. Although the husband was older among most young couples, the gap between ages was narrowing.[32] According to Auclair, when the couple was of the same age, one risked a situation where the wife would be forced to take charge of the household, especially since women were better at adapting to difficult living conditions than men, and *"cela n'est pas normal."*[33] The Communist women's organization, the UFF, also believed marital equality was more likely if the spouses were of the same age, but they viewed this positively and associated it with women's ability to choose whether to enter the workforce or not and the young wife's belief, if she chose to stay home, "that what she accomplishes in the home is a job like any other and should be conceived of as such."[34] Whether they saw it as a frightening or exciting prospect, commentators assumed that even if women chose the same lifestyle as their mothers, it was the result of a new, modern mindset.

For many, the right to vote and right to work granted in the constitution seemed to be evidence that women's liberation had created equality in marriage.[35] In fact, women's legal rights were severely restricted, especially within the family. French law maintained that husbands were *chef de famille*, meaning that they had the legal right to make decisions "for the good of the family," including choosing where the family lived and how the children were educated. Until 1965, a husband could stop his wife from working or pursuing an education, and had control of family property.[36] In spite of this, most sociologists, journalists, and policy-makers

[31] Auclair, "Faut-ils vous marier," 39.
[32] Girard, "Situation de la famille," 9.
[33] Auclair, "Faut-ils vous marier," 43.
[34] Martine Monod, "Je t'aime, tu m'aimes, nous nous aimons..." *Heures claires des femmes françaises* 4 (1957): 4.
[35] See Jane Jenson for analysis of women's rights in the Fourth Republic. Jenson argues that while the vote and the right to work were recognized in the constitution, women's gains were restricted by a national discourse stressing their role as mothers as well as the continued legal subordination of women in the family. Jenson, "The Liberation and New Rights."
[36] Andrée Michel and Geneviève Texier, *La condition de la française d'aujourd'hui* (Paris: Éditions Gonthier, 1964), 79–85. Dorothy McBride Stetson, *Women's Rights in France* (New York: Greenwood Press, 1987), 88. Control of property depended on the "matrimonial regime" under which a couple married, but the vast majority of couples

continued to define the modern couple as equal and young – qualities that they saw as mutually reinforcing.

Young marriage was perplexing, as living conditions were still difficult in the early 1950s, and social commentators sought to understand just why so many young people were deciding to marry, and what they hoped to gain out of marriage. "Never before had France had so few single people," wrote feminist sociologist Evelyn Sullerot, herself a young mother in the 1950s, "Everyone got married. We spit on marriage, but we got married."[37] The marriage-rate from 1946 to 1950 was the highest ever recorded, which was no doubt in part because couples had been forced to wait by the war, but nevertheless it remained high through the 1950s.[38] In contrast to prewar generations, young people proved themselves psychologically willing and ready to have children, despite hardship. Family allocations were helpful, but statistics show that couples were not having the very large families that allocations were meant to support. Instead, more couples were willing to have one, two, or three children than in the past.[39] In fact, to many people it seemed that couples were having children because living conditions were difficult and they sought stability in the family and home.[40]

The nuclear family and private home figured as a refuge from war, political upheaval, and economic hardship. The sociologist interviewed by Marcelle Auclair for *Marie-Claire* noted that it was in these circumstances that the tendency toward young marriage was strongest. Auclair wrote, "The temptation is strong to seize the moment with the sentiment that we will be stronger, as two, and should take a chance. The sentiment is false, because

married under the "*régime de la communauté légale*" which gave the husband control even over property his wife brought into the marriage. Michel and Texier, 83–85. In 1965, marriage reform gave women much more control over their own property and made it possible to go to school, take a job, and run a business without consent, but the designation "*chef de famille*" lasted until 1970. Stetson, *Women's Rights*, 88.

[37] Evelyne Sullerot, "La démographie en France," 83.

[38] Claire Duchen states that the rate from 1946–1950 was 9.7 per 1000; then stabilized at around 7 per 1000 until the 1960s. Duchen, *Women's Rights*, 97.

[39] See Rioux, *The Fourth Republic*, 353, on average size of French families and Drouin, "Pour le meilleur," on how couples were having children even in the midst of the housing crisis. A 1947 survey by the *Institut français d'opinion publique* found that 36 percent of respondents felt that three children was the ideal number, whereas 22 percent believe that two was ideal. *Sondages* 41 (December 15, 1947): 620.

[40] This is a stunning contrast to the reaction to the First World War, which, as Mary Louise Roberts has argued, included the fear that women were abandoning their responsibility to bear children and becoming like men. Mary Louise Roberts, *Civilization without Sexes: Reconstructing Gender in Postwar France, 1917–1927* (Chicago: University of Chicago Press, 1994).

two is soon three on a tiny budget, then four, etc."[41] Women's magazines
wavered on the question of who was responsible for impulsive decisions
to marry. In 1946, Françoise Giroud chided young men in *Elle* for wanting
to marry because their apartments were cold in the morning, and the food
shortage and lack of domestic help reduced them to substandard meals,
but others explained the situation by pointing to the new independence of
young women and their parents' inability to stop them from marrying.[42]
Emancipation, it seemed, led directly to marriage and family.

In Pierre Drouin's exposé on young marriage, he discerned the phenomenon of the "marriage of refuge." These young men and women were
the children of the war and exodus, "who were severed from tenderness."
They were sometimes also children of divorce, "entering marriage
precipitously in order to find an equilibrium of affection."[43] A young person reaching age twenty in 1950 would have been born at the start of the
Depression and would have reached adolescence during the war and occupation. With over two million men, 800,000 of them husbands, absent
in POW camps during the war, chances are that most marriage partners
would have had little experience with stable family life.[44] Surprisingly,
few commentators on marriage noted that by the mid-1950s France was,
in fact, at war again, this time in Algeria. This might be attributable to
the fact that while almost two million French men were drafted to serve
in Algeria, they were not all called up at once, lessening the impact on the
marriage and birthrates.[45] Susan Weiner has also pointed to the inability
of the mass media, due to government censorship, to address the seeming
contradiction of fascination with consumption at home while so many
young men were absent.[46]

According to Drouin, in the early 1950s young people faced difficult
economic conditions and some of them believed "that it is easier to get by

[41] Auclair, "Faut-ils vous marier," 41.
[42] Françoise Giroud, "Aujourd'hui ce sont les garçons qui veulent se marier et les jeunes
filles qui hésitant," *Elle* 13 (1946): 7. Auclair, "Faut-ils vous marier," 39.
[43] Drouin, "Pour le meilleur."
[44] See Fishman, *We Will Wait*.
[45] The French also fought a colonial war in Indochina, of course, but did not draft troops
to do so. Francis Ronsin quotes the *Journal Officiel* in stating that 1.8 million men were
drafted for Algeria, of which 128,000 were reservists. For effects of the Algerian war on
the marriage rate, see Francis Ronsin, "Guerre et nuptialité: Réflexions sur l'influence de
la Seconde Guerre Mondiale, et de deux autres, sur la nuptialité des français," *Population*
50 (1995): 119–148.
[46] Weiner states that the Algerian War was the first war to appear on French television, but
"the studied neutrality of these images meant that they were a source of neither news nor
opinion." Weiner, *Enfants Terribles*, 157–158.

together during a difficult time" and also were aware of the social security benefits they would receive if married.[47] As Sullerot later noted, these couples were different from their children (the baby boomers) in that they wanted to find comfort, but were very much children of "the society of penury." Though defined by the desire to consume, they had not grown up in a society of mass consumption.[48] As people quickly grew frustrated with the inability of the governments of the Fourth Republic to make good on the promises of justice and equality made at the Liberation, some commentators also pointed to the role of the political situation in contributing to the importance of marriage.[49] In her study of working-class families living in furnished hotel rooms, Andrée Michel asserted that working-class men felt shut off from both political influence and economic advancement, and turned to the family instead, as an arena of personal expression.[50] The family was "a social refuge permitting one to fight against isolation in the crowd, particularly during times of trouble," wrote urban ethnologists Paul-Henry and Marie-José Chombart de Lauwe in 1960.[51] Fifteen years after the war, the family still figured as a space for solace, now from the anomie of postwar industrial society.

Along with youth and equality, a belief in the importance of happiness and self-fulfillment in marriage was considered a hallmark of the new family. The decline in worries about the birthrate helped strengthen the notion that family and marriage existed for love and happiness, not merely procreation – a belief reinforced by the celebration of children and family in the popular press during the late 1940s and 1950s.[52] Among Catholics, the view that sexuality was not just a weakness of men, but an important component of happy marriages, spread.[53] Some commentators implied that many young couples had been sexually active before marriage. They married quickly when the woman became pregnant, however, and despite

47 Drouin, "Pour le meilleur."
48 Sullerot explained that she got her first refrigerator at age thirty-four, her first car at age thirty-five. Sullerot, "La démographie en France," 82.
49 The governments of the Fourth Republic were hampered by an inability to create lasting coalitions and governments. Between 1944 and 1958, France had twenty-five different governments, each lasting an average of seven months. Jobs, *Riding the New Wave*, 40.
50 Andrée Michel, *Famille, industrialisation, logement* (Paris: Centre national de la recherche scientifique, 1959), 226. Despite increasing prosperity in France, Jean-Pierre Rioux notes that the typical industrial worker had little chance for advancement. In 1958, the son of a worker had a three in five chance of remaining a worker himself. Rioux, *The Fourth Republic*, 393.
51 Paul-Henry and Marie-José Chombart de Lauwe, "L'évolution des besoins et la conception dynamique de la famille," *Revue française de sociologie* 1(1960), 406.
52 Rioux, *The Fourth Republic*, 357.
53 See Prost "L'évolution," 11–12. Also, Prost and Vincent, *A History of Private Life*, 80.

a high number of infants born less than eight months after marriage, the
illegitimacy rate was lower than during the prewar years and remained
so for twenty years after the war.[54] Sociologists and journalists asserted
that as marriage became less of a national and social responsibility, the
couple's relationship was more important than ever before. A representative of the MRP, former MPF activist, and minister of population
during the Fourth Republic, Robert Prigent wrote that, "before being
spouse, father, mother, for the good of society, the participants in the
modern couple want to be all of these, but for their own good, above
all."[55] Though laws forbidding birth control, as well as any information
that could be construed as birth control, were in place until 1967, sociologists and journalists speculated openly that couples were limiting the
number of children they had. Sociologists observed the use of birth control among all social classes and noted that the "Anglo-Saxon" notion of
the "wanted child" was becoming more and more common in France.[56]
Birth control was still controversial for Catholic couples, but Catholic
doctors and church representatives had begun advocating, when necessary, the "Ogino-Knaus" or "rhythm" method, in part out of recognition
of difficult material conditions and the overwork of mothers.[57] Much of
this discourse about birth control was not about women's emancipation,
but about creating happy families.[58] Commentators assumed that couples
were using birth control for the family – to advance its social position

---

[54] Alain Girard noted that in 1951, 23 percent of first legitimate babies were born less than
eight months after the couple married. Girard, "Situation de la famille," 9. Claire Duchen
states that the illegitimacy rate was always lower than the prewar years and from a high
of 7.6 percent in 1946–1950, stabilized between 6 and 6.5 percent for the next twenty
years. Duchen, *Women's Rights*, 97.

[55] Robert Prigent, "Notion modern du couple humain uni par le mariage," in *Renouveau
des idées sur la famille*, ed. Robert Prigent (Paris: Presses Universitaires de France, 1954),
305. The "couple" as the basis of the family was an innovation. Evelyn Sullerot noted
that in her own research on the family, she did not find the word "couple" used before
1945. Sullerot, "Mariage et famille," 93.

[56] Robert Boudet, "La famille bourgeois," in *Sociologie comparée de la famille*, 146.

[57] Ibid., 145. Drouin, "Un nouveau type de couple," *Le Monde*, April 4, 1953. Drouin also
implied that non-Catholic couples were using condoms, noting their reliance on "methods used for combating venereal disease." Catholic officials saw the rhythm methods
as suitable in difficult, but temporary, situations, but argued that it should not be used
with the goal of preventing childbirth indefinitely. See Marc Oraison, *Union in Marital
Love: Its Physical and Spiritual Foundations* (New York: The Macmillan Company,
1958), 47–48.

[58] That birth control should be legal in order to reduce the number of abortions, which
was estimated at between 700,000 and 800,000 a year in the 1960s, was also claimed by
proponents of family planning. See Stetson, *Women's Rights*, 57–61.

or raise the standard of living – and it therefore reinforced the family structure rather than suggesting a modification of gender roles.

Creating a family was a choice, and the couple had become the center around which the family revolved. Somewhat ironically, the increasing importance of the marital relationship was blamed for the rise in divorce as well. Spouses expected more out of each other, and of marriage, and would end the relationship, even when children were present, if they were not sufficiently emotionally fulfilled.[59] In his exposé, Pierre Drouin noted that young people saw marriage as the start of a great adventure. Notions of a *"grand amour"* had been reconciled with marriage, so that young people believed that true love thrived in marriage, not outside of it.[60] On the one hand, the belief in true love in marriage mean that, as historian Philippe Ariès asserted, extramarital liaisons had become "more shameful" and *"démodé."*[61] On the other hand, as Drouin noted, this sentiment and the increase in young marriages was creating an increase in young divorces. From 25,000 divorces in Paris in 1938, the number had stabilized at around 35,000 by 1953.[62]

French society celebrated the couple and family at the same time that it fretted about its fragility, and despite the fact that the divorce rate remained stable, the increase in importance of the couple, and the perceived threat of divorce led both secular and religious organizations to introduce marriage counseling and preparation in the 1950s. This "Anglo-Saxon" concept born in the United States had achieved favorable results in Britain.[63] Pierre Drouin reported on the spread of such programs in France in 1953. He cited one or two-day marriage preparation courses organized by the JOC and *Jeunesse agricole chrétienne* (Young Christian Farmers, JAC), the corresponding AC group for young rural Catholics.[64] As part of the course, a social worker explained family legislation, a priest talked about the sacrament of marriage, a JOC representative explained the role of family in the working-class community, a doctor presented on sexual problems, and young couples shared their own

---

[59] Boudet, "La famille bourgeois," 145. Paul-Henry and Marie-José Chombart de Lauwe worried about the fate of children in marriages revolving around the couple, especially since women were more liberated than in the past. "L'évolution des besoins," 420.

[60] Drouin, "Pour le meilleur."

[61] Philippe Ariès, "Familles du demi-siècle," *Informations Sociales* 9 (1954), 1269.

[62] Drouin, "Peut-on lutter contre la contagion du divorce?" *Le Monde*, April 7, 1953.

[63] Boudet, "La famille bourgeoise," 145. Prost and Vincent, *A History of Private Life*, 80.

[64] The "milieu" specific groups were created because of the difficulty of creating a united Catholic community across class lines. See Gerd-Rainer Horn, *Western European Liberation Theology*, 51.

experiences and difficulties. Drouin found especially notable the activities of the bishop of Strasbourg, who held three evening marriage preparation sessions every month, usually with between twenty and fifty couples in attendance. He separated the men and women during the evening, and Drouin explained, "They speak to the men about women's psychology; a doctor does an exposé on the anatomy and physiology of marriage, not shying away from raising the question of the conditions necessary for a happy '*conjonction amoureuse.*' For young women, he orients his teaching toward the problems of maternity."[65] Catholic organizations had also begun marriage counseling for those in danger of divorce and Drouin interviewed the head of a family group in Lille to attempt to understand this phenomenon. The leader, who was a professor at a Catholic university, met with one or both members of the couple, then consulted with the members of his "matrimonial consultation" team, who discussed the couple's problems and presented them with a proposed solution. "Never before," concluded Drouin, "have we been so occupied with the couple," suggesting that marriage and family seemed to be at risk, as well as sought after.[66] The new standards of happiness and fulfillment in marriage had been recognized by those most concerned with preserving the family. At the center of that family was the modern couple, which was widely recognized as a postwar creation. Having lived through the war, and now dealing with housing shortages and economic crisis, young people were seeking stability in marriage and family, and, in the process, creating new kinds of family dilemmas as they hoped for a better future.

DEFINING NEW NEEDS AND DRIVING ECONOMIC CHANGE

Whereas the legacy of the war and occupation assumed a prominent place in depictions of the new family, so did the promise of comfort and affluence associated with mass consumer society. These families were formed in hardship, but longed for better living conditions and saw the creation of a comfortable, pleasant home with modern conveniences and commodities as essential to family harmony. The social commentators who defined the new couple and family also defined its material and psychological needs, which were very different from those of the past. Luc Boltanski has described the collusion between sociologists, in

[65] Drouin, "Avec les métallos et les ruraux qui fondent un foyer," *Le Monde*, April 3, 1953.
[66] Drouin, "Peut-on lutter contre." See also Girard, "Situation de la famille," 8.

particular, and modernizing reformers beginning in the 1950s. Scholarly studies, which described needs that could only be met through modernization, were often more prescriptive and proscriptive than descriptive, presenting consumer society as the only possible option for a modernizing France. The social sciences grew in importance in the postwar decades, in part because state planners depended on the information their research provided, something which spurred the creation of quasi-governmental, quasiacademic institutions in the 1950s and 1960s. The information these bodies and scholars provided was not merely valuable for describing conditions in France, but for shaping the present and future as scholars identified which population groups would succeed and which changes would be durable.[67] As scholars described and tabulated people's lifestyles and needs, they also asserted their own definition of modernity, lending prestige to what they defined as "modern" and creating understandings of modernity that appeared salient in a population that looked to them as experts.

Throughout France, scholars' studies showed, families were developing new needs. For scholars and planners, the adoption of a mass consumer lifestyle, including a nuclear family home with a housewife engaged primarily in consumption, was evidence of modernity. At the same time that this lifestyle defined the modern family, family needs drove modernization and the development of mass production and consumption because of the widespread insistence that this family could only be truly happy and fulfilled, its main purposes, in comfortable, modern living conditions. Further, with gender roles seemingly in flux, consumer society provided the means by which men and women remained different, but equal, as it ostensibly created a managerial position for newly emancipated women.

If the family and home provided refuge, it was because they provided *intimité*, or intimacy. Intimacy was an important theme of the women's press and evoked comfort, warmth, privacy, and the nuclear family household. During the occupation, the French government politicized the household, strictly defining gender roles and calling on women to be mothers for the French nation.[68] Whereas the governments of the Fourth Republic expanded the economic incentives for parenthood, the 1950s also saw a discursive shift from pronatalist policies intended to bolster reproduction

---

[67] Luc Boltanski, *The Making of a Class: Cadres in French Society* (Cambridge: Cambridge University Press, 1987), 148–162.
[68] Miranda Pollard, *Reign of Virtue*; Francine Muel-Dreyfus, *Vichy and the Eternal Feminine: A Contribution to a Political Sociology of Gender* (Durham: Duke University Press, 2001).

and national stability, to profamily policies intended to support individual families and help them maintain a traditional family structure.
Somewhat paradoxically, the acceptance of the essentially private nature
of the family coincided with expanded state economic support, the recognition of the UNAF as the official voice of families, and state intrusion
in the form of required prenatal visits and the right to remove children
from the family home.[69] Despite being a publicly funded institution at
the center of policy debates and public discussion, the family came to be
seen as a matter of personal fulfillment, and voices throughout society
asserted that this kind of fulfillment could only be found in the private,
comfortable home. Furnishing and decorating the home was presented as
a private enterprise – not a means of displaying status. This notion was
wrought with tension, however. As we have seen, women's, family, and
consumer groups emphasized the importance of women's consumer decisions for the nation, as well as their own families. Furthermore, the line
between public display and private comfort was never distinct, nor was it
necessarily clear which commodities or home improvements were meant
for utility, status, or, perhaps most commonly, both.

In 1955, *Marie-Claire* devoted an entire issue to intimacy, both giving
advice on creating an appropriate atmosphere in the home and decrying
the fact that many young couples were unable to experience the pleasures of home because of the housing crisis. "No matter how charming a
mother-in-law is, or how excellent a father-in-law, since biblical times the
tribal life has held more inconveniences than advantages," asserted *Marie-
Claire*.[70] The "*vie à deux*" was impossible for many couples, despite the
fact that "for those who love, there is no joy without intimacy."[71] Despite
current problems, Marcelle Auclair urged parents to be discrete and try
to allow the younger generation its privacy, which would, in turn, help
them preserve their own intimacy, "because the intimacy of a man and
woman who have so many memories together is as precious as that of
the young couple that has only its love."[72] That a fulfilling family life
required a sufficient amount and a particular kind of space was a theme
trumpeted by women's magazines, journalists, and sociologists. Privacy
needs were influencing how families spent money on the home, and *Elle*
noted in 1952 that French women were becoming "*coquettes*" for their
interior, paying the most attention to the "essential functions" of hygiene,

---

[69] Prost and Vincent, *A History of Private Life*, 76. Duchen, *Women's Rights*, 102.
[70] Marcelle Auclair, "Intimité," *Marie-Claire* 5 (1955), 48.
[71] Ibid., 48.
[72] Ibid., 48.

rest, and relaxation in the places "one does not see," rather than areas for reception or keeping up appearances. Soon, French "bathrooms will be palaces" and "kitchens salons," but "your living room, no matter how comfortable it may be, will be deserted...."[73] For the author, home décor was important, but for comfort – not for public representation.

Intimacy in the home was not only a matter of privacy and space, but of atmosphere. *Marie-Claire* identified three techniques for creating a desirable ambience: lighting, color, and placement of furniture. A round table, for example, was more intimate than a square table, correctly placed lamps created warmth, and creating a *"coin"* for eating or reading made a room more pleasant.[74] The fact that many young couples were living with parents increased the allure of the private, nuclear family home. As late as 1964, 900,000 French couples lived with the parent of one of the spouses, and 650,000 lived in furnished hotel rooms, another source of dissatisfaction.[75] Women's magazines dispensed practical advice to these families. One could "create an atmosphere of smiling intimacy" in a one-room apartment through the use of judicious lighting, colors (bright colors, rather than somber woods), and plants.[76] The creative force at work was a woman, and the emphasis on comfort and consumption also provided a solution to the dilemma of creating strong, stable families while acknowledging women's presumed equality in the modern marriage. As domestic consumers, women assumed an elevated position in French society without upsetting gendered divisions of labor at home or in the marketplace.

By attaching so much importance to the kind of space, and the commodities in that space, that the family needed, social scientists, journalists, and policy-shapers helped define what was "necessary" for French families. The needs they identified reflected France's position as an emerging mass consumer society even while consumer goods and modern homes were still in short supply. Despite the shortcomings of existing housing, Chombart de Lauwe found that the working-class families he interviewed in the early 1950s felt an attachment even to their meager surroundings and dreamed, however vainly, of transforming them into

[73] Daisy de Goureuff, "Une Grande enquête d'Elle: Joies, espoirs et 'plan de bataille' des femmes pratiques," *Elle* 326 (1952): 17, 57.

[74] Marcelle Auclair, "Équipe 55 vous donne 3 moyens de créer chez vous l'INTIMITE," *Marie-Claire* 5 (1955): 108–110.

[75] Louis Houdeville, *Pour une civilisation de l'habitat* (Paris: Les Éditions Ouvrières, 1969), 143.

[76] Carine, "J'ai trouvé une chambre à louer," *La femme nouvelle* 13 (1946), 13.

the home that women's magazines and other purveyors of comfort glorified in the 1950s. Chombart de Lauwe pointed out that often families could not decorate their own apartments, a fact he found to have adverse psychological effects.[77] Many of the families he and his team interviewed were disappointed that they had not been able to choose the color of paint for their walls, a decision commonplace for bourgeois families. Also, many of them lived in furnished rooms and so could not choose their own furniture, or if they did, could not afford to be selective.

That people felt attachment to the home was apparent even in the worst of conditions. When asked if they liked their home, 55 percent of those interviewed by Chombart de Lauwe said "yes," but 26 percent of those with positive responses appended them with, "but it's too small" or "but we don't have gas" or "but the bathrooms are shared and the floor is in bad shape" or "but it's too little and too humid" or "it's a chateau compared to other workers, but it's cold and in a shambles, because the owner has let it go...."[78] Chombart de Lauwe reflected that, "Among the causes of dissatisfaction, the smallness, the bad conditions, the absence of elementary comfort are the reasons most often stated, but also the fact that one cannot fix it up as one likes, the fact that one cannot arrange the furniture to one's liking, that one is not at home.... Satisfaction comes above all from the effort of having made a personal creation."[79] The people that Chombart de Lauwe interviewed placed a high value on making their lodging a *chez soi*, or home.

Chombart de Lauwe's studies of families and housing were important for stressing the link between comfort at home and family happiness. He argued that housing must be designed both to provide isolation and privacy, and to allow interaction with the outside world when desired. Only in housing with the proper floor plan and domestic equipment could women and children find "liberation" and "prestige" while the man of the house could find "material and moral" relaxation. Good housing meant happy families, and even the disposition of a family kitchen could affect a family's relationships.[80] Although the housing was far from perfect, Chombart de Lauwe found that the families he encountered in a study of three new housing developments stated that they were much happier in their new housing, and that the father of the family spent more

[77] Chombart de Lauwe, *La vie quotidienne*, 86–87.
[78] Ibid., 87–88.
[79] Ibid., 88.
[80] Paul-Henry Chombart de Lauwe et al, *Famille et habitation II: Un essai d'observation expérimentale* (Paris: Centre national de la recherche scientifique, 1960), 14.

time with the family than in their previous housing.[81] Social commentators had long decried the fact that working-class men spent their money and time in the café, rather than at home. Andrée Michel explained that the men in her study of families in furnished hotel rooms turned to the café because of the lack of space for relaxation at home. In two families that she studied, the lack of privacy meant that the husband and wife refrained from sexual activity – the husbands committed adultery in both cases. Michel argued that new housing could keep families from disintegrating, as it would prevent adultery, alcoholism, and the frequentation of cafés.[82]

The dilemma of balancing women's liberation and equality with the traditional family structure sought resolution in the new importance attached to home comfort, which came in part through the purchase of modern consumer durables. Women's magazines created, as sociologist Nicole Benoît termed it, "the myth of conjugal happiness amidst mechanized abundance."[83] Images of the mechanized home celebrated the creative power of women consumers, even though, as Roland Barthes pointed out, this home was an achievement entirely dependent on men, and women's journals constantly reminded readers that they were wives and mothers first.[84] Contemporary commentators rarely acknowledged the limitations inherent in this role and the disadvantages of women's legal position in the family, instead emphasizing the increased responsibility involved in running a household in a mass consumer society and creating an image of equality in difference in the role of domestic consumer. As Robert Prigent wrote in 1954, the emancipation of women was a fundamental mark of the modern couple. This did not mean that women had become like men, but that women should have a social role outside of the home and that women's position in the home had been exalted. "We

---

[81] Ibid., 92. See Nicole Rudolph, "At Home in Postwar France" and "Domestic Politics: The *Cité expérimentale* at Noisy-le-Sec in Greater Paris," *Modern and Contemporary France* 12 (2004): 483–495 for how housing would solve the "social question" of the late nineteenth and early twentieth centuries, in part by encouraging working-class men to stay at home rather than in the café. Rudolph points out that some fathers may have spent more time at home because new developments were often isolated and far from cafés, and few working-class families owned cars.

[82] Michel, *Famille, industrialisation, logement*, 228–229.

[83] Nicole Benoît, Edgar Morin, and Bernard Paillard, *La femme majeure: Nouvelle féminité, nouvelle féminisme* (Paris: Éditions du Seuil, 1973), 43. Benoît is specifically referring to the journal *Elle* in this quote. She notes that this myth was created by *Elle* in 1945, a point at which abundance clearly did not exist in France.

[84] Barthes was referring to *Elle* in these comments. Roland Barthes, *Mythologies*, trans. Annette Lavers (New York: Hill and Wang, 1972), 50–52.

are seeing," wrote Prigent, "an important proportion of women prepared for professional life, and sometimes capable of important administrative, scientific, or technical work, abandoning after marriage, by choice, their professional activity in order to devote themselves totally to their tasks as wives and mothers."[85] These women were not, however, submitting to the domestic slavery of the past, and "This call is so strong that our century has seen the birth of an important industry entirely consecrated to the research, production, and perfection of household appliances. And woman has lifted her daily work to the level of a new art, the annual exaltation of which requires the honor of a 'Salon.'"[86] Since in 1954 less than 70 percent of French homes had running water, Prigent's comments reveal more about his hopes for the future than about actual family life in the 1950s.[87] His thoughts were part of a current of expert opinion that looked forward to the day when mass consumer society could answer the tensions created by women's emancipation. Like government modernizers and planners, scholars and public officials presented this vision of society as the future of France, both predicting the future and shaping the present.[88] Women's new domestic position was tied to an evolving mass consumer society that seemed to reconcile women's emancipation with the structure of the French family. Women could find a kind of liberation in material comfort, and this, as well as the fact that women were choosing to devote themselves to the home, were signs that France was becoming a modern mass consumer society.

Even before being liberated through home modernization and consumer durables, the female half of the modern couple could be exalted in her new role as citizen consumer and director of the family economy. This consumer role was hardly new: historians have written extensively on women's roles as consumers for family and nation in the nineteenth and early twentieth centuries. Despite this, journalists and sociologists declared that women's management of the family budget was another hallmark of the modern couple. This role required not only a talent for the tasteful and rational selection of goods, but the ability to make financial decisions in straitened economic circumstances. As Michel noted, couples living in hotel rooms were united in their desire to leave, and therefore "the

---

[85] Prigent, "Notion modern," 315.
[86] Ibid., 315. The "salon" Prigent refers to is the annual *Salon des arts ménagers*.
[87] Statistic from Fourastié and Fourastié, *Histoire du confort*, 110. In 1954 around 5.5 percent of French homes had central heating, a private bathroom, and a shower or bathtub with hot and cold water. Fourastié and Fourastié, *Histoire du confort*, 111.
[88] Boltanski, *The Making of a Class*, 150.

happiness of the household is controlled by the wife because she's the one who 'holds the purse strings' and on her competence depends either the stagnation of the household in the hotel or the hope of getting out of it."[89] Once in new housing with higher rent, after having incurred the major expenses needed to equip the apartment, only the daily expenses associated with running a household were "compressible" or "elastic," again making women's consumer skills important for maintaining an acceptable standard of living.[90] Drouin cited statistics showing that generally women controlled family finances, and they did so in greater proportion in young couples than in those who had been married for twenty or thirty years. He interpreted this as a sign of women's new equality, since women now had at least as much responsibility for the household as men did.[91]

The question of who made the buying decisions in the family and how couples negotiated which purchases to make with limited resources was a complicated one that both sociologists and market researchers pondered in the 1950s and 1960s. Rochefort's heroine, Josyane, recounted how after purchasing a washing machine and then a television, her father asserted his right to a car: "… mother would have liked a fridge, but father said that it was finally his turn to have some well-being, not always his wife," and he needed the car to travel from one suburb to another for work.[92] Certain consumer items, like the car, were still associated with men, but market researchers wanted to know how couples prioritized their consumer needs.[93] In the 1955 study directed by the *Commissariat general du Plan*, researchers asked couples to select the top three items or categories they felt "deprived of," from a list of ten choices. Nineteen percent of families chose a personal means of transport, while 44 percent selected household appliances and 24 percent furniture.[94] Researchers knew, however, that even with a higher salary families would not be able to buy everything they wanted, so they next asked their subjects what they would do with 20 percent more income. For the 62 percent of families who would spend either all or part of that additional money on large purchases, 10 percent would spend it on home appliances, 10 percent on

---

[89] Michel, *Famille, industrialisation, logement*, 227.

[90] Niaudet, "L'évolution de la consommation," 17.

[91] Drouin, "Un nouveau type de couple."

[92] Rochefort, *Les petits enfants*, 21.

[93] This is despite the fact that much interwar advertising featured women and cars. See Roberts, *Civilization without Sexes* and Emily Rosenberg, "Consuming Women: Images of Americanization in the American Century," *Diplomatic History* 23 (1999): 479–497.

[94] *Enquête sur les tendances*, 31.

improvements to the home, 7 percent on furniture, and only 5 percent would spend the money on a car.[95] This did not necessarily mean, of course, that families did not want cars or that only women were dictating buying decisions, since the researchers estimated that with increased income a family would still need to save for fifteen months to buy a home appliance, versus thirty-one months to buy a car.[96] The relative price of different items made it difficult to determine what families really wanted or who made buying decisions, despite their efforts to create a hierarchy of family needs.

For the most part researchers concluded, perhaps influenced by dominant notions about women and consumption, that couples made buying decisions together, but that usually, in the case of home equipment, it was the wife who decided which appliances were necessary and which model best suited the family.[97] Michel, in her efforts to determine positions of power in couples, examined buying decisions in urban families in the mid-1960s. In her study of 550 couples, she found that in most couples, the budgeting was done either by the wife or the wife and husband together, and that in both of these situations couples tended to make decisions about purchases together.[98] The journal *Marie-Claire* described the desire of men to purchase things that would make their wife's life easier as a characteristic of "The New Husband." The author of the *Marie-Claire* article, Manuela Andreota, also asserted that an essential characteristic of the new husband was a "sort of guilt complex" at seeing his wife, who he considered his intellectual and cultural equal, overwhelmed by her household tasks.[99] The new husband wanted to come home to a human

---

[95] This in itself was a complicated question as only 48 percent would put all of the income into either daily expenses (12 percent chose this), big expenses (22 percent), or savings and investments (14 percent). Of the 49 percent that chose a mix of these categories, 22 percent chose a mix of daily and big expenses, and 10 percent chose saving and big expenses. Ibid., 55, 64.

[96] Ibid., 68.

[97] When the electric industry's UNIMAREL studied the rural population, for example, they argued that whereas men made decisions having to do with the business side of the farm, decisions about domestic purchases were made in the family with the wife proposing and selecting what to buy. The wife had even more say in the families of hired laborers on farms where "as in the great majority of worker's households, she has control of the money." UNIMAREL, *La prospection du marché rural de l'électricité: Cadre psychologique* (Paris: UNIMAREL, 1959), 20.

[98] Andrée Michel, *La sociologie de la famille* (Paris: École Pratique des Hautes Études and Mouton, 1970), 283. For more information on the research, which was part of a project comparing France and the United States, see Andrée Michel, "Comparative Data Concerning the Interaction in French and American Families," *Journal of Marriage and Family* 29 (1967): 337–344.

[99] Manuela Andreota, "Les nouveaux maris" *Marie-Claire* 194 (1968): 12–13.

being – not a "zombie exhausted by her household chores."[100] Responses to a survey by *Marie-Claire* showed that in 62 percent of couples, big purchasing decisions were made in common.[101] Andreota argued that couples were becoming more egalitarian, even though only 25 percent of the survey's responses indicated that men did the dishes, and this was as late as 1968.[102]

Evidence showed that men supported their wives' decisions to buy labor-saving equipment and appliances, but it was the women who used them. That the money-saving qualities of appliances were often touted in journals and advertisements may have been in part an attempt to equip women with arguments for their necessity when proposing and selecting family purchases.[103] Indeed, the journal *L'Express* advised women to make a preliminary visit to the annual *Salon des arts ménagers* exposition on their own to collect information, before bringing their husbands directly to the stands where they hoped to buy. With tongue-in-cheek, the journalist then advised women to let their husband talk to the seller so, "he will have the impression of buying for himself rather than for you. He'll be convinced once and for all that women don't know anything about motors or mechanics."[104] This 1958 washing machine advertisement implied that a loving couple had made their buying decision together, but while he appreciated the machine's efficiency, size, and quiet operation, she was the one who valued how it "saved time and energy." She was practical and he was technical, but the qualities listed in the ad also indicated that for him, the home was a space for relaxation, whereas for her, it remained a workspace (Figure 3.1). Other advertisements in women's journals showed men surprising their wives with home appliances, and Boris Vian poked fun at how this subverted romantic ideals in his 1950s hit *"Complainte du Progrès."* In the past, the lover "offered his heart" to show his ardor, whereas today it was instead "a frigidaire, a pretty motor scooter, a blender, a latex foam mattress, a cooker, with a glass stove...." The purchases might have been made by the man (and more likely, despite Vian's song, the couple in common), but they were intended for the woman.

The modern wife could only be truly liberated and happy in a home with modern conveniences and consumer durables that could serve to

[100] Ibid., 13.
[101] Ibid., 15.
[102] Ibid., 12.
[103] I want to thank Sarah Fishman for suggesting that this might be behind some of the language in advertisements.
[104] "Quelques conseils pratiques," *L'Express*, March 8, 1957, 32.

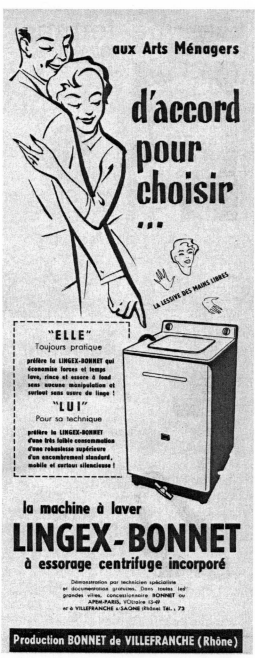

FIGURE 3.1. The happy couple in agreement about their selection of the Lingex-Bonnet washing machine.

Source: Elle 636 (1958), 35.

© ELLE / SCOOP

lighten her workload. This was accepted as early as 1953, when such a home was available to very few, and Drouin found, like Chombart de Lauwe, that women were exhausted by attempts to balance domestic and professional work. "You talk about liberation!" explained one worker "... I have two kids. My wife is obliged to work to help make ends meet. When she gets home from the factory she makes dinner, does a little housework, and after supper, her sewing.... If that's women's emancipation!... If we could buy a washing machine and a water heater, after that we'll talk about it." [105] Revealingly, despite his sympathy with her plight, a sentiment similar to that described by Andreota fifteen years later, the solution to his wife's problems was not his sharing in the housework, but domestic appliances, "the only path to the emancipation of the married woman," according to Drouin. [106] These commodities, though still rare, were already perceived as necessities. Along with lessening the burdens of housework, the possession of domestic equipment would add to the happiness of the whole family, because if her household tasks were easier, the housewife would have more time to spend with her children or go out with her husband. [107] In contrast to those intellectuals who criticized consumer society and Americanization, scholars and journalists concerned with the family rarely portrayed domestic appliances as luxuries and trifles, instead lauding their laborsaving qualities and their benefits to women and families. [108] Jean Fourastié penned a text with his wife Françoise on the state of housing in France and the need for increased comfort. According to the Fourastiés, home appliances were a necessary economic investment, and only the leisure they provided could help the housewife nurture her own intellectual, artistic, and moral development, as well as the education of her children. [109] Again, mass consumer society offered a type of emancipation, but one found in the home.

THE DESIRE FOR DURABLES AND STRUCTURAL CHANGE IN RURAL FRANCE

The connection between women and consumer society, the insistence that home comfort meant much more than in the past, and the assertion that

[105] Drouin, "Un nouveau type de couple."
[106] Ibid.
[107] See, for example, Jacques Doublet, "Parents et enfants dans la famille ouvrière," *Sociologie comparée de la famille contemporaine*, 161–162.
[108] For the reaction of French intellectuals to American culture, see Kuisel, *Seducing the French*.
[109] Fourastié and Fourastié, *Histoire du confort*, 78.

consumer needs were changing the family were also stressed in studies of rural France in the 1950s and 1960s. Conditions in rural France varied by region and were often so different among the regions and from urban areas that nationwide analyses were difficult to undertake. However, a number of academics and journalists were interested in how rural life changed with home and farm mechanization and began noting changes to rural families in the early 1950s. As in studies of urban France, they often focused on new patterns of consumption and attitudes toward domesticity as indications that rural areas were becoming modern.[110] By the 1960s, individual scholars and research teams were undertaking more studies of rural France because the peasantry seemed to be disappearing, because state planners were increasing their emphasis on regional development, and because the French countryside provided a kind of "laboratory" for examining how societies modernized.[111]

Sociologists were particularly interested in rural societies "in transition," accepting that modernization necessarily entailed the adoption of the lifestyles and products of mass consumer society, including the role of woman as domestic consumer and manager. As Henri Mendras wrote in 1965, studying consumption was also studying the "way of life" of a community. Evaluation of the consumption of food, clothing, domestic equipment, and leisure activities revealed "penetration of urban models" in rural communities. Approaching rural society with this in mind, scholars tended to emphasize signs of transition and change, again, shaping the present as they predicted the inevitable future. They often identified a desire for the way of life associated with mass consumer society as a reason for structural change in rural communities and families. Even here, the desire to consume defined young families, and young women in particular. This held specific consequences for rural communities and families, because the attraction that modern homes and consumer durables held for women was prompting them to flee the countryside.

---

[110] See Henri Mendras, "L'étude comparée du changement dans les sociétés rurales françaises," *Revue française de sociologie* 6 (1965): 26.

[111] See Henri Mendras, "The Invention of the Peasantry: A Moment in the History of Post-World War II French Sociology," *Revue française de sociologie* 43 (2002): 157–171; Mendras, "L'étude comparée du changement;" and Henri Mendras, *The Vanishing Peasant: Innovation and Change in French Agriculture* (Cambridge: MIT Press, 1970). For analysis of some of the forces for and consequences of the regional thrust of 1960s planning, see Ellen Furlough and Rosemary Wakeman, "La Grande Motte: Regional Development, Tourism, and the State," in *Being Elsewhere: Tourism, Consumer Culture, and Identity in Modern Europe and North America*, eds. Shelley Baranowski and Ellen Furlough (Ann Arbor: University of Michigan Press, 2001), 348–372.

The difference in conditions among regions, and even among different villages in the same area, made it difficult for scholars to draw general conclusions about change in rural France.[112] About 130,000 people left the French countryside each year after 1955, but living conditions and the rate of departure varied starkly by region.[113] Near Paris, profitable, industrialized farms dominated. In Brittany, where 45 percent of rural homes had earthen floors in the late 1950s, the countryside was still "overcrowded," and in Alsace, many farmers both worked the land and worked in industry.[114] Despite the fact that some farming was profitable, most scholars emphasized the low standard of living in the countryside, where polyculture, or production of more than one crop, remained widespread and the average farmer had at his disposal only about 35 acres of land.[115] The difficult living conditions of the peasantry differed little from the past, but were felt sharply as the gap between standards of living in rural and urban areas increased and farmers felt that they were not benefitting from national economic growth. Even though the urban population continued to suffer with problems like inadequate housing, the economy did expand rapidly in the 1950s, and the housing crisis began to abate in the early 1960s. The peasantry was largely left out of this national prosperity. Although composing 25 percent of the active population, they made only 12 percent of national income during the Fourth Republic.[116]

Scholars and journalists stressed the fact that the needs and norms of the urban population and its nascent mass consumer society had infiltrated the countryside, usually via women. These new norms created discontent because whereas the standards were accepted as necessary, they were rarely possible for rural families. The women's press was widely available and popular in rural areas; the celebration of family and home in it and other media, and the hope for comfort in the nuclear family home were noted by scholars and journalists writing on rural families in the 1950s and 1960s. In Drouin's exposé on young marriage in *Le*

[112] One important example that highlights the diversity between regions, even into the twentieth century, is the discovery by researchers from the *Groupe de sociologie rurale* of the variety of local rules for the transfer of land between generations, despite the fact that this had been, theoretically, nationally regulated and standardized by the Napoleonic Code. Mendras, *The Invention of the Peasantry*, 167.

[113] Rioux, *The Fourth Republic*, 385.

[114] Mendras, *The Vanishing Peasant*, 9, 173. Statistic about floors in Brittany from Rioux, *The Fourth Republic*, 386.

[115] Mendras, *The Vanishing Peasant*, 9, 12.

[116] Rioux, *The Fourth Republic*, 383.

Monde, he devoted considerable space to the rural family and was surprised to find among the young peasantry "a desire to bring to the home a pleasant allure with things that did not exist for earlier generations. It is no longer uncommon to find pretty curtains on the windows, flowers on the doorsteps, etc."[117] He described the presents at a village wedding, noting "you no longer find the statue of Sainte Thérèse ... or the two or three traditional barometers, but an electric iron, a machine for filtered coffee, or dishes. The taste for decorating an interior, for cuisine, a better understanding of the needs of a home, are spreading throughout this generation."[118]

Commentators were surprised by this desire to create a welcoming home in rural areas because there, more than anywhere else, they perceived the home to be a work space, and not a source of personal fulfillment. That women, in particular, wanted to become full-time housewives and consumers, rather than producers, they interpreted as a sign that they had adopted the standards of modern mass consumer society. In the late 1950s, social scientist Marie Moscovici found that peasant women on newly mechanized farms separated work and family functions, creating homes like the urban middle classes. When modern appliances entered the kitchen, farmwomen had more spare time and "the farm ceases to be principally a workplace; it becomes a home."[119] In their quest to be modern, argued sociologist Edgar Morin, farm families longed to separate home and work, offering women the chance to be full-time housewives. In his 1964–1965 study of a commune in rural Brittany, Morin called women the "secret agents of modernity" and asserted that although the traditional tendency to put money into the farm first, rather than the home, remained, women's dissatisfaction with country life was driving change as men attempted to modernize the farm in order to modernize the home.[120] In the mid-1960s, this process was far from complete and a young farmer, asked about his ideal domestic arrangement explained, "The husband in the fields and the wife at home, but unfortunately it's necessary [the wife sighs] that she work the fields, too."[121] The young peasant was now less likely to see investment in the home as money wasted, but the fact that

---

[117] Drouin, "Un nouveau type de couple."
[118] Drouin, "Avec les métallos."
[119] Marie Moscovici, "Le changement social en milieu rural et le rôle des femmes," *Revue française de sociologie* 1 (1960): 317.
[120] Edgar Morin, *Commun en France, la métamorphose de Plodémet* (Paris: Fayard, 1967), 167–8.
[121] Ibid., 168.

women changed more quickly than men still had the potential to create conflict within families as "while she metamorphosed into a bourgeoise in her home, the farmer remained a peasant on his farm."[122] Despite the incongruity between sociologists' notions of modern lifestyles and the living conditions that still prevailed in many parts of France, Morin and others presented the acceptance of new understandings of domesticity and the need for consumer durables as inevitable. Women would not go back to the old ways because "the conflict between the new feminine personality and the peasant condition is insurmountable."[123] The norms and necessities of mass consumer society were catching on before the lifestyle itself was possible.

For many sociologists, modernity in the countryside was evidenced by the desire for nuclear family homes in which the wife was a housewife and consumer – not a producer. Morin explained that, in the 1950s, families began adding onto homes in order to give young families their own space, and now young families hoped to build their own houses to fully separate the generations.[124] In the early 1950s, young rural couples hoping to create a home were perhaps even more frustrated than those in search of apartments in the city. It was still common for a young man to bring his bride into his parents' household, especially since, despite the rural exodus, there was a shortage of farms in many areas. The young women Drouin interviewed were frustrated at their inability to modernize the household that their mothers-in-law ruled.[125] The desire for the nuclear family household kept some couples from marrying without the possibility of a new situation. Drouin described one commune in the Manche, population four hundred, where seven couples waited to find a suitable farm so that they could marry – one of these had already been waiting for five years.[126]

The nuclear family household, with modern amenities, if at all possible, was considered necessary for nurturing the new families being formed after the war, and commentators noted that the concept of the couple had become important in rural areas as well as urban. One observer explained to Drouin that young peasant couples were spending their Sunday afternoons together, rather than, as in the past, "the husband leaving to play cards at the café while the wife chats with the neighbors

[122] Ibid., 168.
[123] Ibid., 169.
[124] Ibid., 171.
[125] Drouin, "Ménages sans toit, foyers sans soleil," *Le Monde*, April 5–6, 1953.
[126] Drouin, "Avec les métallos."

or takes the baby for a stroll."[127] The shifting boundary between consumption for personal satisfaction and public representation is apparent
in Drouin's observation that having a presentable home was important
for young couples who traveled from farm to farm to visit each other.
Products of the utmost utility also served to show to others that one was
in step with the times. UNIMAREL, which investigated the attitudes of
the peasantry for the electrical industry, found that along with its utility,
electricity was seen as a "factor of *progress* and modernization" and that
it gave the peasant "the impression that he is *like everyone else* (that is
to say, like people in the city)."[128] Ownership of a small appliance like
the electric coffee mill was a "symbol of participation in modernization"
that instilled the feeling of "marching in step with one's century."[129]
Despite finding these inclinations among the rural population, however,
UNIMAREL advised that publicity should emphasize profitability, time
gained, and practicality, and although it was a good idea to evoke the
word "comfort," one needed to guard against giving the impression of
"luxury." Advertisers also needed to keep in mind the real conditions of
rural homes and avoid creating the image of an ideal home in which the
rural family could not recognize itself.[130] This cartoon from the paper
France-Soir showed the discrepancy between the ideal promised in ads
and women's journals and actual rural living conditions. (Figure 3.2.)
The warning was thus eminently practical, especially considering that of
the population concerned by the UNIMAREL study, 59 percent lived in
homes more than one hundred years old and only 9 percent lived in homes
less than twenty years old.[131]

Morin found that young people in rural villages, like the young bourgeoisie, had more freedom from parental control in choosing a marital
partner than they had in the past and sought romantic love in marriage.
Girls seemed to evidence this more than boys, who demanded only "an
agreeable, pleasant, level-headed wife." Girls posed a list of qualifications
that included, "amorous inclinations, social promotion, recognition of
their authority in the home, and a suitable house."[132] The desire for a
pleasant, and modern, home for the amorous couple had the potential to
permanently change life in the countryside. Many contemporary observers

[127] Drouin, "Un nouveau type de couple."
[128] UNIMAREL, *La prospection du marché rural de l'électricité: Cadre psychologique* (Paris: UNIMAREL, 1959), 24. Emphasis in original.
[129] Ibid., 29.
[130] Ibid., 35.
[131] Ibid., 40.
[132] Morin, *Commun en France*, 170.

RETOUR DU SALON DES ARTS MENAGERS :
— Ça doit être pratique, ces machines-là, quand on a l'électricité...
(Dessin de Pierre.)

FIGURE 3.2. "I'll bet these machines are real practical if you have electricity...."
Source: *France-Soir*, March 6, 1960.

noted that young women were leaving the farm to seek better living conditions in the cities. Despite myriad economic reasons for deserting the countryside, commentators often pointed to changes in the attitudes of women as the motive force behind this exodus.[133] Morin asked an elderly

---

[133] Roland Maspétiol, "Sociologie de la famille rurale de type traditionnel en France," and "Débats," *Sociologie de la famille contemporaine*.

peasant why young people were leaving and before he could respond his sixteen year-old grand-daughter exclaimed, "liberty."[134] He identified changing attitudes toward the home as just the first step toward finding fulfillment outside of the home. For young women, according to Morin, "the aspiration to live her life in the home," had created "the aspiration to live in the world." This was leading young women to seek employment in the city and leaving those who were tied to the farm to be victims of "a general frustration."[135]

Moscovici also wrote that women on nonmechanized farms grew frustrated with their difficult living conditions. One woman envied industrial workers, noting, "if a man earns a certain amount per month, one knows: This year I'll redo the house, the year after I'll buy a Frigidaire, after that new furniture...."[136] Mothers were not encouraging their children to go into agriculture, and unmarried women were opting out of marrying farmers.[137] Mendras found in his study of four regions, including Brittany, Alsace, Béarn, and the Auvergne, that in all of these regions farmers hoped to have one son carry on the farm, but the majority encouraged their daughters to leave the land. He also cited an *Institut français d'opinion publique* (IFOP) survey that said that only 13 percent of farmwomen encouraged their daughters to marry farmers.[138] In her work on the Aveyron, Susan Carole Rogers found that so many women deserted the countryside in the 1960s that farm families had to devote money to modernizing their homes if they were to attract a bride and assure the family's future.[139]

While many social scientists implied that the rural exodus and other growing pains associated with the modernization of rural areas were inevitable, Pierre Bourdieu's work on his home village in Béarn, in the southwest of France, was moving in its depiction of the pain resulting from the clash of urban and rural civilizations. Bourdieu pointed out, as did many scholars, that women were leaving the countryside more quickly than men. In the mid-1950s, six women and four men left the village each year, on average. In the countryside around the village,

[134] Morin, *Commun en France*, 169.
[135] Ibid., 169.
[136] Moscovici, "Le changement social," 321.
[137] Ibid., 320–321.
[138] Mendras, *The Vanishing Peasant*, 173.
[139] Susan Carol Rogers, *Shaping Modern Times in Rural France: The Transformation and Reproduction of an Aveyronnais Community* (Princeton: Princeton University Press, 1991), 163.

almost 56 percent of the men between the ages of thirty-one and forty were single, and not by choice.[140] Bourdieu used the concept of *habitus* to explain the way that the de-valorization of the peasant lifestyle came to be embedded in the very bodies of the young peasant men who were now "unmarriable" because young women had absorbed the ideals of urban France and judged peasant men according to criteria they could never fulfill. The male peasant was forced to view himself as others did, and so became "*empaysanné*;" his body and bearing marked by his peasant status.[141] Bourdieu described a village dance at which young men of marrying age stood around the edges of the room, watching young women and men from the village and nearby cities dance, embarrassed by their own bodies and clothes and aware that they could not compete with the other men. Bourdieu's work is revealing in that he stresses how, for the peasants of Béarn, the inability of men slated to inherit their family property to marry was the most "glaring symptom of a society in crisis."[142]

Bourdieu determined that the rural crisis was not simply caused by the fact that women no longer wanted to be peasants – the common explanation provided by the people he interviewed – but that traditionally the eldest sons in farming families had been privileged, as they stood to inherit the farm and therefore had good marriage prospects, whereas their younger brothers and sisters either left the farm or stayed, but without marrying. The declining prestige of agriculture meant that eldest sons were now underprivileged compared to men in the village and cities, and even to their younger brothers, who were free to leave the farm and find work in industry.

Like many other sociologists, Bourdieu emphasized the greater ability of women to adapt to urban lifestyles and accept urban norms and standards, many of which were associated with new habits of consumption. "The city is, above all, for the *paysanne*, the *grand magasin*," or department store, wrote Bourdieu.[143] Through the women's press, young peasant women learned about lifestyles, hairstyles, and fashion in the cities.[144]

[140] Pierre Bourdieu, "Célibat et conditions paysannes," *Études Rurales* 5/6 (1962): 68, 62. For analysis of Bourdieu's work on Béarn and the simultaneous study he did of Kabyle peasants in Algeria, see Loïc Wacquant, "Following Pierre Bourdieu into the Field," *Ethnography* 5 (2005): 387–414.

[141] Bourdieu, "Célibat," 101.

[142] Ibid., 32.

[143] Ibid., 105.

[144] Drouin also pointed to the influence of the women's press. He interviewed a member of a rural family movement who told him about a hamlet where five farmer's daughters read together seventeen women's magazines per week. Drouin, "Avec les métallos."

The hold of parents over young women had also loosened, and the number who continued their studies after the primary years increased, so they had many job opportunities in the cities. The city represented the "hope for emancipation." The attraction of "new products and new techniques of comfort," as well as urban ideas about manners and entertainment, led rural women to place all their hopes in marrying a man from the city. "Putting all their hopes in him," Bourdieu wrote, "they are strongly motivated to change themselves and adopt the appearance of the city girl."[145] The country boy was incapable of a similar change.

Bourdieu questioned whether the inability to find a wife was a result of declining conditions on the farm, or if forced celibacy led to decline because the owner had simply given up.[146] The inability to marry caused unique problems for farming families, as one economic imperative was to keep property intact and to pass it on to the next generation. This economic crisis occurred in a national cultural context that celebrated young marriage and children, and in which the overall rate of marriage in the nation was higher than ever. These young families had new consumer needs, however, and rural communities suffered, in particular through the flight of young women, because of their inability to fulfill them.

SPENDING MONEY ON THE HOME

Regardless of whether one lived in a rural or an urban area, the desire to purchase new commodities was often thwarted by the need for a home in which to put them. At the end of the war, the French housing supply was not large enough to shelter existing families, much less the future families hoped for by pronatalists across the political spectrum. Roughly two million homes had been damaged or destroyed during the Second World War, worsening a prewar housing deficit.[147] Various studies done in the late 1940s cited the need for between three and four million new residences over the next ten to fifteen years, numbers that represented almost a quarter of existing housing.[148] Immediately after the war, the provisional government created the *Ministère de la reconstruction et de l'urbanisme* (MRU) to respond to the crisis. Despite the ministry's early efforts, housing activists, family organizations, and women's organizations

[145] Bourdieu, "Célibat," 103–104.
[146] Ibid., 107.
[147] Peggy A. Phillips, *Modern France: Theories and Realities of Urban Planning* (Lanham: University Press of America, Inc., 1987), 80. See also Voldman, *La reconstruction des villes*.
[148] Houdeville, *Pour une civilisation*, 106.

repeatedly lamented the lack of attention to family needs on the part of the national government and political parties.[149] Although all parties professed commitment to providing housing for the population, they rarely followed through on their promises when other national issues arose. As Premier René Pleven told the National Assembly in January 1952, "It is clear that the more that we have given to defense, the less we have given to construction."[150] Colonial wars in Indochina and Algeria distracted attention from domestic consumer issues; in 1947, war costs even forced the government to halt construction underway, cancel new projects, and delay payments to construction companies.[151] Louis Houdeville, an activist in the campaign for affordable modern housing, claimed that the war in Indochina had cost three trillion francs, roughly the equivalent of Marshall Plan aid. He asserted that while West Germany had invested its aid in reconstruction, the French government had largely ignored the housing needs of its population.[152]

In 1953, the government announced initiation of the *Plan Courant* that provided subsidies and low interest loans from the *Crédit Foncier* to companies willing to build low cost family housing according to government standards.[153] In the early 1950s, France's construction record was still poor, but the state was finally devoting significant funding to housing, and by the mid-1950s reconstruction had shifted to new construction. In 1957, the rate of construction was 270,000 housing units a year, and in 1958 the name of the *Ministère de la reconstruction et de l'urbanisme* was changed to the *Ministère de la construction*, suggesting that France had entered a new phase in housing development.[154] By 1960,

---

[149] For extensive discussion of postwar housing reconstruction, see Phillips, *Modern France*, Voldman, *La reconstruction des villes*, and Newsome, *The Struggle for a Voice*.

[150] Quoted in Houdeville, *Pour une civilisation*, 109. See also Newsome, *The Struggle for a Voice*, 89.

[151] Newsome, *The Struggle for a Voice*, 89.

[152] Houdeville, *Pour une civilization*, 110. A 1953 report by the *Conseil économique* came to some of the same conclusions. They stated that the total number of housing units either newly constructed or reconstructed in 1951 was 75,920, and reached a high of 81,390 in 1952, achieving only a quarter of what was needed to eventually reach the government's goal. The study found that France compared very unfavorably to most other Western European nations in housing construction, most notably to West Germany, where 435,000 housing units were constructed in 1951 alone. In the number of rooms per inhabitant constructed in 1951, France ranked behind Norway, West Germany, the Netherlands, Britain, and Italy. Conseil économique, *Le problème du logement* (Paris: Presses Universitaires de France, 1953), 6–7.

[153] See Wakeman, *Modernizing the Provincial City*, 83. The housing units constructed through the plan were called Logements Économiques et Familiaux, or LOGECOS.

[154] Rudolph, "At Home in Postwar France," 222, 228.

the rate of construction had reached 300,000 units a year – more than four times the number built just a decade earlier.[155] Housing was finally booming in France, principally in the form of the *grands ensembles*, huge new apartment blocks that included more than one thousand housing units in a single project. These were determined to be the quickest, most rational way to shelter the large number of families looking for housing. The baby boom only intensified the need for shelter, and the creation of millions of new consumers, and the need to equip millions of new homes, could only increase consumption in France. The glorification of home and family in media like the women's press was supported by a new willingness on the part of the French population to spend unprecedented amounts of money on the home, something of course made more possible by rising incomes.

This change in spending habits was crucial. One reason frequently cited when discussing France's poor construction record until the 1960s was the lack of profit in building and then leasing housing space. In 1953, whereas a three-room apartment in Paris cost, on average, 2.7 million francs to build, and maintenance costs per year were 1 percent of the value, or 27,000 francs, average rent for the same size apartment was 18,120 francs per year.[156] The situation had few clear solutions. Representatives of the working class found lifting the rent cap unthinkable without a corresponding raise in salaries. Understandably, few investors were willing to take on the construction of housing without the hope of a profit. In 1950, the French devoted 3 percent of their spending, on average, to housing.[157] This did not necessarily mean that families were unwilling to spend more, because better quality, more expensive housing was rarely available, even for those families who could afford it. The percent of a family's budget devoted to housing had, in fact, declined through the first half of the century, as in 1914 the French were spending about 15 percent of their money on housing.[158] Over the course of the postwar years, however, French families showed that they believed that better housing and equipment were necessities, and that they would spend money to acquire them.

New housing was desirable, even if it was more expensive. While the price of consumer durables dropped over the postwar decades, the price

---

[155] W. Brian Newsome, "The Rise of the *Grands Ensembles*: Government, Business, and Housing in Postwar France," *The Historian* 66 (2004), 812.
[156] Conseil Économique, *Le problème du logement*, 10.
[157] Ibid., 17.
[158] Voldman, *La reconstruction des villes*, 330.

of rents gradually rose. As late as 1959, rent represented less than 5 percent of family budgets, and ranked seventh in the hierarchy of family
expenses. By 1968, rent was 8 percent of family budgets and fourth on
the list of expenses. In 1968, the rise in rent prices was 72 percent higher
than the general increase in prices in France.[159] A number of factors contributed to housing inflation, including immigration, especially after the
end of the Algerian War, speculation, and urbanization, but the amount of
money families were willing to pay in order to enjoy the comforts of modern housing also shows a new recognition that these comforts were necessities, not luxuries.[160] Jacqueline Niaudet, writing for *Consommation* in
1968, noted that the rapid rise in spending on "embellishment and equipment of the home," compared to the much slower evolution of spending
on things like entertainment outside the home, showed a "preference for
a lifestyle centered on the home."[161] Her statistical research on spending
confirmed the declarations of the women's press about the shift in aspirations among French women and families in the postwar decades.

   Along with paying for better housing, French families showed that
they were willing to pay for home appliances and furnishings and, as we
have already seen, resort to credit to do so. The new family was defined
by its need to consume, and given the opportunity, consume it did. In
1950, the French spent 91 million francs on refrigerators; in 1960, 822
million. In 1950, 46 million francs on washing machines; in 1960, 577
million. In 1950, 32 million francs on vacuums and floor polishers; in
1960, 119 million. (See Table 3.1.)[162] Granted, there were bouts of very
high inflation during the decade, but the numbers are impressive nonetheless. The number of appliances sold each year steadily increased over the
decade. In 1950, 125,000 refrigerators sold; in 1958, 578,000. In 1950,
55,000 washing machines; in 1958, 480,000. In 1950, 210,000 vacuum
cleaners; in 1958, 349,000. (See Table 3.2.)[163] Thus, the first big burst of
consumption occurred in the mid-1950s, even before housing construction reached the rapid pace of the late 1950s and early 1960s.

[159] Niaudet, "L'évolution de la consommation," 59.
[160] The end of the Algerian War would increase immigration to the metropole. For the
     unique history of Algerian families in the housing system see Amelia Lyons, "Invisible
     Immigrants."
[161] Niaudet, "L'évolution de la consommation," 30.
[162] INSEE, *Annuaire statistique de la France* (Paris: Presses Universitaires de France,
     1961): 451. All of the monetary amounts are in new francs.
[163] Acquier, J., "Le matériel ménager dans les foyers français (parc et achats),"
     *Consommation: Annales du Centre de recherches et de documentation sur la consom-
     mation* 4 (1959), 68.

TABLE 3.1. *Annual Spending on Appliances*
(in Millions of New Francs)

	1950	1960
Refrigerators	91	822
Washing Machines	46	577
Vacuums and Floor Polishers	32	119

Source: INSEE, *Annuaire statistique de la France* (Paris: Presses Universitaires de France, 1961): 451.

TABLE 3.2. *Number of Appliances Sold (1950 and 1958)*

	1950	1958
Refrigerators	125,000	578,000
Washing Machines	55,000	480,000
Vacuum Cleaners	210,000	349,000

Source: Acquier, J., "Le Matériel ménager dans les foyers française (parc et achats)," *Consommation: Annales du Centre de recherches et de documentation sur la consommation* 4 (1959): 68.

The French population only continued to increase its domestic consumption throughout the 1960s. At the beginning of 1960 about 25 percent of French households had refrigerators; at the beginning of 1968 almost 70 percent had them. For washing machines, the jump was from 24 percent to 48 percent. As early as the mid-1950s, public laundromats were appearing in urban areas, which meant that more families had access to a machine, even if they did not have one at home.[164] Purchases for home entertainment were also growing: whereas just over 12 percent of French households had a television in 1960, almost 60 percent had one by 1968.[165] The spread of televisions by the late 1960s indicates the willingness to incorporate new products, even those whose labor-saving value was not apparent, into current conceptions of comfort and necessity. Statistics cannot tell us how French families felt about the items they bought, but they do suggest that new conceptions of necessity, which

[164] There were one thousand laundromats in France as early as 1952, and that number was growing every day. Jean Rey, "Les centres de lavage ont rapidement conquis leur place dans la vie française" *Productivité française* 3 (1952), 22.

[165] In 1968, 58.9 percent of households had a television. Fernand Pascaud, "La consommation des ménages de 1959 à 1972," *Les collections de l'INSEE*. Série M. Numéro 134 de collections. 35 (1974), 25.

were discursively created but sprang from the materiality of postwar reconstruction and the housing crisis, had been accepted widely enough that a broad base of French families was willing to spend unprecedented sums of money on living conditions and commodities that were considered luxuries less than twenty years before.[166]

LIBERATION THROUGH DOMESTIC CONSUMPTION?

Just as tensions existed within the notion that domestic consumption entailed private spending, as opposed to spending devoted to public representation, the notion that all French families deserved a certain standard of living that required modern housing and appliances, created frustration, because not all families, in either urban or rural areas, had access to these comforts. In addition, although urban planners and government officials determined that the *grands ensembles* were the most rational means of sheltering the French population, it soon became apparent that even when providing modernity, these apartments did not necessarily provide happiness. Sociologist Nicole Haumont conducted a study on the *grands ensembles* in the late 1960s, and argued that despite the fact that the apartments were modern and fulfilled the functional needs of their inhabitants, designers often ignored factors that were necessary for making people truly satisfied in their home, needs such as separating the public and private, and creating a space "entirely of your own tastes, to remake it for yourself."[167] Haumont also addressed the problems that arose when families moved into new, modern housing, but could not afford to equip it. She cited a study on a section of the thirteenth arrondissement of Paris, which had been renovated and its occupants moved into new apartments. For those who could afford their more expensive rent, the apartment became "more than a shelter for the family; the proof that one is finally able to take one's place in society, to provide one's own with some comfort and happiness, to appreciate as much as anyone else those new items that are celebrated in advertising." Once again, the shifting line between public representation and private enjoyment is apparent in her assertion that this housing solidified one's social position, but that to buy new

---

[166] For a call to use quantitative sources in interpretive cultural histories, see William Sewell, *Logics of History: Social Theory and Social Transformation* (Chicago: University of Chicago Press, 2005).

[167] Nicole Haumont, "Habitat et modèles culturels," *Revue française de sociologie* 9 (1968), 182.

products "corresponds more to a desire to affirm oneself, to be 'modern', than the desire to acquire objects that show one's 'standing.'"[168]

Haumont pointed out that consumption of material goods was more important in the new, modern, housing, as the old social structure of the neighborhood was gone. In the past, the separation between home and street was less strict, as the neighborhood had a lively street culture. The modern lifestyle was more private, with the division between interior and exterior clearly defined. Those families who could not afford to equip their interiors, especially now that their rent was more expensive, felt deeply the loss of the old relationships between neighbors, and felt "isolated, lost, and discontent" being unable to embrace the new lifestyle even as the old disappeared, while their neighbors with money accepted, on the other hand, the "models and lifestyles of the middle classes."[169] Haumont's comments, which were based on research analyzing the social change that accompanied urban renovation, indicated both the inability of many to afford the lifestyle celebrated by women's journals and defined by sociologists as modern, and the potential difficulties of adjusting to housing that was replete with modern conveniences, but could not fulfill all the needs of its inhabitants.[170]

The president of the UFCS pointed to some of these same problems in an address to UNESCO in 1960. The UFCS asserted that providing new housing was important to women, above all, and that they strongly appreciated the comfort that new housing provided, despite its inconveniences, noting that the arrival at a modern apartment was marked by a "sense of euphoria." Despite the euphoria, the problems of the *grands ensembles* included isolation, the fact that the concentration of families with young children did not recreate the variety of a real community, poor insulation that meant that buildings were noisy, and elevated rents that made equipping and decorating the apartments difficult. Worried about the temptation to equip them no matter what the cost, the UFCS advocated the reigning in of door-to-door salesmen, or at least requiring the signatures of both husband and wife for credit purchases. A women's organization that vaunted the influence of the woman consumer, the UFCS at the same time doubted the ability of individual women to resist

[168] Ibid., 189.
[169] Ibid., 189.
[170] Haumont cited research by H. Coing in her study. W. Brian Newsome has written extensively about the inability or unwillingness of government planners and architects to listen to the opinions of inhabitants of postwar housing complexes. See, especially, Newsome, "The Struggle for a Voice in the City."

temptation when faced with an expensive washing machine, refrigerator, or television.[171]

The complaints about the *grands ensembles*, the most widespread means of providing housing with modern conveniences in postwar France, reveal tensions within the notion that concentrating on family in a well-equipped home was the answer to women's fulfillment in postwar France. As W. Brian Newsome has pointed out, by the mid-1960s, the residents of these housing complexes increasingly voted against the Gaullist government to express their dissatisfaction with this solution to the housing deficit. In the events of 1968, the postwar generation would focus not on the fulfillment modern conveniences provided, which the UFCS had pointed to even while suggesting that the *grands ensembles* had major faults, but on how these complexes represented the anomie and alienation of mass consumer society.[172] These were different complaints from those of the generation that had lived through war, occupation, and postwar economic dislocation in the midst of a severe housing shortage; the earlier generation expressed dissatisfaction with the housing solution while at the same time showing appreciation for the standard of living it allowed.

A second tension inherent in the notion that mass consumer society could fulfill the family and provide women with emancipation in the home, was that women were increasingly expressing dissatisfaction with the role of full-time homemaker and mother, especially in the early and mid-1960s. Indeed, as home comfort became more widespread, so did women's complaints about being isolated in the home. Even the UFCS, which still held fairly conservative positions regarding women's place in the home and society, asserted that women's isolation was one problem in the *grands ensembles*. They blamed this situation, however, as well as the torment caused by money worries, and even infrequent cases of women's "depression and immorality," at least in part on the fact that many of these women were not properly educated to assume their role in the family after marriage.[173]

Complaints about isolation in modern homes received little sympathy in the mid-1950s. In 1956, *Marie-France* printed an article called "Don't Say 'I'm Unhappy at Home'." The article told the story of Véronique D., a young mother with three children. Her husband was a civil servant and

---

[171] "Les femmes dans les grands ensembles," *La femme dans la vie sociale* 302 (1960), 2.
[172] See Newsome, "The Rise of the *Grands Ensembles*."
[173] "Les femmes dans les grands ensembles," 2.

she lived in a nice apartment; thus, this was not the story of "a woman fighting step by step against misery and struggling under twenty hours of work a day." Véronique's case was poignant, however. She spoke of the monotony of her days, her isolation while her husband was at work, the never-ending housework that she dared not let lapse, her impatience as she waited for her husband to return, and then his desire for calm, not conversation, and his annoyance at her sharing of her menial concerns. "Why should I tell him about the number of towels I need to mend and change?" Rather than finding fulfillment and strength in her marriage, she feared that she and her husband were "losing one another."[174] The journalist sympathized with Véronique, but offered few options for changing her situation. In few cases did the author find it acceptable to take on professional work when one had young children, but Véronique could enroll in a homemaking class, or follow the example of women who had taken on charity work, pen pals, correspondence courses, or reading and theatre groups.[175]

The case of Véronique exhibited some of the tensions in the notion of the liberation of women through consumption in the modern home. Véronique did not find fulfillment in her domestic role, and while her husband did find relaxation in their home, her need for stimulation was putting her family at risk. By the late 1950s, *Elle*, while still including articles celebrating home, family, and children, had begun to frequently print articles about women dissatisfied with marriage, both men and women committing adultery, and women's rejection of the role of full-time homemaker. The notion of fulfillment through marriage and mass consumer society seemed under attack. In 1959, the magazine published the results of a study by IFOP called *"La française et l'amour."* One of the articles in the series was titled "One woman in three: conjugal love deceived me." The article asserted that women needed to admire the men that they loved, and now that women had discovered that they could succeed in the workplace and that many women had, in addition to their responsibilities in their marriage, "another profession, a true profession," marriages were subjected to new strains.[176] When women had focused on the home, they had admired their husbands simply for being their husbands, regardless of whether they had any special talent or succeeded in their careers. *Elle* quoted a young woman who worked in the same field

---

[174] Francine, "Ne dites plus: 'Je m'ennuie chez moi'," *Marie-France* 8 (1956): 42.
[175] Ibid., 45.
[176] Jean-Jacques Delacroix, "Une femme mariée sur trois: L'amour conjugale m'a déçu," *Elle* 729 (1959), 62.

as her husband, and upon finding out that she was better at her job than he was, she was no longer attracted to him. She now had much higher standards for the ideal husband – he needed to be "sure of himself" and successful, but also consider her "as an associate" as she, of course, would continue to work professionally.[177]

Whereas in 1956, *Marie-France* had dissuaded young Véronique from taking a job outside of the home, in 1965, *Marie-Claire* printed a series of articles called "*La femme libérée*," based on readers' responses to an eight-question survey on women's liberation. To the question of whether the role of "*femme au foyer*," or full-time homemaker, was ideal for women, 68 percent of *Marie-Claire's* respondents, the majority of whom were between the ages of twenty-five and forty, said "no."[178] From the women's replies, *Marie-Claire* chose the "best" letter, that of a twenty-seven-year-old wife and mother from Le Creusot. The writer, Denise Roux, was married to a worker, and so kept her job as a secretary after having a child because the family needed her income. Despite the fact that financial necessity prompted her decision, she also stated that a life in the home "no matter how beautiful, no matter how useful, no matter how absorbing it may be, does not fully satisfy me."[179] While feeling the desire and the need to work outside of the home, Denise still associated the responsibilities of caring for and consuming for the home to be women's, noting that daily expenses were "indisputably the jurisdiction of the woman."[180] The young woman who wrote to *Marie-Claire* held that the role of the housewife as domestic consumer and manager was a valid formula for women's satisfaction, but argued that she also needed something beyond this to be fulfilled.

The recurrence of articles on adultery, divorce, and marital woes in women's journals in the 1960s reveals the tensions in the notion that mass consumer society could reconcile the traditional family structure with women's desires for independence and equality. Ironically, one of the women that Nicole Haumont quoted in her article on the *grands ensembles* asserted that her sister-in-law and her nieces were unhappy with the modern flooring in their apartment because it was too easy to clean; "all they have to do is polish it, it's always clean, and so after that, what do they do? They just look at one another."[181] The claim that life was

[177] Ibid., 100.
[178] "La femme libérée," *Marie-Claire* 138 (1965), 60.
[179] Ibid., 63.
[180] Ibid., 63.
[181] Haumont, "Habitat et modèles culturels," 182–183.

too easy for women in modern housing was unusual, and contradicts the ample research showing that women's domestic work actually expanded with modernization and appliances because their standards were higher, but it is interesting in its rejection of the notion that women could only be fulfilled in this kind of housing. Clearly, this notion had problems even as it dominated public discourse in the 1950s.

The notion of liberation through consumption was increasingly under attack in the 1960s. The *Mouvement de libération des femmes* (MLF) was not created until 1970, and many historians associate the feminism of the next generation with women's dissatisfaction with the events of 1968, but evidence suggests a weakening of the postwar discourse on family and marriage by the early 1960s.[182] Whereas birth control was often construed as a tool to be used in support of the family, rather than evidence of women's independence from the family, the more open discussion of limiting births in the 1960s does show a weakening in the notion that women's destiny was found in motherhood. Birth control was still illegal, but the *Mouvement français pour le planning familial* began opening centers dispensing advice and referring women to prescribing doctors in 1961. These rapidly spread, indicating the government's unwillingness to try to punish the offenders. The realization that 63 percent of the electorate for the first presidential elections of the Fifth Republic was female helped make birth control an important campaign issue. François Mitterrand took the step of placing legalization of birth control on his presidential platform in 1965, and the Neuwirth Law legalized contraception in 1967.[183]

Perhaps more germane to the faltering notion of emancipation through mass consumption was the new complexity in discussion of women's employment in the early 1960s. The government's Armand-Rueff committee advocated increasing recourse to women's labor as part-time workers, and even organizations like the UFCS began to accept this as a way for women to combine professional work and devotion to family and home.[184] The 1965 marriage reforms ended the husband's ability to stop his wife

---

[182] On 1968, see Michelle Zancarini-Fournel, "Genre et politique: Les années 1968," *Vingtième Siècle* 75 (2002): 133–143.

[183] Sylvie Chaperon, *Les années Beauvoir, 1945–1970* (Paris: Fayard, 2000), 301–306, 315, 323. The first center for Family Planning was opened at Grenoble in 1961. By 1966, there were 123 of them in 72 departments. Chaperon, 279–280.

[184] Ibid., 288–289. For analysis of changes in the UFCS's attitudes, changes that partisans of the movement argue have been overlooked because of the movement's conservative and Catholic origins, see Doneaud and Guérin, *Les femmes agissent, le monde change*.

from working, and the same year the government created a Committee for Study and Liaison for the Problems Concerning Women's Work under the labor ministry. Though it had no budget and only an advisory role, it did show an attempt to determine the specific constraints women faced in the workforce.[185] More radical ideas about women's place in society and culture began circulating after 1964. Simone de Beauvoir's *Le deuxième sexe*, which had been widely condemned when it was published in 1949, began to attract more attention. Geneviève Texier and Andrée Michel's influential *La condition de la française d'aujourd'hui* appeared in 1964, and Betty Friedan's *The Feminine Mystique* was translated into French by Yvette Roudy.[186] These would be important for inspiring women working for a very different kind of emancipation from that found in mass consumer society.

The belief in emancipation through mass consumer society was weakening by the mid-1960s, but that does not change the fact that consumption was central to defining the new couple and family of the postwar decades. New standards of living and new commodities were accepted as necessities, not luxuries, and the expanding population of young families, many of them in new housing by the 1960s, helped drive mass production of consumer durables and, thereby, economic expansion. The discourse of journalists, the popular press, public figures, and sociologists asserted that the home provided a refuge from the horrors of war, economic dislocation, and the alienating affects of industrial society. The couple and family that figured so prominently in postwar French society needed the space of the home in which to meet not just the social and national responsibility of reproduction, but to find personal fulfillment, happiness, and security, and these depended on home modernization and the development of mass consumer society in France. At the same time, the family drove mass consumer society and economic expansion with its growing list of needs, including new housing and the commodities that went in it. Mass consumer society also seemed to potentially reconcile women's emancipation with the widespread desire for "normalcy," the definition of which usually included the need for women to devote themselves to home and family. Just as the role of citizen consumer implied a new responsibility for influencing the national economy, the role of domestic consumer and manager included new responsibilities and skills, even while women remained confined to the home.

---

[185] Chaperon, *Les années Beauvoir*, 323–331.
[186] Ibid., 323–331, 292–3.

Nowhere were new consumer needs more apparent than in the young couples marrying and forming families in the late 1940s and 1950s. They all seemed to be retreating to the comfort of their nuclear family households, or hoping to, in any case. As Pierre Bourdieu's work on consumption in 1960s France shows, as French society grew more affluent, it became more important for individuals and families to display their social status through consumption.[187] For most of the commentators writing on domestic consumption in the 1950s, when many families were still in search of new housing and when the rural population, in particular, had not yet experienced the benefits of postwar prosperity, domestic consumption was often portrayed as private, not public or status-seeking. But as is clear from the young peasant couples who needed to decorate because they enjoyed visiting their neighbors' homes, or the image of modernity associated even with small items like the electric coffee mill, the line between private comfort and public representation was never clear, even in the most modest of homes. Regardless of these mixed motives, young people retreated to the home, commentators explained, to escape the upheaval of war and economic crisis. They were both scarred by the past and hopeful about the future, seeking stability in the family and looking forward to the time when they could create their own comfortable homes. This stability, therefore, rested on the promise of mass consumer society, which also served to define the roles of French men and women, the modern couple, and the new family.

---

[187] Pierre Bourdieu, *Distinction: A Social Critique of the Judgment of Taste* (Cambridge: Harvard University Press, 1984).

4

"Can a Man with a Refrigerator Make a Revolution?"

Redefining Class in the Postwar Years

In March 1957, as the *Salon des arts ménagers* hosted its annual exhibition of home appliances, domestic arts, and national reconstruction plans, the journal *L'Express* gathered four scholars and intellectuals to discuss the future of France in light of the great demand for consumer durables. With all of the needs facing France, the *L'Express* host wondered, was it really healthy to turn production toward home appliances? Was perhaps a bit of "austerity" preferable? And what did this mean for working-class demands, he wondered, asking, "can a man with a refrigerator make a revolution?"[1] The possible effects of mass consumption, credit, and comfort on the French class system were open to debate in the 1950s and 1960s. During the interwar period, economic conditions in France had made household technology and home modernization virtually unattainable for working-class families, and this had enabled socialists and intellectuals to insist that needs were class based: a worker with the same amount of money as a member of the bourgeoisie would spend it in different ways.[2] Both socialists and elite intellectuals clung to this belief, as discarding it would entail modifying their notions of bourgeois taste or working-class radicalism.

The great demand for home modernization and new commodities that accompanied French economic expansion in the 1950s and 1960s poked

[1] "La machine à laver, tourne-t-elle dans le sens d'histoire?" *L'Express*, March 1, 1957, 14.
[2] For opposition to the notion of a "standard of living" see De Grazia, *Irresistible Empire: America's Advance through 20th Century Europe* (Cambridge: Belknap Press of Harvard University Press, 2005) and Coffin, "A 'Standard' of Living? European Perspectives on Class and Consumption in the Early Twentieth Century," *International Labor and Working-Class History* 55 (1999): 6–26.

holes in the thesis of limited needs and class based consumption. The French public had determined that the ability to consume was vital to the new families being formed in the wake of war and occupation, and those families were spending large sums of money, sometimes on credit, to fulfill new needs. In this atmosphere, public officials, scholars, and intellectuals debated how these new consumer demands affected the revolutionary potential of the working class, as well as the lifestyle of its class-conscious bourgeoisie. That people of all backgrounds would accept, and, indeed, demand, mass-produced consumer goods challenged notions of taste and class in a society in which the bourgeoisie had, since the nineteenth century, used household consumption to distinguish itself and in which those on the political left had embraced notions of working-class austerity. For critics, mass consumer society seemed to portend the arrival of an American-style, comfortable, but standardized and even banal, society.

Further complicating the situation for those who wished to hold onto the belief that consumer desires were determined by class was the fact that the growing French economy depended on an expanding sector of middle managers, engineers, and white-collar service workers. These employees put the class structure in flux because they seemed to fit into neither the old bourgeoisie, nor the sector of independent petit bourgeois shopkeepers and artisans, nor the working class. They were a new "middle class" that prospered and grew along with mass consumer society. In the end, the development of the postwar French economy and the challenge of mass consumer society reshaped both the structure of French society and understandings of social class as the French population came to accept that domestic consumption was not necessarily a primary indicator of class status. Women in working-class family organizations, members of the Communist women's organization, and women journalists shaped these new perceptions of consumer durables and class, portraying home appliances and other commodities as tasteful, modern, practical, and necessary. Such beliefs were crucial for creating mass consumer society in France. Consumer goods were appropriate for all families and, thus, domestic consumption became a less effective means of defining class status as the lifestyles, purchases, and homes of families across income ranges and class barriers came to resemble one another much more than they had in the past.

STANDARDIZED LIVING IN THE CLASSLESS SOCIETY

The notion that mass consumption would erase class distinctions stemmed in part from popular understandings of life in the United States, the world's pre-eminent mass consumer society at the end of the Second World War. As Victoria de Grazia has argued, American-style Fordist consumption with its cheap, mass-produced goods seemed threateningly democratic in interwar Europe, where class-stratified consumption was a pillar of what she labels the "bourgeois" regime of consumption.[3] Though cheap consumer goods were not widely available in France in the 1930s, images of them, and of the American "way of life" flooded France via American films, sparking much discussion of mass consumer society.[4] The characterization of America as an empty, materialist, standardized society emanated from Catholic intellectuals, Communists, and Socialists in the 1930s. This discourse continued in the postwar years, but was increasingly claimed by the political Left, which opposed Marshall Plan aid and American interference in French political and economic concerns.[5] To intellectuals and politicians, American mass society threatened French taste and individuality; consumer comfort was not worth the sacrifice of French history and culture. As elite, and for the most part male commentators, they saw no value in becoming, as Communist poet Louis Aragon termed it, "a civilization of bathtubs and Frigidaires."[6]

Despite intellectual resistance to the "American way of life," there is little evidence that this sentiment was widespread among the French populace, and it seems that most people found consumer durables desirable. Women's magazines, in particular, spread the gospel of mass consumer society, appealing to a population that, perhaps, saw more value in "bathtubs and Frigidaires" than did Louis Aragon. Immediately following the war, with the presence in France of GIs making American wealth and power all the more apparent, women journalists glorified this classless society, which had seemingly eliminated the drudgery of household

---

[3] De Grazia, *Irresistible Empire* and "Changing Consumer Regimes in Europe, 1930–1970: Comparative Perspectives on the Distribution Problem," in *Getting and Spending: European and American Consumer Societies in the Twentieth Century*, eds. Susan Strasser, Charles McGovern, and Matthias Judt (Cambridge: Cambridge University Press, 1998), 59–83.

[4] Richard Pells explains that by the mid-1920s, about 70 percent of films shown in France were American. *Not Like Us: How Europeans have Loved, Hated, and Transformed American Culture Since World War II* (New York: Basic Books, 1997), 15. Victoria de Grazia describes how this trend continued after the war. The 1946 Blum-Byrnes agreement ended the prewar import quota on American films in France by replacing it with a screen time quota, which helped American filmmakers to overrun the French industry by 1947. See Victoria de Grazia, "Mass Culture and Sovereignty: The American Challenge to European Cinemas, 1920–1960," *Journal of Modern History* 61 (1989): 53–87.

[5] See Kuisel, *Seducing the French* and Philippe Roger, *The American Enemy: The History of French Anti-Americanism* (Chicago: University of Chicago Press, 2005).

[6] Quoted in Kuisel, *Seducing the French*, 38.

labor for women. The image that epitomized abundance, equality, and the absence of class tension, in part because of the success of American motion pictures, was that of life in California. In 1946, the women's journal *La femme* printed an article titled, "The Land of the Stars is also an Earthly Paradise: The Life of Three Households in California." The article described the lifestyles of three families at different income levels who had been featured in the American review, *Life*. The article began, "Life in the open air, in an eternal summer, high salaries combined with low priced merchandise, urbanism and ultramodern comfort in a new country unencumbered by its past, these are the characteristics of life in California, the ideal life for every American."[7] The article portrayed the life of each family, including that with the smallest budget, the family of a firefighter, as comfortable and modern.

La femme reported that the firefighter, who was married with two children, lived in a six-room house that he owned. His wife, Mrs. Loeffler, had a refrigerator and a washing machine. The family went "everyday, in their Dodge, to swim in the Pacific, forty kilometers away."[8] Like the Loeffler family, a sales director's family had no domestic servants, but had eliminated most housework through the acquisition of domestic appliances. *La femme* reported that the Campbell daughters "accomplish in three hours and thirty minutes the washing of the entire household: two hours in the washing machine and one hour and thirty minutes of drying in the sun."[9] Only the richest family, that of a famous composer, had domestic servants: "their life differs very little, however, from that of all the other Californians."[10] The portrayal of the United States as a society devoid of class differences and tensions was common in the French women's press, and the absence of domestic servants in well-to-do families, a very different organization of labor from the traditional French bourgeois household, provoked comment in this and other articles.[11] According to women journalists, modern consumer goods, and labor-saving domestic appliances in particular, had an equalizing effect.

---

[7] "Le pays des stars est aussi le paradis terrestre: La vie de trois ménages en Californie," *La femme* 30 (1946): 4.

[8] Ibid., 4. The family's home ownership was notable as in the mid-1940s in Paris, its suburbs, and the twenty-eight largest cities in France, only an average of 23.3 percent of the population owned homes. Newsome, "The Struggle for a Voice," 63.

[9] Ibid., 4.

[10] Ibid., 5.

[11] See, for example, Berthe Bernage, "Recevrons-nous quand même?" *Le Petit Echo de la Mode* 40 (1947): 2.

Modernizers in the French government, and their American supporters, pushed the view that mass consumer society, free trade, and increased
productivity would ultimately make American-style living conditions
available to all, which would in turn end adversarial relations between
labor and management in France. In 1951, the journal *Rapports France-
États-Unis*, a French language magazine published by Marshall Plan representatives in Paris, printed an article by a French journalist traveling
in the United States. He observed that after visiting the homes of both
"bourgeois" Americans and working-class Americans, "There aren't any
major differences. In one and the other, one finds the inevitable *icebox*,
the freezer, the washing machine, the television set. The American worker
lives almost exactly like his boss; perhaps that's the secret to the harmony
that, in general, reigns in relations between management and workers." [12]
The United States government used the high standard of living and wide
availability of consumer durables in its working-class homes to build
support in Europe for the benefits of free trade. The American government, through the United States Information Agency (USIA), sponsored
exhibits at the *Salon des arts ménagers*, including a 1954 presentation of
the "The House without Borders." This home included mass-produced
items from twelve different countries in an effort to show how economic
cooperation and free trade could raise the standard of living for everyone. [13] Mass-produced goods were available to everyone in the United
States, because, as the author in the *Rapports France-États-Unis* article
claimed, in that country there was actually little difference between the
salary of the worker and the manager. In the Soviet Union, he claimed, the
engineer usually made three to four times the salary of the laborer. [14] As
Pierre Laroque pointed out in 1962, to the "superficial observer" of the
United States, it was difficult to identify different social classes because

[12] Pierre Ferenczi, "Aspects de la vie ouvrière aux États-Unis," *Rapports France-États-Unis*
54 (1951): 55. Icebox is in English in the text.
[13] La maison sans frontières. CAC 19850023 article 120. These kinds of exhibits were not
limited to France, nor even Western Europe. Robert Haddow notes that by 1960, the
American commerce department sponsored ninety-seven exhibits in twenty-nine countries. Haddow, *Pavilions of Plenty: Exhibiting American Culture Abroad in the 1950s*
(Washington: Smithsonian Institution Press, 1997), 15. For analysis of these same kinds
of programs in Eastern Europe, see Walter Hixson, *Parting the Curtain: Propaganda,
Culture, and the Cold War, 1945–1961* (New York: St. Martin's Press, 1997).
[14] Ibid., 57. For more on Marshall Plan information in France, see Kroen, "Negotiations
with the American Way." Kroen points out that Marshall Plan information about the
United States almost always portrayed workers as consumers, rather than part of the
production process, in an effort to de-emphasize union organization and belligerency as
a means to prosperity. See also McKenzie, *Remaking France*.

the dependence of American industries on a wide mass of consumers led to a situation where the grand mass of citizens had "the same style of living, the same housing, the same type of clothing, the same elements of comfort...." In this context, he noted, other distinguishing features, including race, religion, education, income, profession, and social connections became more important in defining social status than was consumption.[15]

The equalizing effects of mass consumption clashed with a French culture of consumption in which bourgeois women, in particular, consumed in a way that confirmed their taste, distinction, and class status. The notion of a "standard" of living – in which needs and purchases are not determined by class status – was not widely accepted in prewar France. In his 1933 work, *L'évolution des besoins dans les classes ouvrières*, sociologist Maurice Halbwachs had considered consumption patterns and class. His findings were controversial because he insisted that the needs of working-class families would expand with income rather than being defined by their class status. This differed from the views of other sociologists, as well as his own earlier work, which insisted that needs were class based, and therefore, housing was a need that was very differently conceived of by the working class and bourgeoisie. To assert that the working class aspired to live in the same comfortable conditions, with the same commodities, as the bourgeoisie, offended cultural conservatives, because it challenged their notions of a hierarchy of tastes. At the same time, it angered socialists who feared the end of a radical working-class culture as workers became depoliticized, satiated consumers.[16]

Both of these sets of concerns had to be confronted as France gradually became a mass consumer society. Producers needed bourgeois consumers, since they were the first potential market for consumer goods. Difficult living conditions and the decline in bourgeois savings after two world wars made consumer goods attractive to bourgeois women, but the efforts of women's journals and advertisers were also important for demonstrating the fitness of consumer goods, and home appliances in particular, for wealthy families. Also important was the rapidly expanding new "middle class" – the tertiary sector employees, managers, and other white-collar

---

[15] Pierre Laroque, *Les classes sociales* (Paris: Presses Universitaires de France, 1962), 82–85.

[16] Halbwachs' 1913 study argued that workers never changed the amount of money they spent on housing, even when their income increased. By 1933, and after a stint in the United States, Halbwachs had become convinced that needs were ever-expanding. See Coffin, "A 'Standard' of Living?" and De Grazia, *Irresistible Empire*.

workers so important in an expanding technical and industrial economy. These workers seemed to live and work in a way that set them apart from both the old bourgeoisie and the working class and they were, in a sense, both created by and creators of mass consumer society as they provided a vast market for consumer durables. For their part, working-class women's and family organizations would quickly appropriate consumer durables into their own political platform, demonstrating that mass consumption was compatible with working-class radicalism and notions of solidarity. They demanded access to mass consumer society as citizens contributing to reconstruction and economic growth through their labor, but unable to purchase the very goods they produced.

THE NEW MIDDLE CLASS

In 1951, American economic historian David Landes wrote a piece addressing the question of why Marshall Plan aid had not immediately achieved the levels of productivity its supporters had expected. In his answer, he focused on the unique attitude of French entrepreneurs and the conditions that kept France from becoming a mass consumer society. Landes pointed out that the two biggest population groups, the working class and peasantry, were unable to afford consumer goods. A further hindrance to development was the bourgeois consumer. Members of the French bourgeoisie were not good consumers. They did not spend as much as Americans, and "those people who are in a position to buy have never been completely willing to accept the standardization implicit in mass production." [17] The wealthy French consumer was interested in individuality, differentiation, and luxury. As sociologist Jesse R. Pitts noted in his work on the bourgeois family, the desire to increase sales by keeping prices down was anathema to the bourgeois notion that perfection was the measure of worth of an item, not price. [18] Landes asserted that the French would not laugh at the stock American joke about two women showing up for a party in the same dress; in France, "it is nothing to

[17] David Landes, "French Business and the Businessman: A Social and Cultural Analysis," in *Modern France*, ed. Edward Meade Earl (Princeton: Princeton University Press, 1951), 344. Robert Frost has pointed out that this was a hindrance to the spread of home technology in the 1930s. Working-class families could not afford home appliances, and the families that could would not accept mass-produced goods. Frost, "Machine Liberation."

[18] Jesse R. Pitts, "Continuity and Change in Bourgeois France," in *France: Change and Tradition*, ed. Stanley Hoffmann (London: Victor Gollancz Ltd., 1963), 246–247.

joke about."[19] Along with sacrificing its individuality, the bourgeoisie had to be convinced to go into debt to buy consumer goods. This was difficult, explained Landes, since the idea of "borrowing against the future" was "heresy in a country where the proverb defines a man who makes $5,000 a year and spends $5,001 as poor, and who makes $5,000 and spends $4,999 as rich."[20] These features: the penchant for high-quality luxury goods and the repugnance of debt, combined with a reliance on servants to do the most onerous of household tasks, were defining features of the bourgeois lifestyle of the late nineteenth and early twentieth centuries. The prestige associated with this lifestyle would have to be rejected in order for France to truly become a mass consumer society. In many ways, this lifestyle declined out of necessity, as reduced bourgeois fortunes meant that few families could afford to pay domestic servants and buy goods that were not mass-produced. If this change was accepted reluctantly by some families, it was the embracing of this lifestyle by the new "middle class" that would both provide the key to economic expansion by constituting a wide base of consumers, and help popularize a "modern" lifestyle that included technologically savvy housewives who did their own housework, with the assistance of quality mass-produced goods in a new kind of home.

The Landes piece was published in 1951, just as France was about to turn the corner from poverty to plenty. Consumption would significantly increase from this point through the 1950s and the 1960s.[21] As wealthy families started buying consumer durables, often on credit, the service sector continued to grow, and as middle managers and other white-collar employees grew prominent in the economy and society, sociologists and commentators started "redefining" the class structure in response. The class categories of the prewar economy seemed to no longer fit the modernizing postwar economy. Given its growing size and income, and its apparent "newness," it was the middle class that inspired the most speculation.[22]

[19] Ibid., 344.
[20] Landes, "French Business," 341.
[21] Georges Rottier estimated in 1956 that French consumption had increased 36 percent in the previous six years, averaging close to 5.5 percent per year. Rottier, "Nourriture, logement ou télévision," *Esprit* (December 1957): 739. CREDOC calculated that the standard of living in France improved by 4.5 percent per year between 1950 and 1957. "La consommation dans l'économie française," *Consommation: Annales du Centre de recherches et de documentation sur la consommation* 2 (1958): 25. From 1956 to 1965, average consumption rose by 40.5 percent. Gabriel Vangrevelinghe, "Le niveau de vie en France, 1956 et 1965" *Economie et Statistique* 1 (1969): 7.
[22] As Luc Boltanski has shown, classes exist largely in the realm of representation, and defining the boundaries of social groups is a political process. Boltanski, *The Making of*

Class boundaries are always discursively created, but the boundaries of the middle class were perhaps more unstable than any other, as they shifted with France's rapid economic changes in the mid-twentieth century. The term "middle class" was first popularized during the labor unrest of the 1930s and reflected the belief that France now had three classes, rather than the two dominant classes of the Marxist paradigm: the working class and the bourgeoisie.[23] The educated middle class sat between the owners and the laborers, working for a salary, but exercising responsibility and passing on family property. In the 1950s and early 1960s, it increased in size with the expansion of the French economy and the growing need for managers, administrators, engineers, and service workers. Thus, this group was closely tied to the modernizing economy, as the expansion of industries required a large number of intermediaries between directors and workers.[24] The most studied and analyzed component of the middle class in the postwar years was the rank of the *"cadres,"* or managers, a group that was then further segmented into the "middle" and "superior" *cadres*. Because of its very pronounced "middleness," directing other workers while following directives from above, the *cadre* was emblematic of the larger middle class, which included a variety of professions and incomes.[25]

By 1962, the combined group of middle and superior *cadres*, liberal professionals, and salaried employees composed almost 35 percent of the population, suggesting both the importance of these kinds of workers to the economy and their importance as a market for consumer durables.[26] Between 1956 and 1965, the number of French households headed by members of this group increased by about 590,000, whereas the agricultural population and the lower ranks of the bourgeoisie declined. By the mid-1950s, the old petite bourgeoisie of artisans and small business owners had been overtaken by this group that depended not on family

---

a *Class*. I am speaking of class not necessarily as a social position defined by one's relationship to the means of production, but as a "never-finished project" that is discursively created. See Geoff Eley and Keith Nield, "Farewell to the Working Class?" *International Labor and Working-Class History* 57 (2000): 1–30.

23 See Boltanski, *The Making of a Class*.

24 In 1952, for example, economist Jacques Lecaillon commented on the need for "an immense army of new men, in charge of technical, administrative, and commercial responsibilities, which the '*patron*' can no longer handle on his own." Jacques Lecaillon, "Le revenue des cadres," *Revue économique* 3 (1952): 206.

25 Kristin Ross argues that the *cadre* was an allegory for the French nation at this moment. The *cadre* sat midway between owner and laborer, just as France was both colonized by the United States and colonizer in Algeria. Ross, *Fast Cars, Clean Bodies*.

26 Mendras, *Social Change in Modern France*, 35.

inheritance, but on income, usually in a large firm, and education for success, and which dominated normative understandings of the middle class.[27] Earning significantly higher salaries than the petite bourgeoisie and other socioprofessional groups, including the still large working class, this middle class was an essential market for the producers of consumer durables.[28]

Because the middle class included a range of incomes and professions, making a coherent identity difficult to pinpoint, consumption helped to unify it as a group, at least in the minds of sociologists, consumer researchers, and social commentators. The modern statistical apparatus created after the war reinforced and defined understandings of class and consumption by using the socioprofessional classifications of superior *cadres*, middle *cadres*, employees, and workers when dissecting and predicting the income and expenditures of the French population.[29] Throughout the postwar decades, studies examining the budgets of households according to these professional categories only reified the structure of the French population according to this new formulation. Consumption helped unify the group, as this new middle class was considered to be consistent in its way of life and spending habits, which differed from those of the old bourgeoisie. The old bourgeoisie had valued thrift; commentators emphasized this both as a feature of the bourgeois family business and the bourgeois household.[30] Until at least the 1920s, the bourgeois family relied more on inherited wealth than income, so the desire to pass on family property trumped risky investment decisions that might have led to economic expansion.[31] However, the Depression, the war, and inflation had caused a decline in bourgeois savings, necessitating new consumption patterns and changing the shape of the family, as the children of many of these families became part of the vast new middle

[27] Vangrevelinghe, "Les niveaux de vie," 8–10. Boltanski, *The Making of a Class*, 111.

[28] Vangrevelinghe includes average salaries for socioprofessional categories. In 1965, the average salary for those in the *cadre supérieur* and liberal professional category was 32,500 new francs (NF), in the *cadre moyen* category it was 20,500 NF, for workers it was 13,000 NF, for unskilled manual laborers 10,400 NF, and employees 14,000 NF. Vangrevelinghe, "Les niveaux de vie," 21.

[29] From the list of categories used in the French census. See Pascaud, "La consommation des ménages," 27. These larger categories were further subdivided – workers, for example, into skilled workers, foremen, etc.

[30] See Landes, "French Business." See Boltanski for discussion of how the objective reality of need for thrift may have been transformed into a moral ideal. Boltanski, "The Making of a Class," 68.

[31] Boltanski, "The Making of a Class," 63–5. Pitts, "Continuity and Change," 253.

class.[32] Consuming on credit, they placed value in the potential capital
of technical training and education, which distinguished them from the
working class, which did not have the same level of training. The middle
class expressed confidence in the expanding French economy and placed
value in productivity and technology, rather than the landed wealth,
government bonds, and family savings of the old bourgeoisie.[33]

The middle class was created by the modern mass consumer economy,
which provided its members with positions. They were also creators of
mass consumer society in the sense that, with their relative wealth and
their willingness to buy, they constituted the broad base of consumers that
drove mass production. A satirical example of this relationship is found
in Georges Perec's 1965 novel, *Les choses* (Things). The main characters,
Jérôme and Sylvie, are children of the petite bourgeoisie. They drop out
of college because "It was not the desire for knowledge that devoured
them," instead it was "the need for a room a bit bigger, running water, a
shower, more varied, or at least more copious, food than that at the university café, maybe a car, records, vacations, clothes."[34] The couple takes
jobs as market researchers, a position stereotypical of the new careers in
the modern French economy. In this position, they work to understand
and create consumers, taking surveys on products, asking others: "What
do you think of your washing machine? Are you satisfied with it? Does
it create too many suds? Does it wash well? Does it damage your linens? Does it dry them? Would you prefer a washing machine that also
dries?" and so on.[35] "But money," explains Perec, "creates new needs"
and Jérôme and Sylvie become tied to unfulfilling jobs as they strive to
attain the lifestyle they dream of.[36] They are creators of mass consumer
society even as it comes to define, and for Perec, confine them.

As Kristin Ross has argued, the postwar press also helped make a
cohesive group of the disparate range of professions within the middle class.[37] Ross stresses the importance of popular news journals like

---

[32] See Chapter 3 for discussion of how this decline changed marriage and family.

[33] See Jesse R. Pitts for discussion of bourgeois attitudes to saving and property and how
these were challenged in the postwar period. Pitts, "Continuity and Change." For the
importance of education and training in defining the *cadres*, see Jean Marchal and
Jacques Lecaillon, "Is the Income of the *Cadres* a Special Class of Wages? A Study in the
Light of French Experience," *The Quarterly Journal of Economics* 72 (1958): 166–182.

[34] Georges Perec, *Les choses: Une histoire des années soixante* (Paris: René Juillard,
1965), 30.

[35] Ibid., 34.

[36] Ibid., 38.

[37] Ross, *Fast Cars*, 104–144.

L'Express, but the women's press was particularly instrumental in creating the image of the new middle-class housewife who managed a household full of mechanical servants that had replaced the real-life servants of the prewar period. The journals, and the advertisements they contained, promoted an image of consumer society that could appeal to both the old bourgeoisie and the new middle class. In this image, new home technology, in particular, was neither luxurious nor cheap and shoddy. It was rational, necessary, and modern. Whereas the images could appeal across classes, both *Elle* and *Marie-Claire,* two of the most successful journals, drew the majority of their readers from the growing middle class, and had a readership that was slightly more educated than the general population, and of which just over half of the readers were under the age of thirty-five.[38] The representations in advertisements, photo spreads, short stories, and advice columns were clearly aimed at women marrying and raising children in postwar France.[39] Women with husbands in the rising group of professionals serving the mass consumer economy were probably most likely to see themselves in the modern homes and with the consumer durables that were slowly arriving in France. The journals taught these women, who had lived through war and economic dislocation but now experienced the very gradual arrival of mass consumer society, how to be technocrats in the home just as their husbands were technocrats in the modern French economy.

The interwar years had seen the introduction of a number of fashion journals that grew in popularity with the spread of high fashion to the streets and the increasing use of cosmetics.[40] In 1937, Marcelle Auclair revolutionized the genre by introducing *Marie-Claire,* which combined practical advice and fashion, aspiring to be "the Vogue of the poor."[41] The magazine was heavily influenced by American magazines in its colorful photos and its portrayal of women who were optimistic, confident, and

[38] Nicole Benoît, "La nouvelle féminité," 42–43. In 1970, about 53 percent of *Marie-Claire's* audience and 58 percent of *Elle's* were in this middle class.

[39] See Weiner, *Enfants Terribles* and "Two Modernities: From *Elle* to *Mademoiselle.* Women's Magazines in Postwar France," *Contemporary European History* 8 (1999): 395–409 for her discussion of how *Elle,* in particular, had difficulties moving beyond this audience of women to their daughters. *Elle* launched *Mademoiselle* in 1962 because this fantasy of glamorous domesticity did not appeal to young women.

[40] See Samra-Martine Bonvoisin and Michèle Maignien, *La presse féminine* (Paris: Presses Universitaires de France, 1986) and Roberts, *Civilization without Sexes* and "Samson and Delilah Revisited: The Politics of Women's Fashion in 1920s France," *The American Historical Review* 98 (1993): 657–684 for discussion of mass production of fashion between the wars.

[41] Evelyn Sullerot, *La presse féminine* (Paris: Armand Colin, 1963), 52.

modern. The rubrics created by *Marie-Claire* and other journals spawned new publications after the war, and in 1948, the national press printed about seventy million journals per month; of these, twenty-four million were women's journals. This number reached twenty-nine million in 1950 and thirty-one million in 1951. In 1952, the number of women's journals sold in France equaled that of the political, economic, technical, financial, agricultural, union, artistic, and sporting press combined.[42] Despite intellectual, political, and moral opposition, women's journals remained extremely popular until the mid-1960s. By the end of the 1950s, *Echo de la Mode, Nous Deux*, and *Confidences* sold over one million copies per week, with *Marie-France, Elle*, and *Marie-Claire* close behind in popularity.[43] In fact, when *Marie-Claire*, which had been suppressed at the Liberation because of its links with collaborationist journals, reappeared in 1954, it sold out its first 500,000 copies in several hours.[44] Hélène Gordon Lazareff, who spent the war years in the United States, started *Elle* in 1946, and by 1955 an estimated one-sixth of French women read the popular monthly journal.[45] Less flashy than either *Elle* or *Marie-Claire, Le Petit Echo de la Mode* was often cited as a conduit bringing the mass consumer lifestyle to rural women, and remained extremely popular into the mid-1960s.[46]

This press was instrumental in shaping the new discourse on the home. The new home was not explicitly connected to a particular class, but was described as "American" immediately following the war, and by the early 1950s was increasingly labeled simply "modern." This kind of home was appropriate to all social classes, though only really available to the wealthy, and it was a comfortable, private, household in which modernity had replaced luxury and machines had replaced servants. In 1957, for example, the journal *Marie-France* made this transition explicit in an article called "But of course, Madame, you can have 7 servants ... thanks to ARTS MENAGERS 1957."[47] These items of steel, plastic, and

[42] Figures from Mattei Dogan and Jacques Narbonne, *Les françaises face à la politique* (Paris: Cahiers de la Fondation nationale des sciences politiques, 1955), 67. Susan Weiner points out that the number of journal readers was likely higher than the number sold, as women shared magazines with friends and family. See, "Two Modernities."

[43] Rioux, *The Fourth Republic*, 442.

[44] Weiner, *Enfants Terribles*, 28.

[45] Ibid., 33.

[46] The journal dropped *Le Petit* to become *Echo de la Mode* in 1955. Bonvoisin and Maignien, *La presse féminine*, 16.

[47] Jeanne Chavant and Anne-Marie Seigner, "Mais oui, Madame, vous pouvez avoir 7 domestiques ... grâce aux ARTS MÉNAGERS 1957," *Marie-France* 12 (1957): 52–69.

aluminum were servants one could keep forever; they required no social security taxes; and they only had to be fed electricity. The article included a spread with prices of appliances at the annual *Salon des arts ménagers* exposition, and compared them to the social security fees and salary of a servant performing the same tasks that the machines could do. An electric washing machine, dishwasher, and vegetable cutter could eliminate the need to hire a woman to do the most onerous household tasks, saving the family 23,000 francs in monthly wages and 8,370 francs a trimester in social security charges. The washing machine discussed was top-of-the-line from Bendix, and would cost around 198,000 francs, but *Marie-France* also included a section on buying appliances on credit in the same issue.[48] The article finished with a section on clothing, including patterns for a cap and apron that the housewife could wear while preparing her meal, then remove in time for her guests to arrive.

The question of how to entertain guests in this household was an important one, as an important task of the bourgeois housewife of the nineteenth and early twentieth centuries was to represent her family to outsiders through her household and the commodities in it.[49] New technology could help middle class housewives entertain on their own. *Le Petit Echo de la Mode* broached the subject in 1947 in an article called, "Let's Receive Guests All the Same." The author stated that some people, accustomed to a *savoir-vivre traditionnel* were insistent that "one could not, in a certain milieu, simplify to the point of having people serve themselves. It just isn't done." She noted that in America, servants were uncommon, and hosting was accomplished *sans cérémonie*. With an electric stove you could keep one course warm while eating another, and with modern furnishings, you could even entertain in the kitchen instead of the dining room.[50] That the author mentioned eating in the kitchen was telling, as the eat-in kitchen was often pointed to as an equalizing characteristic of new homes in the 1950s. Traditionally, the working class and peasantry had eaten in the kitchen, but not the bourgeoisie.[51]

Despite the fact that this kind of hosting was *sans cérémonie*, it was important that the housework accomplished by the modern middle-class housewife not be drudgery. Along with being productive, as the discourse

[48] Ibid., 68–69 for prices. See 120–127 for information on credit.
[49] See especially Auslander, *Taste and Power*.
[50] Berthe Bernage, "Recevrons-nous," 2.
[51] See *De la 4 CV à la vidéo* for discussion of the *coin repas*. For women's demands for the eat-in kitchen and the classless nature of this kitchen, see Newsome, "The Struggle for a Voice," and Rudolph, "At Home in Postwar France."

on credit showed, it was technical and scientific. Like her husband, this housewife was part of the new France, the modern France. She was a technocrat in the home, with a laboratory kitchen and a scientific approach to cleaning. The modern home was rational, healthy, and boasted a standard of cleanliness that greatly contrasted with that of the past, according to the women's journals. Cleanliness was associated with health, an issue of great importance at a time when a national priority was producing and raising healthy children, just as it had been since the late nineteenth century.[52] Even if the time spent in household labor remained equal, the character of that labor changed significantly if one had appliances, and that fact made it acceptable to a broader swathe of the population. The elimination of the work of climbing up and down stairs to fetch fresh water, boiling clothes on the stove, and scrubbing them by hand changed the quality of housework even if women were still kept busy.

Although immediately following the war, the American household had provided the model for modernization, journalists and women's organizations were not uncritical in their evaluation of American labor-saving methods and lifestyles, even if they wholeheartedly embraced modernity in the home. Journalists often expressed displeasure with ready-made foods, for example. The implication was that while American-style appliances could help the French housewife, there were certain standards of taste that could not be jeopardized. Likewise, the early postwar period saw a slew of articles denigrating American fashion. An article in *La femme* announced in 1945, "Alert in Paris ... New York Attacks ... this summer, on all of the beaches, American style has triumphed."[53] The photos of American "fashions" that illustrated such articles were often ridiculous – *Marie-France* featured a woman in white top and striped skirt, an outfit they called "women's prison" – but the message was serious.[54] American fashion posed both a cultural and economic challenge because of the economic importance of the fashion industry in Paris.[55]

The ability to embrace American modernity while also rejecting features that did not fit the pattern of French life was common among

---

[52] See Susan Pedersen for background on the French government's social programs to promote health, and thus natality. Pedersen, *Family, Dependence.*

[53] "Alerte à Paris... New-York attaque: Cet été, sur toutes les plages, la mode américaine a triomphé" 66 (1946): 6–7.

[54] "Fanfreluches et falbalas. U.S.A. La mode de demain nous viendra-t-elle d'outre-Atlantique?" *Marie-France* 38 (1945): 8.

[55] On challenges to the French fashion industry during and immediately after the war, see Nancy L. Green, *Ready to Wear and Ready to Work: A Century of Industry and Immigrants in Paris and New York* (Durham: Duke University Press, 1997), 95–101.

other groups concerned with household technology. A group of domestic science experts, for example, made adverse comments after touring a series of experimental prefabricated homes created by the French government in its efforts to house the population quickly. The group criticized the American-built homes because they did not have attics or basements. One woman visitor noted, "The Americans have almost no washing to dry (they throw away dirty linens and replace them with new). They are much less conservative than we are ... therefore, no attic." Likewise, the use of canned food meant that Americans did not need to store fruits or vegetables. Almost all of the women visitors also rejected the "American and English system of a WC in the bathroom," something they found was much too inconvenient for families with children since it meant that the toilet was unavailable while a family member was bathing.[56] The comment about linens reveals how widespread, and exaggerated, was the notion of American wealth at this time, and the suggestions for change show that advocates of home modernization also hoped to modify the features of the American home to better suit French lifestyles.

Despite being selective in the time-saving methods they advocated, journalists were explicit in their insistence that the housewife who "hired" appliances rather than people to do these tasks, was not lowering her social status, but modernizing her home. Women's magazines were rife with advertisements featuring modern life and the modern woman, touting everything from household appliances to Tampax. Pyrex was the way to "modernize your pots and pans"; Airwick was the "modern deodorizer"; and everyone needed the four elements of "modern comfort": the gas stove, water heater, heat, and washing machine.[57] Susan Weiner notes how advertisements for "modern" products often showed young women getting the better of their elders.[58] This theme worked for advertisements for margarine, for example, because of the tendency of older people to associate the product with the shortages of the war. A 1955 ad in *Marie-Claire* featured a young woman preparing lunch for a male friend. She is a bit disconcerted when he decides to relax in the kitchen while she works, instead of retiring to the sitting room. Juliette goes to work, all

---

[56] Compte rendu des inspectrices d'art ménager de la Caisse de compensation, Mme Rohaut. CAC 19771078 article 1. For more on the housing units, see Nicole Rudolph, "Domestic Politics."
[57] Pyrex ad in *Marie-Claire* 17 (1956): 144. Airwick ad *Marie-Claire* 6 (1955): 118. Gaz de ville ad *Marie-Claire* 5 (1955): 89.
[58] Susan Weiner, *Enfants Terribles*.

the while wondering how Alain will react when he sees the margarine. When he does, he cries,

"Juliette, you're not going to make me eat margarine, are you?"

There it is! She thinks for several seconds and then continues the conversation calmly:

—Ok, you're a modern young man, but you're prejudiced against margarine?

—It's not a question of being modern. Margarine is a replacement product that you only use to save money.

—Very good! Well, to be frank with you, I find your opinion ridiculous! Have you ever tasted it?

—No! But its low price doesn't inspire confidence.

—Ah la la! So you think that a reasonably priced product can't be good! I could give you a thousand examples that prove the opposite. But I'll content myself with proving to you that Astra can make a cuisine that's worthy of you.

Alain, of course, enjoys his meal and the ad proclaims "Try it for yourself! Astra will convince you." Juliette shows that a "cheap" product is now "modern" and proves herself an intelligent and skillful consumer.[59]

The connection between modern lifestyles and private comfort was reflected in the floor plans of new housing constructed in the late 1950s and 1960s. Many new apartments included only a *coin à manger*, not a separate dining room or formal *salon*. Having a *salon* was important for entertaining guests, as was a dining room, which meant "kitchen smells avoided, better presentation of food, of which the preparation remains invisible," according to a domestic science expert.[60] The contrast between the modern middle-class home and the homes of the prewar bourgeoisie was one of the factors leading political scientist André Siegfried to write that the bourgeois "way of life" no longer existed in the 1950s. He argued that at the beginning of the century there was a clearly defined bourgeois way of life that included a home with a traditional *salon* for receiving guests, domestic help, educational goals for children, and constant control of the family future through careful accounting that allowed families to accrue reserves of money. In the late 1950s, he wrote, middle-class families lived on their earnings, not reserves. From this he concluded there no longer existed either a bourgeoisie or a bourgeois way of life.[61]

Marguerite Perrot's 1961 sociological study of bourgeois family budgets found that for the first time since the late nineteenth century,

[59] *Marie-Claire* 5 (1955): 88.
[60] Compte rendu des inspectrices d'art ménager.
[61] André Siegfried piece in Marguerite Perrot, *Le mode de vie des familles bourgeoises, 1873–1953* (Paris: Librairie Armand Colin, 1961), 461–463.

bourgeois families recorded having no domestic help. For those who did have help, one-third dedicated less than 2 percent of the family budget to paid domestic labor, often hiring a woman who came in several times a week, rather than a live-in domestic servant.[62] The decline in bourgeois fortunes was not the only cause of this situation. Perrot also attributed the change to the availability of home appliances which, she concluded, "has led many housewives to dedicate themselves to the home without fear of social decline that was associated, in other times, with a bourgeois woman performing the most unpleasant household tasks."[63]

Affluent families were embracing a new lifestyle that entailed earning and spending money in different ways. The belief that bourgeois families should steer clear of mass-produced items was disappearing, and this was an important change, for without these families providing the first market for mass-produced consumer durables, France could not become a mass consumer society. As Victoria de Grazia's work on models of distribution in Europe and the United States shows, mass distribution eventually thrived in Europe precisely because wealthy families were cognizant of how to make their lives better, knew how to save money, had cars to drive themselves to new shopping centers, and had refrigerators at home to store food. The supermarket was the primary example in France of Fordist distribution, which entails low market costs, standardized goods, high turnover, and consumer choice.[64] In the 1950s, the French government and consumers discussed ways of promoting this paragon of modern enterprise in France. The Commission on Commerce at the Plan noted that while 59 percent of young people seemed favorable to increasing this kind of retail operation, older people did not like the idea of self-service shopping. They suggested including "hostesses" in supermarkets to make them more attractive.[65] Domestic science experts also preached

---

[62] Perrot, *Le mode de vie*, 137.

[63] Ibid., 138–139. Nicole Rudolph points out that the number of women working as domestic servants had not actually declined, but the number working as live-in servants had. In 1921, there was one *femme de ménage* (a woman coming in for a certain number of hours a week) for every eleven live-in servants; by 1951, the ratio was one to four. Rudolph, "At Home in Postwar France," 119. See also Louise Tilly and Joan Scott for statistics on the declining number of live-in domestics relative to the number of cleaning women in Paris between 1921 and 1951. Tilly and Scott, *Women, Work, and Family*, new edition (New York: Routledge, 1987), 154.

[64] See De Grazia, "Changing Consumer Regimes in Europe, 1930–1970" and *Irresistible Empire*.

[65] Commissariat Général du Plan de modernisation et d'équipement, "Rapport de la Commission du Commerce, Troisième Plan de modernisation et d'équipement" (May 1957). CAEF Library.

the benefits of this kind of shopping to their future homemakers.[66] The French government encouraged the growth of supermarkets by eliminating taxes that protected small shopkeepers and discriminated against large chains. The first supermarket opened in France in 1957 and from 1962 on, the number of the stores increased by at least one hundred a year. The first hypermarket, or store with over 2,500 square meters of retail space, opened in 1963.[67] If the new middle class had not made the choice for mass-produced goods, the supermarket would not have been nearly so successful. In doing so, they acknowledged mass consumer society as modern, rational, and necessary, and rejected the bourgeois regime of consumption as a relic of the past.

WORKING WOMEN: "THIS MACHINE, SHE'S A SOCIALIST"

As the use of credit spread and it became increasingly clear that working-class families were willing to go into debt in order to buy consumer durables, social commentators pondered what this meant for the politics and identity of working people. As historian Gary Cross has shown, by the 1940s and 1950s, workers in Western Europe had made a choice in favor of consumption; instead of calling for a reduced working week, they saw vacation time as the proper space for relaxation and would work longer hours the rest of the year in order to earn the wages that gave them access to consumer society.[68] Commentators wondered if this meant that workers would no longer strike, for fear of losing money. As we have seen, credit posed a particular risk because it meant committing to a series of future payments – another reason to avoid a loss of income by going on strike. Not only would workers worry about their financial obligations, but they would become capitalists themselves, better rationalizing and regulating their own spending, as they were absorbed into the consumer marketplace.[69] The desire to consume could, conversely, portend increased radicalism, as new needs only added to frustration and the desire for salary revision.[70]

[66] See Chapter 5.
[67] William James Adams, *Restructuring the French Economy: Government and the Rise of Market Competition since World War II* (Washington, DC: The Brookings Institution, 1989), 220–221.
[68] Gary Cross, *Time and Money*.
[69] Ibid. See also Gelpi and Julien-Labruyère, *Histoire du crédit*, 188.
[70] "La machine à laver," 15.

The 1957 *L'Express* article concerning consumption and France's future included a discussion of women's "taste for sacrifice" and unwillingness to accept modern appliances that reveals some of the problems with the contemporary discourse on class and consumption. The moderator raised the issue of anxiety among women over the question "of what use am I if a machine does my work for me? A humble woman might be proud of her quality washing. And if it seems the machines work as well as her...."[71] His questions point to key gaps in intellectuals' understanding of these consumer issues: a tendency to think of workers only as men, an ignorance of women's demands, and a lack of awareness of the tangible benefits home appliances and modern living conditions offered women. The one woman in the discussion, Colette Audry, noted that the washing machine was the most demanded of appliances because it was "truly the task of doing laundry at home that makes a woman a *femme de peine*" and makes her condition similar to the "African woman" subject to the hardest labor.[72] Despite Audry's explanation, the group would be drawn into a discussion of the need to modernize women, hypothesizing that women's magazines could be a method of spreading belief in the benefits of technology, particularly among the peasantry. At the same time that these intellectuals pondered how to modernize women, sociologists were finding that peasant women were deserting the countryside in search of better living conditions in the city and working-class women were organizing washing machine cooperatives to gain access to an appliance they could not afford.

The inability of scholars to recognize the unfulfilled needs of working-class families also stemmed from their focus on the workplace as the exclusive site for working-class identity formation, to the detriment of the neighborhood, the household, and working-class family organizations. Unaware of the challenges working-class women faced, they turned a deaf ear to very real demands for modernization and instead often assumed that "workers" were not interested in these trifles. They drew a distinction between male labor and political issues, and female consumer issues – seemingly unaware that the two could be conflated.[73]

---

[71] Ibid., 14.
[72] Ibid., 14.
[73] In doing this, they ignored the important working-class cooperative movement that started at the end of the nineteenth century and was successful through the 1930s. See Ellen Furlough, *Consumer Cooperation* and Helen Harden Chenut, *The Fabric of Gender*.

As Mme J. de la Taille, a woman who submitted an angry opinion letter to *L'Express* in response to the journalist's question about whether
"austerity" might be better for France at this moment stated: "Women
don't know the forty-hour week (sixty hours at a minimum) and when
it seems possible to ameliorate their working conditions you think right
away about 'austerity': The question shouldn't even be raised. Home
appliances bring not just comfort, but above all rest; the simple rest to
which every worker aspires and has a right."[74] Mme de la Taille's letter
echoes some of the common arguments for home improvement made
by women's organizations, family organizations, and individual women
journalists: Women were workers, too, regardless of whether they
labored in the factory or the home, and modernizing the home was not a
luxury, but a necessity. Such language challenged constructions of class,
notions of consumption, and characterizations of consumer goods, as it
first, incorporated consumer demands into working-class demands and,
second, portrayed domestic consumption, particularly consumption of
home appliances, not as luxurious, wasteful, and conspicuous, but as
rational, practical, and just. Such ideas were prominent in the publications of two important segments of the working class: the Communist
women's organization and the working family groups born in the interwar AC movement. Furthermore, while home consumption was often
figured as a private matter in the popular women's press, these working-
class organizations revealed that the question of why some families were
able to equip their homes, while others were not, was also inherently
political. Workers were citizens in a consumer-driven economy, laboring
for reconstruction and economic expansion, but unable to enjoy the lifestyle and goods they produced and therefore unable to fully participate
in that modern economy.[75] Furthermore, as the women of the UFF and
the working family movement demanded access to mass consumer society, they dedicated themselves to aiding the working family, practicing
yet another form of consumer citizenship, this time a citizenship in the
service of the working class.

The publications of the *Union des femmes française* (UFF), the
Communist women's organization, show the ability to appropriate consumer durables into working-class demands. These journals portrayed

---

[74] *L'Express* letter section, March 15, 1957, 35.
[75] See Charles F. McGovern's work on the United States for discussion of how, in a consumer-
driven economy, consumption itself becomes a form of citizenship. Charles F. McGovern,
Sold American: Consumption and Citizenship, 1890–1945 (Chapel Hill: University of
North Carolina Press, 2006).

mass-produced consumer durables not as trifles, but as a means of relieving women from the onerous burdens of housework and providing families with a comfortable home life. Their position differed little from the mainstream women's press, and the attraction of journals that glorified this lifestyle was, in fact, one of the reasons that the UFF launched its magazine, *Heures claires des femmes françaises*, after the war.[76] *Heures claires* was meant to be a recruiting tool that would appeal to women in the same way other popular journals did, but also open their eyes to the political reasons for difficult conditions in France. *Heures claires* would "awaken the consciences, the sentiments, of women." Rather than being a journal of "action," a role filled by other UFF publications, it spoke to women "where they are right now."[77] Despite its many similarities to popular journals, the UFF consistently drew attention to the specific problems that working-class families faced in attaining home comfort. In 1954, *Heures claires* glowingly described home technology, but asserted that "all of these machines, fruits of modern technology, these comfortable pieces with their clean lines, this young, practical, and rational ambience that can simplify and embellish our lives, is only accessible to the privileged." The author went on to print photos of modern furnishings "in the hope for a better future."[78] The UFF participated in the dream of comfort that accompanied consumer society, but decried a social and political system that made it inaccessible to working-class families.

Unlike male, often Communist, intellectuals who associated mass consumer society with the United States in their wholehearted rejection of this model as a vision for France, the UFF rejected American influence without rejecting the products and comforts of mass consumer society. The UFF reacted to the article in *Rapports France-États-Unis* about American workers soon after its publication, asserting that all of the consumer goods listed in the article were available only to those with a high salary. They argued that, despite the journal's claims, 60 percent of the working-class population did not have the necessary financial resources to buy such products. The UFF journalist wrote, "Yes, the legendary American worker, with all of these modern comforts, including the refrigerator and television, exists, but he is a minority; 30 percent of the population lives quite normally, a very small minority is fabulously rich, and

[76] Sullerot, *La presse féminine*, 67.
[77] Claudine Chomat, "Rapport sur Heures claires des femmes françaises," *La vie de l'Union des femmes françaises*, New Series 5 (1958): 3–4.
[78] "Le dernier salon où l'on parle... ménage... et ameublement," *Heures claires des femmes françaises* 104 (1954): 8–9.

the rest of the population is very poor."[79] The journalist went on to note that there were no *allocations familiales* in the United States and that poor Americans had fewer social programs to turn to than impoverished families in France or Britain.[80] The UFF attacked claims that the United States made about affluence and the standard of living, but this was not a negative characterization of mass consumer society, only a recognition of the fact that consumer durables and modern homes were not really available to all.[81]

That working-class families were denied consumer comforts was all the more lamentable considering that their labor was the driving force behind reconstruction. The journals of the UFF stressed not just consumption, but production, as necessary for ending inflation and improving standards of living, thereby linking the quest for consumer products to the "battle of production" that the Communist party declared immediately after the war.[82] Theorists of consumption have argued that in mass consumer societies, production becomes divorced from consumption; people construct their identities through the latter, rather than basing it on their position in the production process.[83] In the early postwar years, France was in the process of becoming a mass consumer society and the need for increased productivity was at the center of national discourse. In this context, the UFF and other working-class organizations balanced women's dual roles as consumers and producers, in particular by asserting that productivity was the answer to scarcity and that producers should be able to consume the products they made. The UFF recognized no contradiction between the desire to consume the products they considered necessities, not luxuries, and working-class identity. Anger at living conditions was one of the central issues motivating the Communist women's organization. The UFF frequently criticized the amount of money being spent on colonial wars and lamented the

---

[79] "La sécurité sociale dans les pays étrangers," *Les cahiers de l'Union des femmes françaises* (January/February 1952), 16.

[80] Ibid., 16.

[81] See also Marianne Milhaud, "Femmes américaines," *Heures claires des femmes françaises* 12 (1946): 6–7, for an attempt to debunk the myth that life was perfect for American women.

[82] See, for example, Marcelle Barjonet, "Comment éviter l'inflation. Economiser, produire!" *Les cahiers de l'Union des femmes françaises* 9 (1946): 20–22.

[83] See Robert Bocock, *Consumption* (New York: Routledge, 1993), 77–79. Jean Baudrillard argued that in affluent societies consumption is "miraculous"; goods are not experienced as coming from work or a production process, but as blessings or miracles. Baudrillard, *The Consumer Society: Myths and Structures* (London: Sage Publications, 1998), 31–32.

money not being spent on housing, claiming in a 1952 article on mass production of furniture, that "one day of the war's budget would be enough to build 2,000 homes."[84] The UFF also challenged the definition of workers as men and blurred the line between work performed in the home and work performed in the factory and marketplace. The organization consistently argued against the notion that the healthiest family structure was one in which only the husband worked outside the home, asserting that many women found fulfillment and independence in their careers. At the same time, they recognized the value of work performed in the home and mobilized women around domestic issues. Thus, the UFF valorized women's work in both spheres, consistently objecting to the claim that women belonged in the home, but also acknowledging that domestic labor was important and arduous and could be ameliorated through modernization and consumer goods.

The tendency to focus on women as both workers and mothers meant that the Communist party in general, and the UFF in particular, had a difficult time reacting to the debate on birth control that erupted in the 1960s, something they originally considered a bourgeois vice. For a long time, the UFF had concentrated on the need for working-class women to be able to freely choose to become mothers, advocating *crèches* and aid to working mothers, so it was difficult to embrace the notion that women might also choose to not become mothers. At the same conference in 1965 where the UFF voted to support changes to the 1920 law on birth control and abortion, the vice-president of the organization ended the conference with a speech in which she insisted, "To say yes to a child is to say yes to peace."[85]

The UFF's celebration of women's work outside of the home contrasted with the claims of working-class family organizations born in the *Mouvement populaire des familles* (MPF). By the early 1950s, the MPF had become the *Mouvement de libération du peuple* (MLP) and had split with the *Mouvement de libération ouvrière* (MLO). The journal *Monde Ouvrier* continued to publish articles about the problems facing working families and the work of these activists, many of whom were still motivated by social Catholic teaching, despite the movement's deconfessionalization in 1949.[86] A good portion of the working family movement's membership

---

[84] Annette Houzet, "Avenir du meuble ... et meubles de l'avenir?" *Femmes françaises* 80 (1952): 4.

[85] Quoted in Chaperon, *Les années Beauvoir*, 322.

[86] Given the multitude of groups that emerged from the MPF and the many points of commonality between them, I have followed the lead of Geneviève Dermenjian and

was women, and the movement counted the desire to liberate the working-class woman among its goals. These organizations believed strongly that women, even if they did not labor outside the home, were members of the working class, and extended the working-class struggle from the workplace and wages to include family and living conditions, focusing special attention on the needs and responsibilities of working-class women. For the working family movement, women and men had complementary roles and the liberation of women meant improved working conditions, men's salaries high enough to enable women to stay home with their children, and good, comfortable housing with modern conveniences. The working family movement continued the interwar struggle for the family wage, but included new demands related to modernization and consumer society.[87] Liberated from her domestic burdens, the working-class wife could fulfill her social role outside the home by participating in MPF meetings, organizing in her neighborhood, demonstrating before the public authorities, supporting striking workers, and doing anything else that would help her advance her family and her class.

Despite the working family movement's valorization of the male breadwinner model, the experience of the war, in which many women took on new responsibilities, the right to work guaranteed women in the constitution of the Fourth Republic, and the awareness that many working-class families could not survive on one salary prompted the MPF to both recognize women's rights as workers and stress how relieving women of their responsibilities in the work force was necessary to their liberation.[88] The working family movement recognized women's right to work, and in various articles demanded child care, sick leave for children, and maternity benefits. At the same time, they stressed the risks to women's health posed by the double burden of work at home and in the factory.[89] The

Dominique Loiseau, who speak of the original MPF and its successors at the *mouvances MPF*, or MPF movements or circles, despite the split. I also use the phrase "working family movement" to refer to the multiple organizations. See Dermenjian and Loiseau, "La maternité sociale," 93.

[87] Laura Levine Frader shows how French industries avoided instituting the family wage by granting family allowances. These allowed them to answer the demands of fathers and pronatalists without raising wages for everyone. Frader, "Engendering Work and Wages: The French Labor Movement and the Family Wage," in *Gender and Class in Modern Europe*, eds. Laura Levine Frader and Sonya Rose (Ithaca: Cornell University Press, 1996), 142–164. See also Susan Pedersen, *Family, Dependence*.

[88] The women of the MPF, in particular, were actively organized during the war, especially in their efforts to help POW wives. See Dermenjian and Loiseau, "La maternité sociale," and Fishman, *We Will Wait*.

[89] See, for example, "Femmes – Jusqu'ou les mènera l'augmentation folle de la vie? Alerte à la santé des mamans," *Monde Ouvrier* 32 (1947): 4.

real answer to women's problems lay neither in equal pay for equal work nor in men's participation in household labor. The solution to the worries of working-class women was for industries to pay their husbands enough to support their families, so that women could return to their homes and their true calling as mothers. Thus working family associations hoped to liberate married women from the work force, but also acknowledged the especially acute problem of women raising families on their own. Obviously, single women could not be saved from their dilemma even if men's salaries were higher.[90]

The difficulty in obtaining food and other basic necessities in the economic conditions of postwar France made the double burden even heavier. The shortages of the war lasted for years after the Liberation, and the productivity drive that members of these working families participated in was focused on heavy industry, not the consumer durables that families needed. When businesses did increase the manufacture of consumer durables, the goods were often too expensive for working-class families. In these conditions, working family organizations initially concentrated on obtaining more affordable and higher quality food, but also began to include the right to enjoy the fruits of a society of mass consumption, in particular through access to labor-saving appliances, among the needs of working-class families.

In 1947, a journalist for *Monde Ouvrier* commented on the inability of working-class families to achieve the modern lifestyle on exhibit at the *Foire de Paris*, an exposition of modern technology. The journal printed a cartoon of a man being choked by a machine next to an article about the *Foire*. The caption read, "THE GREAT INVENTOR – Approach, ladies and gentlemen.... I give you the greatest and most useful invention of modern times: A machine that cuts the appetite."[91] The author marveled at the material used for all of the appliances and at their incredible prices. One manufacturer explained that he could only make about one hundred of his machines, and so had to charge exorbitant prices to get his money back. It is clear that the author found the exhibited goods desirable, but he lamented the fact that they were an impossibility for working families,

[90] Dermenjian and Loiseau have noted the importance of single women in the MPF and explained that the notion of "social maternity" gave them the opportunity to be mothers in the community if not in their own homes. See "La maternité sociale." For discussion of the problem of single women, in this case widowed and abandoned mothers, see, for example, "Honorer les mères, c'est de leur permettre de vivre," *Monde Ouvrier* 366 (1953): 3.

[91] Jacques Cru, "La Foire de Paris," *Monde Ouvrier* 52 (1947): 1.

concluding, "Certainly, this [the *Foire*] is a door that opens on the world. A door that workers have created, through the force of their technique and their sweat; convenient, comfortable, perfect. But a world that workers cannot use...."[92] He regretted the inability of producers to buy the products they had made.

Whereas the early postwar efforts of the MPF were mainly aimed at subsistence consumption, by the early 1950s, the organization and its successors turned their efforts to accessing consumer durables. These groups, and their women's committees in particular, included the acquisition of labor-saving household appliances as a family necessity in their goal of liberating working-class women. In "The Memoirs of a Washing Machine, as a Little Birdie Told me," a journalist described the beginnings of a washing machine collective and its importance for women of the working class.[93] The "washing machine" described was selected by the women of a family association. While surrounded by the women, the machine heard the words "collective management" and the affirmation that, "These days, this machine, she's a socialist."[94] The machine was not a sign of individual affluence, but the fruit of collective organization.

The machine explained that she "responded to a precise problem (as says... my 'manager') that of the buying power and household equipment of the great majority of working mamas" and that her manager often said, "we must unite, each person in his or her own neighborhood should not enclose herself within her own personal problems, the promotion of the mamas of the neighborhood can commence with the washing machine...."[95] The machine concluded, "I know that I'm more than 'fill with water to the mark and agitate for four minutes,' I am the little washing machine with a spin dryer for a head caught in the current of worker's liberation."[96] The working family associations latched on to the washing machine as the household appliance most able to provide immediate relief for women. In so doing, they included access to consumer durables among consumer demands, creating a discourse in which the washing machine was "socialist," rather than "luxurious."

[92] Ibid., 2.
[93] The French title of the article is "Les mémoires d'une machine à laver racontés par mon petit doigt," but this translation seemed to convey the sentiment of the title better than a literal translation could. *Monde Ouvrier* 450 (1955): 5.
[94] Ibid., 5.
[95] Ibid., 5.
[96] Ibid., 5.

A contributor from a small town described the process through which her local associations began a collective. The group began with a machine demonstration in one of the women's homes. "We were enraptured," the woman explained, "in a short time the clothes were done without fatigue, and even the most stained working blues were clean."[97]

The local CAF helped the group obtain a loan to pay for the machine, after which they bought the appliance, a new Hoover, for 51,000 francs. They also bought a long cord so that families who needed to could plug the machine into the cellar or the washing room, ensuring that each family could run the machine on its own electrical supply. With twenty families included in the machine's circulation, the women were able to do their laundry for sixty francs per wash. *Monde Ouvrier* asked Jeannette W—, a mother of six, about her experience with the machine. "Am I happy?" she exclaimed, "What do you think?" Before the machine she dedicated an entire day to doing laundry for her six children and was "stiff all over" for two days afterward. Now, she explained, "It's simple: I started at 10:00 and now it's quarter after eleven – look at the pile of clothes already washed! I'll be finished before noon. And see how clean my laundry is! Washing has become child's play. And look, with the machine installed in my kitchen I can attend to other work. I can fix my meals, take care of my two littlest ones."[98] Jeannette admitted that there were problems in scheduling her washing with the other women in the cooperative but concluded that, "With a little bit of understanding, you always manage. Anyways, it's not the business of one woman, we're all in this together."[99] The journalist agreed, concluding, "I left my friend Jeannette, thinking of what would be possible if all women gave a hand in building, together, a world that is more humane, more fraternal."[100] For *Monde Ouvrier*, the provision of domestic equipment, a product of mass consumer society, was part of the struggle to liberate both women and the working class in general.

The use of washing machine collectives was not limited to urban society. In 1952, an article in the UFC bulletin spoke of collectives organized among rural families in the Maine-et-Loire, a department in west-central France. Groups of five or ten families would buy a machine together, and each would have a day or half-day per week to do laundry.

[97] "Réalisation de l'AFO à Exincourt," *Monde Ouvrier* 366 (1953): 4.
[98] Ibid., 4.
[99] Ibid., 4.
[100] Ibid., 4.

The novelty of the washing machine is clear in the problems encountered and solutions offered by the collective. The idea of creating a central location for the machines, to which each housewife could bring her own laundry, had been broached, but was unpopular because the rural members of the cooperative were very independent and wanted to use the machine only in their own homes. Thus, the machine was placed in a cart and rolled from farm to farm. Unfortunately, rural roads did not always allow easy passage of the machine. For this, an attachment had been added to allow a man to carry it on his back to the next farm, and if need be, across the fields.[101] The desire for consumer durables was strong enough to inspire creative means of accessing them before they were easily available.

The Communist women organized washing machines cooperatives as well, and as in its vision for the journal *Heures claires*, the national organization advocated them as a recruiting tool. At the national council meeting in 1961, one member noted that washing machine collectives had provided an important service to the families of miners in her district; ten new women had joined the UFF and some of them were now reading *Heures claires*.[102] A woman from Reims explained in an article on recruitment how a washing machine cooperative had been an effective way of increasing membership in her canton. The group now had four machines that circulated among women's homes so that different women could use a machine in the morning, afternoon, and evening. Each machine was, of course, accompanied by a UFF member who collected money and shared information about the organization. The machine had inspired thirty-five new memberships and earned enough money to send a local delegate to the national congress. The washing machine service had revealed a new side of the UFF to the women in the canton and led them to ask, "How was it that an organization that helped mothers was not their own organization, and why shouldn't they come and expand its ranks so that it could do so many more good things?"[103] Initiatives such as these helped the UFF show women, very tangibly, how the Communist party was working to improve their lives.

[101] "Une coopérative de machines à laver en Maine-et-Loire," *Union fédérale de la consommation: Bulletin mensuel d'information* 8 (1952): 23.

[102] "Pour améliorer les conditions de vie quotidienne des familles et assurer l'avenir des enfants," *La vie de l'Union des femmes françaises*, New Series 20–21 (1961): 37.

[103] "Le recrutement," *La vie de l'Union des femmes françaises* 42 (1954): 5. For discussion of how social services more broadly fit into recruitment and showed the efficacy of collective action, see Fayolle, "L'Union des femmes françaises," 79–82.

Buying machines collectively was one means of lowering the price, but, as is clear in the discourse of both the UFF and the working family organizations, only mass production could truly lower prices and, therefore, create mass consumption. That the workers producing these goods could not afford them was lamentable, and would have to change for France to become a mass consumer society. Instead of seeing mass consumption as a destructive force for working-class identity, these women's and family groups saw consumption as merely one more issue to address in becoming a more just society.

THE DEMOCRATIZATION OF MODERNITY

The beginning of mass consumer society did not entail the end of class distinctions in France, but it did mean that purchasing a washing machine, for example, did not necessarily have a bearing on one's social identity. The postwar change in French lifestyles happened gradually and was postponed by the concentration on heavy industry during reconstruction, as well as by colonial wars, the need for new housing, and inflation. Even as the economy grew, increased spending and wealth were unevenly distributed, and a government study from late 1956 and early 1957 found that the percentage of their budget families spent on food differed between 27.2 and 57.6 percent, depending on income.[104] Public officials and researchers often cited "Engel's law," which held that food consumption occupied a smaller place in the family budget the higher the family income. Despite an estimated 4.5 percent increase in the standard of living each year from 1950 to 1957, when a government study from 1955 asked participants whether their living conditions had improved since 1950, 68 percent of engineers said "yes," compared to 13 percent of manual laborers.[105] The purchasing power of a Parisian metal-worker was actually lower in 1955 than in 1937, despite 75 percent growth in that economic sector over the same period. While wages increased, so did prices, resulting in salaries being weighed down until 1961.[106] By 1965, all categories of the population had made significant increases in revenue, but the distribution of incomes and gaps between groups remained in

[104] Georges Rottier and Elisabeth Salembien, "Les budgets familiaux en 1956," *Consommation: Annales du Centre de recherches et de documentation sur la consommation* 1 (1958): 36.
[105] The statistic on the standard of living is from CREDOC in, "La consommation," 25. Government study on improvement is *Enquête sur les tendances*, 27.
[106] Rioux, *The Fourth Republic*, 392.

place.[107] Even the prominence of consuming in one's daily routine varied according to class. As Paul-Henry Chombart de Lauwe explained, for wealthy women, shopping was "as much leisure as necessity" and could occupy the entire afternoon, in contrast to the shopping experiences of working-class women strapped both for time and money.[108]

Even for those with high income, access to increased consumption did not compensate for the housing shortage that was still acute in the mid-1950s and had not been completely resolved by the mid-1960s. The housing shortage, explained a government researcher in 1956, might explain why only 8 percent responded "yes" to a survey asking whether one's standard of living had improved over the last year, despite the fact that national per capita revenue had gone up almost 6 percent over the same period.[109] A washing machine or refrigerator would not resolve the problems of those in overcrowded housing, furnished hotel rooms, or even spacious housing without running water or an electrical supply strong enough to power an appliance. In the *L'Express* article on consumption, a representative of CREDOC suggested that the increase in sales of automobiles and scooters could be attributed to the fact that their housing was so horrible some families sought "evasion" through these other purchases.[110]

Despite the existence of income and spending differences across the population, and the continuation of the housing problem, a change in the culture of consumption and spending on the home over the course of the 1950s and 1960s is undeniable. Between 1950 and 1957, consumption in France grew by 40 percent per person, and the structure of that growth was heavily weighted toward purchases of goods that would provide family comfort. Spending on hygiene, personal care, and electric and mechanical products for personal use increased by between 80 and 150 percent.[111] Although the rise in consumption meant more spending in general, including on basic necessities like food, there had been a disproportionate increase in spending associated with home comfort. Spending on the *"équipement"* or "outfitting" of the home had increased by 110

[107] Vangrevelinghe, "Les niveaux de vie," 8.
[108] Chombart de Lauwe, *La vie quotidienne*, 59.
[109] Rottier, "Nourriture, logement, ou télévision," 742. In response to this question, 29 percent said their standard of living had declined, whereas 63 percent said it had stayed the same. The survey was of several thousand households deemed to be representative of the overall French population.
[110] "La machine à laver," 16.
[111] "La consommation," 23.

percent.[112] The growth continued into the late 1960s, with average consumption again increasing 40 percent between 1956 and 1965.[113] While still a stratified society, a widespread rise in incomes and the standard of living meant, at least by the mid-1960s, that how one lived and who did one's household labor were no longer key indicators of class status.[114]

Home appliances and other consumer durables were still expensive in the 1950s, and many families could not afford them until the 1960s, but with the gradual drop in prices and growth in access to credit, statistics show growth in the proportion of low-income families achieving home modernization even over the course of the 1950s. In 1957, 7 percent of the families of manual laborers and 13 percent of other working families had a refrigerator, versus 31 percent of families of middle managers and 60 percent of families of executives and professionals.[115] Eight and a half percent of manual laborers' families and 18 percent of other working families had a vacuum cleaner, versus 45 and 70 percent, respectively, of the other two groups.[116] The distribution of appliances depended, also, on whether one lived in the country or the city. Those involved in agriculture had a much lower level of *équipement* regardless of income. A study performed by UNIMAREL found that certain appliances were more closely tied to income than others: the washing machine was more "democratic" than the refrigerator because families were more willing to devote money to its purchase, even if their income was low.[117] This is not surprising considering that laundering clothes was one of the most physically demanding of household tasks. Furthermore, women changed their daily shopping routines slowly and many considered the refrigerator merely a means of providing pleasantly cool drinks in warm weather, rather than a way to limit shopping expeditions by preserving food for longer periods. Thus, working-class families owned a greater share of the

[112] Ibid., 34.

[113] Vangrevelinghe, "Les niveaux de vie," 7.

[114] Between 1956 and 1965, the average income for a worker went from 6,000 NF to 13,000 NF per year and a *cadre moyen* went from 9,000 NF to 20,500 NF. Although the increase was striking, it is also important to note that there was high inflation, especially between 1956 and 1959. Vangrevelinghe, "Les niveaux de vie," 21.

[115] UNIMAREL, *La "démocratisation" de l'équipement ménager* (Paris: UNIMAREL, 1959), 2.

[116] Ibid., 2.

[117] In addition, Quyhn Delauney explains that the diversity of living conditions of French families meant that washing machine manufacturers produced a range of sizes and shapes so that families with differing amounts of space or levels of access to electricity, water, or gas could still use a machine. Delauney, *Histoire de la machine à laver* (Rennes: Presses Universitaires de Rennes, 1994), 201–203.

TABLE 4.1 *Percent of Households Equipped (1954 and 1957)*

	Vacuum Cleaners		Washing Machines		Refrigerators	
	1954	1957	1954	1957	1954	1957
Workers	6.3	17	8.5	19	3.3	12
Middle *Cadres*	41	45	16.4	26	15.5	31
Superior *Cadres* and Liberal Professionals	70.5	67	23.4	42	42.8	57

Source: UNIMAREL, *La 'démocratisation' de l'équipement ménager* (Paris: UNIMAREL, 1959), 6–7.

washing machines in existence in 1957, than they owned of the refrigerators or vacuums.[118] Whether one lived in an urban or rural area also helped determine which machines were most desirable. As the number of laundromats grew, more urban families had access to the machine without purchasing one of their own. On the other hand, the purchase of an electric floor polisher or vacuum cleaner was low on the list of priorities for agricultural families.[119]

Some of the most telling statistics for understanding the diffusion of home technology throughout French society are those showing relative growth of appliance use among different social groups. Between 1954 and 1957, the percentage of families owning appliances grew among all sectors of the population. For example, whereas 3.3 percent of working families owned refrigerators in 1954, 12 percent owned them in 1957. For washing machines, the figures were 8.5 percent and 19 percent. For middle *cadres*, the figures were 15.5 percent and 31 percent for the refrigerator, and 16.4 percent and 26 percent for the washing machine.[120] (See Table 4.1.) More indicative of the diffusion of appliances is the percentage of the total number of appliances owned by each group. Whereas the working-class population owned only 12 percent of the refrigerators in existence in 1955, only two years later it owned 20 percent. After owning 29 percent of washing machines in 1955, it owned 31.5 percent in 1957; for vacuum cleaners the jump was from 12.5 percent to 22.5 percent.

[118] UNIMAREL, *La "démocratisation,"* 5.
[119] UNIMAREL, *Qui possède les appareils électrodomestiques et les téléviseurs? Analyse socio-professionnelle et géographique des clientèles, 1957–1961* (Paris: UNIMAREL, 1962), 3, 16.
[120] UNIMAREL, *La "démocratisation,"* 7.

TABLE 4.2 *Proportion of Total Appliances Held by Socioprofessional Group (in Percentages)*

	Refrigerators		Washing Machines		Vacuum Cleaners	
	1955	1957	1955	1957	1955	1957
Workers	12	20	29	31.5	12.5	22.5
Middle *Cadres*	10.5	10	10.5	8	15	11.5
Superior *Cadres* and Liberal Professionals	23.5	14	12	10.5	21	13.5

Source: UNIMAREL, *La 'démocratisation' de l'équipement ménager* (Paris: UNIMAREL, 1959), 8.

A noticeable decline is apparent in the higher income groups of the French population. Superior *cadres* and liberal professionals owned 23.5 percent of refrigerators in 1955, but only 14 percent in 1957. Middle *cadres* owned 10.5 percent of washing machines in 1955, but only 8 percent in 1957.[121] (See Table 4.2.) For almost every appliance, the sectors of the population with modest incomes had increased the proportion of appliances they owned, and the more wealthy sectors had decreased their proportion. Between 1957 and 1961, working-class families bought by far the largest proportion of washing machines, vacuums, and refrigerators sold in France.[122] This was, of course, because many affluent families already owned them before 1957, but also shows that appliances were "democratizing." By 1961, more than 20 percent of working-class homes had televisions, versus only 6 percent in 1957.[123] The television audience continued to grow, so that by the end of the 1960s, almost two-thirds of the population had a television. This statistic revealed not only a willingness to spend on the home, but the embracing of a home-centered lifestyle as sale of the machines increased and money spent on distractions outside the home decreased.[124] By 1968, more than 72 percent of the population had a refrigerator, an item that just ten years earlier had been considered one of the least democratic appliances, indicating that this kind of domestic comfort had crossed the threshold separating luxury and necessity.[125] (See Table 4.3.)

[121] All comparisons, Ibid., 8.
[122] UNIMAREL, *Qui possède les appareils*, 4–9.
[123] Ibid., 12.
[124] Vangrevelinghe, "Les niveaux de vie," 20.
[125] Niaudet, "L'évolution," 60.

TABLE 4.3 *Percent of Total Households Equipped*
(1960, 1965, and 1968)

	1960	1965	1968
Refrigerators	24.8	52.3	72.4
Washing Machines	24	38.3	50.1
Vacuum Cleaners	28.1	43	50

Source: Jacqueline Niaudet, "L'évolution de la consommation des ménages de 1959 à 1968," *Consommation: Annales du Centre de recherches et de documentation sur la consommation* 16 (1970): 60.

The general rise in incomes and the widespread ascension to a level of home comfort unthinkable at the end of the war meant that the question of whether mass consumer society had ended class distinctions continued into the 1960s. Sociologists skeptical of the equalizing qualities of mass consumer society, Pierre Bourdieu prominent among them, asserted that as consumer "needs" were met, new kinds of consumption distinguished social groups. Now that durables were no longer rare, possession of a certain good was no longer enough to distinguish oneself; one had to instead acquire the highest quality brand of that particular commodity. Bourdieu also pointed to the ways that consumption of art and literature served to define social classes, the wealthy being much more able to write and talk about art and culture than the rest of the population.[126]

Rather than domestic consumption, other categories, such as leisure activities and education, remained markers of status. Though all workers were guaranteed time away from work, in 1964, 84 percent of superior *cadres* and 73 percent of middle *cadres* took a vacation, compared to 43 percent of workers and 9 percent of farmers. In the 1960s, the sale of printed material such as journals, reviews, and books was three times higher among the *cadres* than across the general population.[127] This sort of consumption, in the realm of leisure rather than the home, along with educational achievements and cultural capital, thus still served to define class categories. Wealthy families were more cognizant of the need to get their children into the best public schools, despite the fact that the nationalized curriculum implied uniformity. And at the top of the educational

[126] Pierre Bourdieu's massive study on taste was conducted in France in the 1960s. Bourdieu, *Distinction*. For analysis of the scope of Bourdieu's writing on class and consumption, see Jeremy F. Lane, *Pierre Bourdieu: A Critical Introduction* (London: Pluto Press, 2000).

[127] Vangrevelinghe, "Les niveaux de vie," 20.

pyramid sat the *grands écoles* – which continued to produce the professional and political elite.[128] Finally, while the middle class was growing and, to some extent, peopled by the sons of the working class, more than one-third of the men in the ranks of the *cadres*, liberal professionals, and businessmen married the daughters of men from this same group, and they rarely married women from the working class.[129] Such distinctions all served to show that class divisions, emulations, and pride remained, even if class was no longer defined by whether one ate in the kitchen, bought home appliances, or did one's own housework.

By the end of the postwar period, mass-produced consumer goods were accepted as appropriate for all families, regardless of class. There was a range of prices within the market for each appliance, for example, but appliances in general were neither "bourgeois" nor "working-class," neither vulgar nor luxurious. Home technology and home modernization were perceived as being egalitarian, even before they actually were. By the mid-1960s, however, French families, across class divides, were living more like one another than they had in the past. They were buying more of the same commodities and devoting more money to their homes without formal dining rooms in which they entertained themselves with their new televisions.

By the 1960s, the middle class dominated the representational field once held by the old bourgeoisie, and now survived off its own income and performed its own household labor. This kind of lifestyle had been accepted, indeed, embraced by this group that grew wealthy as the economy expanded and which provided an important base of consumers of mass-produced goods. Although some features of the middle-class home and lifestyle may have worried those whose vision of French society included the hierarchy inherent in the "bourgeois regime of consumption," class categories were remarkably flexible and France was able to negotiate the arrival of mass consumer society without becoming a "classless" society. Household consumption simply no longer defined one's class position. In the 1950s and early 1960s, class identities, in particular the confrontational position of the working class, remained strong. Consumer society,

---

[128] "Cultural capital" is Bourdieu's term. See Henri Mendras with Alistair Cole, *Social Change in Modern France: Towards a Cultural Anthropology of the Fifth Republic* (Cambridge: Cambridge University Press, 1991), 100, on the need for families to plan ahead – choosing the best *lycée* and pushing their children to take the *baccalauréat* exam as early as possible to have the best chance of entering one of the *grands écoles*.

[129] Only 6 percent married the daughters of workers. Marchal and Lecaillon, "Is the income of the *cadres*," 179.

in fact, by introducing new "necessities," fueled the fires of contestation rather than calming them.[130] By defining consumer goods as necessities rather than luxuries, and modern rather than shoddily produced, French society moved the definition of class out of the realm of home consumption and into other realms of consumption and means of distinction.

[130] Richard Hamilton argued that radicalism increased with national affluence because workers believed that firms had the ability to pay more, but chose not to. Hamilton, *Affluence and the French Worker*, 7.

5

The *Salon des arts ménagers*

Learning to Consume in Postwar France

In the spring of 1950, the *Salon des arts ménagers* welcomed visitors every day, all day, and into the evening from February 23 through March 19. A visitor, likely with husband and perhaps even children in tow, could stroll through the ground floor of the *Grand Palais*, just off the Avenue Champs-Elysées, perusing the sections on Antique Arts in Modern Life, Today's Home, the *Cité* 50, the Rural Domestic Arts, Kitchen Furnishings, and Collective Living. Then she could climb to the first floor and visit the sections on Food, Wine, Furniture, The Room of the Woman and Child, Cleaning Products, and the star of the show, the Home Appliances. Along the way she might pause for dinner at the *Salon's* restaurant, perhaps even scheduling her visit based on which regional specialty would be featured on the night's menu. She might also stop in at one of the twenty-eight conferences held during the exposition, maybe Paulette Bernège's "If Women Designed Home Appliances" or "Joy and Comfort through Color and Light," and on her way out, she could browse the Exposition on Habitation in the gardens and see the latest in collective living, paying particular attention to the exhibit on the new apartment complex designed by Le Corbusier in Marseille.[1]

Depending on her budget, the visitor could buy or order products at the *Salon* or she could compare and contrast and decide to buy something from a local vendor. If her budget precluded both of these, she could turn to a journal like *Le Petit Echo de la Mode*, which advised women on how to imitate the expensive furnishings at the *Salon* using cheaper materials, asking, for example, "You who are going to soon marry, do you

[1] Les arts ménagers 50. CAC 19850023 article 127.

admire at *'arts ménagers'* those superb kitchen installations with their new plastic furnishings, their stainless steel sinks, their electric ovens with clear doors?" For those with modest budgets, the journalist recommended "carefully painted white wood, which creates a clean and smart appearance" in place of the more expensive modern materials.[2] The *Salon* offered inspiration to visitors of every budget.

The *Salon* also exemplified many of the features of France's path to postwar modernization and mass consumer society. As a government sponsored event under the authority of the ministry of education, it revealed the state-driven nature of postwar modernization. Here, as throughout postwar economic planning, state and industry cooperated as government ministries lured potential consumers to the most important event of the appliance manufacturer's year. However, it also revealed demand from the public in the form of throngs of French citizens who attended the event each year, and in the planning for the *Salon* that required the year-round cooperation of government officials and representatives from women's, family, and consumer organizations. Together, these groups worked to create the citizen consumer. They vaunted the role of the citizen consumer and domestic manager, stressing the skills involved in running a household in the modern economy, all the while reinforcing the notion that the home and domestic consumption should be women's primary concern, and that the organizations' own role was to educate women for these tasks. The *Salon* was the perfect site to promote a mass consumer society by teaching women about their responsibilities as citizen consumers, the appropriate and modern use of credit, the new necessities of the postwar family, and the suitability of mass-produced goods and new kinds of housing for tasteful French consumers.

THE EVOLUTION OF THE *SALON DES ARTS MÉNAGERS*

The *Salon des arts ménagers* began in 1923 under the direction of Jules-Louis Breton, the head of the *Office national des recherches scientifique et industrielles et des inventions,* the predecessor of the *Centre national de la recherche scientifique* (CNRS). It remained under the control of the Breton family for much of its life, with Breton's son Paul acting as *commissaire* of the event from 1929 to 1976 and Breton's son André serving as director of the publication *Arts Ménagers.* Members of the *Salon's* directing council came from the CNRS as well as the *Comité*

[2] "Gai! Gai! Cuisons ..." *Le Petit Echo de la Mode* 49 (1948): 13.

français des expositions. In addition to overseeing the *Salon des arts ménagers,* the council cooperated on international expositions and organized a variety of national exhibits at other times of the year.[3] From the beginning, the *Salon* was both an effort to strengthen manufacturing and to educate the public, though the type of education the public needed changed with time. Jules-Louis Breton was the first minister of hygiene for the Third Republic, a socialist, and a strident pronatalist who hoped that the *Salon* would provide a venue that would expose working-class women to new technologies and develop their taste in home furnishings. As in his other efforts to aid families and women, which included creating special train fares for large families and instituting the *"Médaille de la famille française,"* a medal for mothers of many children, Breton hoped that lessening women's household burdens would encourage them to have larger families, and that the hygienic lessons of the *Salon* would result in more healthy French babies.[4] New technologies would provide greater leisure time for the mother and thus strengthen the family – a goal that was both private and public in the pronatalist environment of the French Third Republic.[5]

The *Salon* drew sizeable crowds before the Second World War, but exploded in popularity afterward. The first *Salon* at the *Grand Palais,* in 1926, drew 146,000 people, and by 1939 visitors numbered 608,476.[6] The event was suspended during the occupation, and then was cancelled until 1948 because of a fire in the *Grand Palais* during the Liberation. When it reopened for the first time, people waited in the snow for an hour before being admitted.[7] The number of visitors was 795,113, not much higher than prewar attendance, but the number jumped to 1,313,377 in 1952 and reached 1,402,299 in 1955.[8] By 1954, the *Salon* covered

[3] Paul Breton was director of the 1946 *Exposition des techniques américaines de l'habitation et de l'urbanisme* and the 1947 *Exposition internationale de l'urbanisme et de l'habitation* before the *Salon des arts ménagers* reappeared in 1948. Rouaud, *60 ans d'arts ménagers,* 12.
[4] On the prizes instituted by Breton as minister of hygiene, see Henri Queuille, "Le Salon des arts ménagers, œuvre sociale," *XVIIIe Salon des Arts Ménagers* (Paris: Salon des arts ménagers, 1949), 42–45. CAC 19850023 article 65.
[5] For background on the Salon, including its place in interwar France, see Furlough, "Selling the American Way"; Yvette Lebrigand, "Les archives du Salon des arts ménagers," *Bulletin de l'Institut d'histoire du temps présent* 26 (1986): 9–13; Leymonerie, "Le Salon des arts ménagers"; Newsome, "The Struggle for a Voice"; Rouaud, *60 ans d'arts ménagers;* Rudolph, "At Home in Postwar France"; Segalen, "The Salon des Arts Ménagers, 1923–1983."
[6] Note sur les entrées. CAC 19850023 article 18.
[7] Rouaud, *60 ans d'arts ménagers,* 16.
[8] Note sur les entrées.

36,000 square meters and included exhibits by fifteen-hundred companies and organizations. Despite moving to a larger space at the *Palais de
la Défense* on the edge of Paris in 1961, the *commissaire* was forced to
turn away "serious" manufacturers because of insufficient space.[9] The
Salon was an annual event for popular women's journals, among others, *Marie-France, Marie-Claire, Elle,* and even the Communist women's
Heures claires des femmes françaises printed multipaged spreads on the
exhibition. Its appeal extended beyond the women's press, however, and
articles on the exposition's events, information on fees and daily conferences, advice on attending and shopping at the *Salon*, maps of the
exhibition hall, and reports on sales at the *Salon* appeared throughout
the French local, regional, and national press. The event was difficult to
ignore, and each year's commencement spurred debate about consumption and home modernization. For example, the opening of the event
was the occasion for *Productivité française* to discuss productivity in
the home, whereas for the working-class press, it was an opportunity
to call attention to the pitiable living conditions of working families.[10]
It prompted debate over credit, consumption, and class identity even
while the Communist *L'Humanité* advised its readers, "You have only a
few more days to visit the huge family event that is not only the annual
convergence of modern equipment, appliances, and products, but also
the most important, diverse, and complete exposition on furnishing and
decoration...."[11] Although scores of articles on the inaccessibility of the
portrayed lifestyle for working families appeared in the postwar decades,
the articles on the *Salon* in journals like *L'Humanité, Monde Ouvrier,
Heures claires des femmes françaises,* and many other publications aimed
at the working class portrayed the advertized consumer goods as desirable, though unaffordable, for working families.

For appliance manufacturers and sellers, the *Salon* was the most important commercial event of the year. The character of the exposition and the
audience changed over the years. When the *Salon* reopened in 1948, the
appliances and furnishings presented were not only unaffordable to most

---

[9] Statistics reported in "Le 24e Salon des arts ménagers," *Vente et Publicité* 31 (1955): 64.
Paul Breton reported having to turn away exhibitors who wanted to participate in the
Salon at the *Palais de la Défense* after 1962. Rapport du Commissaire Générale du Salon
des arts ménagers au conseil de direction. CAC 19850023 article 10.

[10] See, for example, Jacqueline Bernard, "La période des inventions" and Yvonne Beuque,
"Quat' pas dans les nuages au Salon des arts ménagers" *Monde Ouvrier* 354 (1953), 1, 4.

[11] For the debate on the working class, see Lise Claris, "Arts ménagers: Êtes-vous pour ou
contre les achats à crédit?" *Observateur*, February 28, 1957. Caption in *L'Humanité*,
March 16, 1955.

visitors, they were unavailable in France. For some appliances, one had to wait from six months to two years for delivery, and some American manufacturers asked for payment in dollars.[12] An advertisement for a washing machine in the 1949 catalogue announced that it would be deliverable by the end of the year.[13] In 1950, *Monde Ouvrier's* article covering the *Salon* was titled, "Alice in Wonderland (New Version)."[14] As early as 1949, however, consumers could buy appliances on credit through *La Semeuse, Gaz de France*, or the CAF.[15] As the credit industry expanded in the early 1950s, more of the visitors to the *Salon* could actually purchase the products on display, either there or elsewhere. In 1953, *L'Équipement Électrique* reported that for the first time since reopening, the *Salon* had fewer visitors than in the previous year. Despite this, there were more sales. Home appliances, refrigerators and washing machines, in particular, "were in extremely high demand, infinitely more than last year." *L'Équipement Électrique* attributed this to the fact that most sales were done on credit, which they deemed, "the only means of developing" the appliance industry.[16] Historian Claire Leymonerie points to 1955 as a turning point in the *Salon's* history, as articles about the *Salon* revealed that visitors, even from working-class families, more frequently intended to buy products, rather than simply enjoy the spectacle.[17]

In 1955, the socialist *Libération* still announced, "Arts Ménagers 55: The 'Happy Home'...a happiness that is not available on all budgets."[18] But by the late 1950s, people had grown accustomed to home mechanization and fewer *Salon* goers were first time appliance buyers. Many visitors were now experienced in techniques for gathering information and came to the *Salon* not to marvel at new inventions, but to weigh the benefits of various models before buying elsewhere. Articles about the *Salon* began reporting that there were few "*nouveautés*" but that

[12] Rouaud, *60 ans d'arts ménagers*, 16.
[13] Advertisement for a Hoover washing machine, *XVIIIe Salon des arts ménagers* (Paris: Salon des arts ménagers, 1949), 3. CAC 19850023 article 65.
[14] Madeleine Durieux, "Visite au Salon des arts ménagers ou ... Alice au pays des merveilles (nouvelle version)," *Monde Ouvrier* 197 (1950): 1, 3.
[15] Rouaud, *60 ans d'arts ménagers*, 17. *La Semeuse* was a company that provided credit to working-class customers starting in 1913. This was a form of credit redeemable at specific stores. See Alain Chatriot, "Protéger le consommateur," 96.
[16] "Moins de visiteurs aux Arts ménagers 1953 ... Mais plus de commandes!" *L'Équipement Électrique* 84 (1953): 16.
[17] Leymonerie, "Le Salon des arts ménagers," 48.
[18] "Arts Ménagers 55: La 'Maison Heureuse' ... un bonheur qui n'est pas à la portée de toutes les bourses," *Libération*, March 18, 1955.

one might visit to see how the "little details" continued to improve.[19] In 1958, the prefect of the Seine noted that the business transacted at the *Salon* itself was only a fraction of that created by the event and that, "In effect, it is more and more common for customers to come and make their selection by profiting from this great annual *confrontation* of all of the latest inventions, and then to make their order from the distributor closest to home, who will deliver the product, install it, and provide service after the sale."[20] Thus, the *Salon* not only profited sellers with exhibits, but the home comfort industry across France experienced an increase in sales during the weeks of its operation.[21] Market research by *Électricité de France* (EDF) found exhibitions like the *Salon* an effective means of advertising. The public responded well to demonstrations and personal contact with sales representatives.[22]

The *Institut national de la statistique et des études économiques* (INSEE) interviewed exhibitors at the *Salon* to keep track of demand for home technology, though the sales stimulated by the event had spread beyond the confines of the *Grand Palais* by the end of the 1950s, as the Prefect noted.[23] The marketing journal *Vente et Publicité* explained that, "The *Salon*, for most enterprises, is the base for commercial and advertising campaigns that flow from it over the following twelve months."[24] The *Salon des arts ménagers*, held each spring, and the *Salon de l'automobile*, held each fall, created veritable buying "seasons" for various products, as consumers knew that new products and innovations would be unveiled at these events, and so waited for the annual exhibition to research their potential purchases.[25] One journalist argued that it was difficult to know how well a manufacturer had done until six months afterward, and that some participants "made their year" off of the customers that they had attracted during the *Salon*.[26] The knowledge of consumer taste, demand,

[19] See, for example, Claris, "Arts ménagers: Êtes-vous pour ou contre."
[20] Emile Pelletier, Préfet de la Seine, La Conjoncture économique dans le département. CAC 19850023 article 26.
[21] Opinions des exposants, Opinions diverses et retentissement du salon. CAC 19850023 article 26.
[22] UNIMAREL, *Expérience d'Orléans: Les effets de l'action commerciale sur le marché domestique de l'électricité* (Paris: UNIMAREL, 1960).
[23] UNIMAREL, *Le marché électrodomestique en 1958, prospectives pour 1959* (Paris: UNIMAREL, 1959).
[24] "À propos du Salon des arts ménagers," *Vente et Publicité* 10 (1953): 1.
[25] "À propos du prochaine Salon des arts ménagers : Les salons spécialisé," *Vente et Publicité* 7 (1952): 29.
[26] "Aux Arts ménagers on a acheté davantage de machines à laver et de réfrigérateurs mais il y a eu moins de visiteurs" *Paris-Journal*, March 24, 1959.

and concerns acquired at the *Salon des arts ménagers* was indispensable for manufacturers and sellers, whereas for consumers the *Salon* made wise research and rational purchasing easier by grouping competing products and sellers in one location.

When it reopened in 1948, a *Salon* survey found that only 14 percent of visitors were from the provinces.[27] To help create a mass consumer society, the *Salon* had to reach an audience beyond Paris, and over the course of the postwar decades, the *Salon* gradually reached out to rural visitors, who marveled, just as working-class visitors did, at the disconnect between their daily lives and the lifestyle presented at the exhibition. As the journal *Libération Paysanne* argued, the preponderance of Parisian visitors occurred not just because it was difficult for rural families to leave their farms unattended, but also because of the lack of attention given to information and exhibits that might interest rural women.[28] In 1950, the ministry of agriculture held a congress on "Relieving Women's Work in the Countryside" to coincide with the *Salon*, which included a rural section for the first time. As for the *Salon* in general, the rural section came about through the cooperation of state representatives and private organizations, including the *Société des agriculteurs de France* and several rural women's and family associations.[29] As the paper *La Croix* explained, although postwar modernization had changed men's work on the farm, the farmer's daughter and wife continued to live as in the past. Events that focused on narrowing the gap between modern working conditions and ancient housing conditions on the farm were necessary as the situation was "one of the principal causes of the rural exodus, and at the very least, of dissension in rural families."[30] Thus, like women's magazines, the *Salon* was a means of spreading the values and lifestyles of mass consumer society, which were chiefly associated with urban living, to women in the countryside. By creating the rural exhibit, organizers balanced the objectives of the Paris-centered modernization campaign with the demands of life in the countryside.

Another means of spreading modernization to the provinces was to bring young rural people to Paris to see the lifestyle and consumer goods exhibited at the *Salon*. The SNCF, the national train company, offered

[27] Rouaud, *60 ans d'arts ménagers*, 18.
[28] "Au XIXe Salon des arts ménagers, le confort rural en valeur," *Libération Paysanne*, January 19, 1950.
[29] "Les jeunes au Salon des arts ménagers," *Libération Paysanne*, February 2, 1950.
[30] "À l'occasion du Salon des arts ménagers, un congrès pour l'allègement du travail des femmes rurales," *La Croix*, February 18, 1950.

special rates and trains for trips to Paris during the *Salon* and associations for young, forward-thinking farmers organized junkets for young men and women to visit Paris, the *Salon des arts ménagers*, and the *Grande Semaine Agricole*, which took place shortly before the *Salon*.[31] In 1956, a group of four-hundred young peasants from the Sarthe signed on to a group trip to visit Paris for the *Salon* and the *Concours Agricole*, the annual agricultural fair. The local paper reported that the young people were able to meet with the minister of education, who told them he understood the problems of young rural people and was counting on them to "contribute to the future of the nation." It also reported that the students were happy to have the chance to visit Paris and its monuments.[32] Though France's "modernity" had been diminished by war and poverty, Paris had long been what Vanessa Schwartz calls "the quintessentially modern city" and the spectacle of consumption both inside and outside of the *Grand Palais* likely impressed rural visitors.[33] The event reached out to the provinces in more than one way: While the *Salon* brought visitors to Paris, it also inspired the creation of several provincial exhibitions on the *arts ménagers*, as well as an event in Algiers.[34]

The *Salon's* exhibits reflected the changing position of France in the global economy as well, by popularizing support for international trade – another concern of modernizers and something that would be particularly important after the creation of the Common Market. Even before that, "The House without Borders," the American exhibit at the 1954 exposition, contained goods manufactured in at least ten different countries and taught visitors how the lowering of trade barriers and increased productivity were the two essential keys to postwar prosperity.[35] Along with exhibits like these, the *Salon* attracted international visitors and international manufacturers. In 1965, Paul Breton reported having

[31] See, for example, "Nous irons à Paris" *La République de Franche Comte (Besançon)*, February 5, 1955. The press clippings in the *Salon des arts ménagers* archives contain hundreds of advertisements for these kinds of trips.

[32] "Les élèves des cours postscolaires agricoles ont été enchantés de leurs visites au Salon des arts ménagers et au Concours agricole. Ils furent également reçus par le Ministre de l'Éducation Nationale," *Le Maine Libéré*, March 13, 1956.

[33] Vanessa Schwartz, *Spectacular Realities: Early Mass Culture in Fin-de-Siècle Paris* (Berkeley: University of California Press, 1998), 3.

[34] As early as 1948, salons were announced in Toulouse and Lille. See newspaper clippings in CAC 19850023 article 567. A salon on *arts ménagers* and radio was also held in Algiers. "Le XVème Salon nord-africain des arts ménagers et de la radio," *Revue de la Région Economique de l'Algérie* 58 (1954) in advertising section.

[35] Press release by the Organisation Européenne de Coopération Economique, "Maison sans Frontières," CAC 19850023 article 120.

given tours to members of diplomatic missions from the United States, Sweden, Switzerland, the Netherlands, Belgium, West Germany, Italy, and Great Britain.[36] In 1962, about 20 percent of the 1,289 exhibitors at the *Salon* were from outside of France, coming primarily from Western Europe, Scandinavia, and the United States, but also from Hungary, East Germany, Tunisia, Morocco, and Iran, among other places.[37] Ads for the *Salon* also appeared in international journals circulating in England, Belgium, Lebanon, and Germany.[38] Along with the manufacturers, the CNRS profited from all of these guests, as 95 percent of the proceeds from the *Salon* went to the CNRS and 5 percent remained in the *Salon* coffers. In 1968, the *Salon* was shortened from eighteen to sixteen days, but still brought in more than a million francs.[39] The immediate profits of the event were less consequential than its role in strengthening an industry essential to economic growth and working to create mass consumer society in France.

CREATING CITIZEN CONSUMERS AT THE
SALON DES ARTS MÉNAGERS

The cooperation between state and industry that characterized French postwar planning was clearly on exhibit at the *Salon*. No less evidenced was the desire to build what UFC president André Romieu called the "market community" in which consumers, producers, and distributers would work together to help the economy function smoothly.[40] With its captive audience of women already interested in the goods and lifestyles associated with mass consumer society, the *Salon* was an important site for educating women about their role in creating the "market community" and thereby strengthening both their own household economies and the national economy. At its debut, the *Salon* served to promote the industries that manufactured domestic appliances, and the focus of the exhibition was primarily on the appliances themselves. As the minister of reconstruction wrote in 1951, "The *Salon* established a dialogue, so profitable for everyone, between manufacturers and buyers. It was an important

[36] Rapport du Commissaire Général.
[37] Note sur les entrées. CAC 19850023 article 18.
[38] Presse, revues, journaux français et étrangers A-Z, Insertions publicitaires, abonnements, correspondances divers, *1927–1982*. CAC 19850023 article 152.
[39] Rapport du commissaire délégué du gouvernement. CAC 19850023 article 9. These are new francs.
[40] André Romieu, Conférence de presse du 4 février 1955.

element in the unceasing progress in the form and quality of these diverse machines that are now so familiar."[41] Though home appliances remained the stars of the exposition, in the postwar period the focus shifted from the items to a more comprehensive celebration of the home – including the house itself, the commodities in it, and the housewife who managed it. At the *Salon*, state modernizers; productivity enthusiasts; and women's, family, and consumer organizations worked to form citizen consumers who were aware of their place in the national economy. This meant teaching women to make rational purchases that helped the economy expand in healthy ways, and also instilling in them the notion that mass-produced goods were necessary, modern, high-quality goods appropriate for families of all social backgrounds.

From its inception, the *Salon* had served to educate the public. The pronatalist goals of Jules-Louis Breton had inspired lessons in health and childcare at the earliest exhibitions. This interest continued through the postwar period, with conferences such as Education in Infant Healthcare and its Repercussions for the Future of the Race (with demonstrations) and Infant Protection in the late 1940s. Events at the *Salon* also reflected changing concerns about the family, and the postwar shift from family as social and national responsibility to self-fulfillment through marriage and family inspired sessions on "the psychology of women and men in conjugal life" by the mid-1950s. Along with the pronatalist and profamily focuses, the number of conferences on, first, using home appliances and, later, making tasteful and intelligent consumer decisions, grew through the 1950s and 1960s.[42] These changes revealed the new emphasis placed on rational consuming skills in definitions of the ideal housewife, as well as recognition of the influence consumers had on the national economy in a modern mass consumer society. As centers for domestic science education thrived and women's and family groups took part in consumer organization and action, the *Salon des arts ménagers* became a school for consumers. Because many men visited the *Salon*, commentators sometimes speculated on whether its "scientific" character appealed to men. Despite this, and the evidence that couples made big purchasing decisions together, women's groups consistently asserted that women were the public's most important consumers. The citizen consumer formed at the *Salon*

---

[41] Eugène Claudius-Petit, "Le Salon des arts ménagers et la maison de bonheur," *Arts Ménagers* 51 (Paris: Salon des arts ménagers, 1951), 41–42. CAC 19850023 article 66.

[42] The conjugal life program is described in Geneviève Dardel, "Le bonheur est un art difficile," *La Croix*, May 6, 1955. For list of conferences, see the placards in Affiches. CAC 19850328 articles 1–3.

was gendered, giving women a new role in economy and society but also tying them to the home.

One of the tasks of the citizen consumer was to direct industries toward the production of goods that would improve family living conditions, and for many women's, family, and consumer groups, that meant affordable, high-quality, mass-produced durables. As we have seen, consumption served to differentiate class in the nineteenth and early twentieth centuries, but the emphasis on health, happiness, and above all, comfort, which permeated the *Salon*, was applicable to all of France's families, regardless of class. In 1948, when none of the French manufacturers presenting at the *Salon* was producing appliances on a large scale, the journal of *Gaz de France* (GDF) expressed the hope that the throng of potential customers at the *Salon* would inspire in manufacturers the "enterprising and hardy spirit; that is to say a taste for risk" necessary to begin mass production while economic conditions were still unfavorable.[43] Informing manufacturers of consumer demand was one part of the equation, but the *Salon* also worked to teach French citizens that inexpensive, mass-produced goods were also quality goods appropriate for everyone. As the minister of industry and energy explained in the catalogue for the 1953 *Salon*, the exhibition fit well within a "French tradition of always combining aesthetics and progress."[44]

Mass production as the means of providing inexpensive, quality goods to all was an ideal shared by women's, family, and consumer groups with diverse perspectives and memberships. In 1952, the Communist UFF's publication *Femmes françaises* interviewed several architects and designers who saw mass production as the solution to providing comfort to working-class families. Housing was still the major obstacle, but a "politics of peace, a politics conforming to the true needs of the French people" would help direct money toward housing while putting pressure on designers and industrialists to produce more goods in series.[45] In 1957, the journal *La maison française*, which was pitched at a wealthy, bourgeois audience, included a lesson on how one could make a room furnished with mass-produced items, such as the rooms on display at the *Salon*, into something distinctive. The journalist noted that the designer,

---

[43] *Journal des Usines à Gaz* 72 (1948), 45.

[44] Jean-Marie Louvel, "Les arts ménagers et l'industrie et le commerce." *Arts ménagers* 53 (Paris: Salon des arts ménagers, 1953), 48. CAC 19850023 article 66.

[45] Annette Houzet, "Avenir du meuble … et meubles de l'avenir?" *Femmes françaises* 80 (1952): 5.

"wanted to prove that it is not necessary to possess exclusive furniture, rare tissues, or collectables to compose a décor that reflects your personality. Personality expresses itself through details." The journal showed how extras such as curtains, a lamp, or a vase of flowers could lend warmth to a room furnished with mass-produced goods.[46]

The immense popularity of the *Salon* seemed to show that resistance to mass-produced goods was waning, and that the exposition had successfully balanced taste and affordability in its selection of goods. The advertising journal *Vente et Publicité* argued that, "If we will not imprudently argue that mass production was born at the *Salon des arts ménagers* ... we are at least convinced that it would not have the audience that it does among all classes of society without the presentations of quality repeated at the *Grand Palais* in the last several years."[47] The *Salon's* organizers were not indiscriminate in what they allowed to be exhibited at the event. They were not interested in promoting every object of mass consumption, but only quality mass-produced goods that met a certain standard of style and were therefore worthy of the *Salon's* support, as one of its goals was to "shape the taste of the public."[48] This desire inspired contests on mass-produced goods as well as competitions in which designers decorated apartments for the public's perusal. In 1955, for example, the *Salon* celebrated the winner of a contest on mass-produced furniture. As a journalist explained, too often when designers created furniture for the new affordable housing springing up around France, they considered only its functionality, "not taking into account its [furniture's] other role, a secondary one no doubt, but still essential, of contributing aesthetically to one's lifestyle." This was both an economic and cultural problem, for if France did not learn to manufacture quality mass-produced furniture, it would lose its "recognized supremacy" in furniture production.[49] The competitors were asked to design furniture for a living room, a parent's bedroom, and a child's bedroom, and had to remain under a designated maximum price for each room. That same year, the *Salon* also hosted a contest on furniture made of plastic, in which the materials could not be painted individually, but must be colored through a mass-production

---

[46] "Une ambiance chaleureuse à partir d'éléments de série," *La maison française* 11 (1956/1957): 28.

[47] "À propos du prochaine Salon des arts ménagers," 29.

[48] Claudius-Petit, "Le Salon des arts ménagers," 41. Ellen Furlough has argued that this upholding of French taste was one of the reasons the *Salon* was successful in the interwar period. See "Selling the American Way."

[49] "Le concours du meuble français de série," *Nous Loger*, March 15, 1955.

process.[50] Such contests showed, as a journalist calling himself "Mr. Everyone" noted, that one could "make practical furniture at affordable prices ... that's tasteful at the same time."[51] To this end, the *Salon's* "Furnishings Section" always featured mass-produced items currently available on the market.[52]

All kinds of domestic items were featured at the *Salon*, but the *"vedettes,"* or "stars," as journalists often noted, remained the appliances. The kinds of conferences dedicated to these items of home modernization changed as the years passed and educational needs evolved. In the immediate postwar years, the use of gas and electricity in the home was relatively new, and the appliances for sale were prohibitively expensive. At this point, education about the base industries that would support the use of appliances was in order. Teachers in the burgeoning field of domestic science led sessions at the *Salon*, and the use of appliances, electricity, and gas were popular topics, as evidenced by sessions on "The Liberation of Women by Electricity" and "The Technique of Using Gas in Domestic Science and Modern Life."[53] As these services and items became less mysterious, the focus gradually turned from the consumer durables themselves, to emphasizing how to be a modern consumer of those goods. This evolved into a full-fledged effort to create citizen consumers. After 1950, the *Salon* organized its conferences into full days of study on particular topics. In 1951, the *Salon* had a "Day of Purchases," in 1952 a "Day of the Housewife Concerning her Purchases and the Markets" and a "Day of the Consumer" organized by the newly formed UFC.[54] As in other efforts to create citizen consumers, the events at the *Salon* suggest the tension inherent in the effort to both empower women consumers and to tame their irrational impulses by disciplining them to make the right kinds of consumer decisions.

The UFC's account of the 1954 "Day of the Consumer" reveals this tension, as well as the level of cooperation among consumer, women's, and family groups, the state, and the *Salon* in creating a society of mass consumption. The secretary of state of economic affairs, a man charged with, as he put it, "defending the interests of consumers" was "detained

[50] "Concours des meubles en plastiques renforcés au verre textile," *Plastiques Information,* April 16, 1955.
[51] M. Renal, "M. Toutlemonde a découvert le bois," *Le Foyer Rural*, March 25, 1955.
[52] According to the Salon's archives, this was true from at least 1956 to 1976. CAC 19850023 article 122.
[53] Affiches.
[54] Conférences grand public au Salon des arts ménagers. CAC 19850023 article 127.

at the last minute" and therefore sent a representative to speak to conference attendees about "his total support of efforts whose goal is to
improve the buying power of consumers, at the same time ensuring they
are provided with quality products."[55] The speeches that followed this
introduction emphasized the involvement of women in consumer activities, expressed the belief that women's consumer acts were important for
the national economy, and reflected the conviction that women needed to
be educated to make proper consumer decisions. Following the introduc-
tory speech, another representative from the economic affairs ministry
spoke to the audience about the new products that had made women's
labor easier, items such as: aluminum, electricity, the washing machine,
and the refrigerator. At the same time, however, he scolded his audience
for complaining about the expense of new appliances stating, "Do you
know that each year in France, 250 billion goes up in smoke and that
15 million French families spend close to 350 billion in wine, aperitifs,
and alcohol, while they spend less than 150 billion on home appliances,
which are, however, as much an investment as an expense? You see that
much is possible for those who know how to choose."[56] The implication
was that the French were not yet good citizen consumers, a problem that
needed to be rectified.

A representative from the food industries used the conference to point
out the problems in women's consumer habits, but expressed hope that
consumers would educate themselves and therefore promote processes
such as wrapping food products in plastic, which would lengthen the life
of perishable goods. "Progress is impossible unless the consumer gets in
the game and looks for the best solutions … It is up to the 'client king'
to determine the success of this or that new mode of presentation."[57] The
solution to this problem was in the hands of women consumers, and as
happened so often in postwar France, the speaker reminded women of
their economic influence at the same time that he called attention to their
need for education.

The consumer also spoke at the conference, through the voice of the
UFCS, which presented on the advice councils that it and other women's
and consumer organizations participated in at department stores. The

[55] "Allocution de M. Genez," *Union fédérale de la consommation: Bulletin d'information*
21 (1954): 3.
[56] "M. Georges Vailly, Les produits nouveaux," *Union fédérale de la consommation: Bulletin
d'information* 21 (1954): 12.
[57] "Exposé de M. Vasnier, Rédacteur en chef de la Presse de l'Alimentation," *Union fédérale
de la consommation: Bulletin d'Information* 21 (1954): 18.

women on the councils advised department stores about their organization, advertising, and merchandise, a kind of consumer organization that epitomized faith in cooperation between retailers and consumers, rather than their inherent opposition. Mme Irène Mancaux, the vice-president of the UFCS, concluded that, "for the first time, the seller has admitted that he does not always know what the client wants and that the best thing is to let him speak ... Experience shows that his advice is profitable for sellers, too."[58] Along with Mme Mancaux, the *journée* included speakers from the government's bureau of repression of fraud, cooperative organizations, an economist, and other government representatives. The UFC noted that the speeches were followed by an active exchange of views from the public.[59]

The UFC continued its "Day of the Consumer" in subsequent years, but also participated in additional "days" on consumer education, such as 1957's "Day of Credit" and 1959's "Day on Expenses for Home Equipment in the Family Budget." There were days on labels, quality control for different appliances, information sessions on shopping for individual appliances, and information on service after the sale. By 1965, the UFC was holding two "Days of the Consumer" at the annual event.[60] All of these were meant to help consumers make rational, intelligent purchases that would help their families as well as the national economy.

Along with conferences at the *Salon*, the minutes of preparatory meetings evidence a great degree of cooperation among the directors of the *Salon*, the UFC, other consumer organizations, and, after it was created, the INC. The *Salon's* directors also worked with the UNAF, the government subsidized voice of family organizations to the national administration. Paul Breton, *commissaire* of the *Salon*, was a regular at UNAF meetings and served as an advisor to the organization when it brought matters of home equipment before the French government.[61] There were close connections between the *Salon* and teachers in the field of domestic science education as well, providing an efficient means of shaping the consumer skills of a new generation of women. Just after the war, Paul

[58] "Exposé de Mme Mancaux, Vice-présidente de l'Union féminine civique et sociale," *Union fédérale de la consommation: Bulletin d'information* 21 (1954): 28. Mancaux used the masculine form of "consumer" despite the fact that most of the organizations on the Conseils de clientèle were exclusively feminine.
[59] André Romieu, "Intro," *Union fédérale de la consommation: Bulletin d'information* 21 (1954): 1.
[60] Conférences grand public.
[61] UNAF file in the Salon des arts ménagers archives. CAC 19580023 article 64.

Breton, as representative of the *Salon*, took part in a project to create a university-level school for domestic science.[62] The program failed, but Breton and the *Salon* continued their cooperation with instructors and schools of domestic science. In addition, thousands of students of the domestic arts toured the *Salon* with their classmates each year. In 1965, a total of 515 student groups, or 16,918 students, visited the *Salon*. The students were from the region of Paris, rural areas of France, and foreign countries.[63]

THE FAIRY HOMEMAKER: THE PERFECT CONSUMER

The *Salon* had particularly close ties with instructors from the domestic science programs directed by the UNCAF, the national network of organizations charged with distributing state family allocations. The UNCAF, in an effort to create "a vast propaganda movement in favor of domestic science education," began a contest in 1947 called the "The National Domestic Science Competition," the winner of which was crowned "The Fairy Homemaker."[64] The UNCAF moved the contest to the *Salon* in 1949 and it became a fairly elaborate affair. The contest reinforced the *Salon's* message that being a good housewife and consumer did not come naturally, but through education. Over time, the need to be educated to assume the responsibilities of the citizen consumer increased in prominence.

The contest was yet another way for the Paris-based *Salon* to reach out to the provinces and shape lifestyles and consumer habits throughout France. Beginning at the departmental level, the contest included elimination rounds to select finalists for the *Salon* in Paris. In 1954, 1,250 students participated at the regional level, 120 made the semifinal at the *Salon des arts ménagers* in Paris, and 20 made the final round to select the Fairy Homemaker.[65] The contest received coverage across France, making successful contestants virtual celebrities. In 1955, a Dijon paper described how in a "superb modern kitchen ... possessing every appliance a housewife could want: gas and electric cookers, fridges," candidates

[62] Création d'une faculté des sciences domestiques. CAC 19850023 article 1. See also Rouaud, *60 ans d'arts ménagers*, 12.
[63] Rapport du Commissaire General du Salon des arts ménagers.
[64] From information on 1962 contest, "La maison, cadre de la vie familiale." CAC 19850023 article 123.
[65] L'Union nationale des caisses d'allocations familiales présent le VIe Concours National d'Enseignement Ménager. CAC 19850023 article 123.

busied themselves around their casserole dishes. "Each dressed in a white blouse," they worked away as, "one stirs a sauce, the other grates cheese or carefully presses a tart crust." The contestants needed to show their skill in creating a "cauliflower dish with béchamel sauce and a lemon tart." The young women had the honor of receiving, during the contest, the attentions of local government officials, leaders of local family associations, the head of the local CAF, local doctors, and social workers. During the afternoon, the young women watched a series of short educational films on "How Rational Home Equipment Can Help the Mother," "Robots, at Your Service," and "The Gas Kitchen."[66] The Dijon paper printed the names of the finalists and photos of the departmental winner, Marguerite Etienney, who would advance to the regional level.

The departmental exam was not limited to a demonstration of skills, but included an essay portion as well. A paper from Rennes published the written questions for its departmental contest.[67] The exam began, "You are married and the mother of a little seven year old boy. At the beginning of the school year you enroll him in a school that is too far away from your home for him to return for lunch and there is no school canteen (though there is the possibility of heating up his packed lunch). Question 1: Describe the contents of his first lunch sack, explaining the reasons for your selections. Price, nutritional value, and ability to reheat."[68] After the departmental and regional levels, newspapers followed local contestants as they made their way to Paris for the finals at the *Salon des arts ménagers*. The winner of the national contest in 1955, seventeen-year-old Bernadette Thielges of the Moselle, defeated 119 other candidates for the title "Fairy Homemaker," and photos of the "slender" young girl "with blue eyes and light brown hair" appeared in papers across France.[69] (Figure 5.1) One paper pointed out that she was not yet engaged, and would bring her winnings, including a Frigidaire and a washing machine, into the *foyer paternal*. Unless, of course, she happened to meet a "prince charming" on the way home.[70]

---

[66] "Mlle Marguerite Etiennay de l'École national professionnelle de Poligny sera la 'fée du logis' jurassienne 1954," *Le Bien Public Dijon*, December 6, 1954.

[67] Note that departmental level competitions were held only in places with enough contestants to make them appropriate.

[68] "Le concours départemental 'la fée du logis'," *Ouest-Matin*, December 8, 1954.

[69] Description of Thielges from "Une Marseillaise, Mme Denise Soubeyran de Sainte-Marguerite deuxième 'fée du logis' 1955," *Le Provençal*, March 6, 1955.

[70] "La 'fée du logis' est une Lorraine, Mlle Bernadette Thielges âgée de 17 ans," *Nice-Matin*, March 6, 1955.

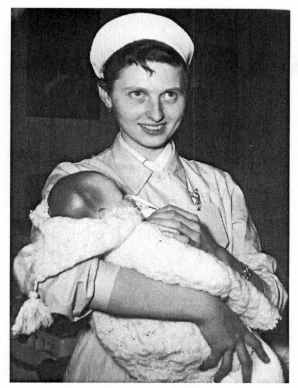

FIGURE 5.1. Bernadette Thielges, winner of the 1955 contest, posing with a doll.
Source: Centre des archives contemporaines, 19850024 article 44.

The questions were more difficult and the atmosphere more tense, of course, at the semifinal and final competitions in Paris. In 1956, a journalist described the "feverish" atmosphere at the finals. One contestant "nervous and crushed by culinary difficulties," had abandoned her efforts after an hour.[71] It was no wonder that the women felt overwhelmed, as they were surrounded by photographers, filmmakers, and judges, and even disturbed by the arrival of the president of the Republic, who came to take his tour of the *Salon* during the competition. The journalist noted that photographers were under strict regulations, as the previous year Bernadette Thielges, "had been photographed taking a taste of sauce with

[71] "À Paris, dans le cadre du Grand Palais, cent vingt concurrentes disputant avec autant de sérieux que d'émotion l'épreuve des demi-finales du concours pour le titre envié de fée du logis 1956," *L'Est Républicaine*, March 3, 1956.

a wooden spoon." This unsanitary gesture, "was a heresy" and the fact that it was printed by many papers in the coming days "set off a slew of indignant protestations."[72] Contestants for the title of Fairy Homemaker were instructed, of course, to uphold the strictest standards of hygiene and neatness. Instructors monitoring the women were told to make sure that all of the students' personal effects were kept hidden from view and that when finished with their cooking, they set their tables in perfect order, washed their dishes, and cleaned their stoves.[73]

An oral exam also took place at both the regional level and during the semifinals in Paris. Topics came from the categories "Domestic Economy," which included questions about modern equipment, organization, and budgeting, "Hygiene," "Nutritional Hygiene," "Cuisine," "Childcare," and "Family Education," the last of which included issues such as "responsibilities of the wife in maintaining equilibrium in the family" and "reciprocal rights and responsibilities of the spouses."[74] In 1955, after passing through a semifinal requiring ironing, cooking, and preparing bottles for children of various ages, those who advanced to the finals were instructed to bake a chestnut cake without a recipe. They were given an array of ingredients that they could choose to use or not use, and a scale; then they were told to present their recipe along with the cake.[75]

The winner was handsomely rewarded for her efforts in surviving these trials. In 1954, organizers awarded the Fairy Homemaker a gas or electric cooker, a washing machine, a sewing machine, a mattress, a set of pots and pans, a steam iron, and an alarm clock as prizes. Each of the twenty finalists received sizeable prizes, the top ten earning a stove, washing machine, water heater, or vacuum. A conference attended by domestic science teachers, social workers, a professor at the *Conservatoire des Arts et Métiers*, and representatives from the UNAF and UNCAF preceded the prize ceremony. That the professor in attendance was productivity enthusiast and modernizer Jean Fourastié reflects the belief that home productivity had an impact on the national economy. The conference title for 1954 asked "Domestic Science Education: What is its role?"[76]

---

[72] Ibid.
[73] "Note à l'attention de Mesdames les Professeurs surveillantes de la matinée ménager." CAC 19850023 article 123.
[74] Programme du Concours National d'Enseignement Ménager. CAC 19850023 article 123.
[75] 7e Concours National d'Enseignement Ménager. CAC 19850023 article 123.
[76] VIe Concours National d'Enseignement Ménager Programme. CAC 19850023 article 123. For more on Fourastié, see Régis Boulat, "Jean Fourastié."

While home modernization and scientific housewifery remained important, the emphasis on rational consuming skills grew increasingly prominent in the selection of the Fairy Homemaker in the postwar years, reflecting the organizers' recognition of the importance of the citizen consumer's decisions for both the family and national economies. In 1961, the theme of the contest was "The Daily Purchases of a Good Homemaker," in 1963, "Food Budget, Family Economy, and Saving," and in 1965, "Knowing How to Buy." In 1965, the students who made the finals were given, in the morning, a publication about the day's prices created by the CNC called "Telex-Consommateurs." Then, they were sent to a local market to purchase items for a meal for five people for which they were told not to spend more than three francs on each person.[77]

In 1968, the Fairy Homemaker contest celebrated its twentieth anniversary. The *Salon* published an information sheet on its winner, twenty-eight-year-old Renée-Claire Larcher, who had green eyes, two young sons, and was married to an airplane mechanic (the information also included her height and weight). Renée-Claire Larcher dreamed of owning a house in the country "with all the comforts." In preparation for the Fairy Homemaker contest in the year of "The Woman Shopper," Madame Larcher, along with students at the other schools submitting candidates for the contest, had taken part in an enquiry asking students to analyze the purchases of a young family with two (or more) children, and also the purchases of a young, single woman with a profession. The students were asked to address both the kinds of stores that the women chose and the method of payment they used. The oral examination in the semifinal in Paris also concerned purchases, and gave the examiners a chance to ask each contestant about the particular economic situation in her home region. Officials trailed the students as they shopped on the *rue des Moines* for the provisions necessary for a meal for four people, which were not to exceed fifteen francs. Next, they asked the contestants to buy linens, and monitored them for their astuteness in discussing the purchase with a salesperson. The contest concluded with an oral exam in which each contestant was interrogated about the circuit of distribution of a product from her home region.[78]

The shift in the focus of the Fairy Homemaker contest to consumer decisions reveals the importance consuming skills now held in definitions

---

[77] These are new francs. Information on each year's theme in file on the Concours de la meilleure ménagère. CAC 19850025 article 123.

[78] These are new francs. Flyer on winner, Renée-Claire Larcher, and information on 1968 contest, "La femme acheteuse." CAC 19850023 article 123.

of the ideal, modern French housewife. This was also apparent in a study the UNCAF, sponsor of the competition, undertook in 1961. Concerned about how young women understood "The Daily Purchases of a Good Homemaker," the organization sent questionnaires to fifty-thousand young women studying in eight-hundred different domestic science courses across France. The UNCAF happily found that 80 percent of the women believed it was necessary to create an annual budget for big expenses, and also a monthly or weekly budget for smaller expenses. They found that young women preferred modern methods of commerce; 85 percent found the personality or likeability of a seller to be of negligible importance, and instead preferred big stores with a wide range of products, and in particular, brand-name products. Seventy to 80 percent of them shopped in chain or large retail stores, a fact that likely cheered modernizers in the French government, who advocated this modern, rational type of distribution and who created new tax laws that encouraged the growth of superstores.[79]

The women questioned preferred brand-name products because they were certain of the quality, and sometimes the guarantee, carried by the name. They showed no aversion to modern advertising, and in fact 52 percent of them said that they expected manufacturers to provide them with information through advertising. The UNCAF found all of this reassuring and concluded, "This wise equilibrium is without a doubt the result of efforts over the past decades to teach and to create our future homemakers. Future homemakers are being instructed more and more in business matters, and are less and less ready to buy or consume without a care. It is probable that after having acquired competence in all the manual skills, the Fairy Homemaker of the years to come will be the best informed homemaker."[80] If women's economic sense had been disrupted by poverty and rationing during the war and occupation, making them incapable of choosing low-priced, but quality, products, the problem had been remedied through education.

In the late 1940s and early 1950s, economic planners had advocated that citizen consumers make wise purchases in order to keep prices of scarce goods low and to direct industrial power toward family need. By the late 1950s and early 1960s, however, the expansion of production

---

[79] Commissariat Général du Plan de modernisation et d'équipement, Rapport de la Commission du Commerce, Troisième Plan de modernisation et d'équipement (May, 1957). CAEF Library. See also William James Adams, *Restructuring the French Economy*.

[80] Les achats quotidiens d'une bonne ménagère. Une épreuve-test proposée a 50,000 jeunes filles. CAC 19850023 article 123.

in domestic appliances had made consumer decisions ever more complicated. The need to rationalize, mold, and shape the citizen consumer to
make decisions for the good of her own family and the nation continued.
An American journalist who visited the 1957 *Salon* explained that "By a
straight count, there were forty-two exhibitors of refrigerators alone, fifty-
seven of ranges, and thirty-six of water heaters. Obviously their products
could not all be good or even comparable to each other," and concluded,
"you really had to know something about the subject and about quality
control before you could even arrive at an opinion or make a purchase
with any guarantee of reliability."[81] Productivity enthusiasts and modernizers saw the planned economy, with roles for government, producers,
and consumers, as necessary for mitigating what one journalist called the
"anarchical" development of the French appliance industry.[82] Consumer
training was to be provided by women's, family, and consumer organizations, domestic science experts, and the national government, and the
Salon des arts ménagers provided a convenient and very popular site for
both the consuming and the training.

In 1963, Organizers of the Tenth International Congress on Domestic
Science issued a press release informing the public of the impending event
and explaining the utility of their work. Their justification for their own
necessity reveals the changing concerns of domestic science educators
moving into the 1960s. Organizers explained that whereas in the past,
domestic science had concentrated on improving and refining traditional
activities, this practice had changed because society's "new conception of
existence is oriented less towards reaching perfection in domestic skills,
than towards comfort and the enjoyment of the greatest number of goods
possible."[83] The release explained that, "The acquisition of more and more
numerous goods, which are constantly recreated, is one of the most tyran-
nical socio-economic imperatives of our society. Newness has become a
virtue in itself and 'to buy' has become an unavoidable obligation."[84]
The writer wondered if the homemaker might become a machine, like
all the others, in the modern home, but not despairing, stated that this
situation made modern domestic science education all the more important. There was an imperative to educate women to be good consumers
and good home organizers in order to encourage "reflection, choice,

---

[81] Peter Muller-Munk, "The Household Arts of Europe," *Industrial Design* 4 (1957): 88.
[82] Jacqueline Bernard, "La période des inventions," 16.
[83] L'esprit de l'enseignement ménager moderne. Xᵉ Congres International de l'Enseignement
Ménager. CAC 19850023 article 64.
[84] Ibid.

resistance of impulse, decision making, and a critical spirit." According to French home economics experts, the growth of production, the use of new consumer durables, and the ever-expanding market of goods in the modern economy made rational consumption the most important trait of the modern homemaker.[85] The rhetoric on women's rational consumption and the importance of creating educated citizen consumers handily made the transition from poverty, in which women monitored prices and controlled inflation, to plenty, in which women weighed the safety, price, and quality of a range of goods while outfitting their modern homes.

THE HOUSEWIFE SPEAKS

The educational functions of the *Salon des arts ménagers* were not limited to the development of modern consumers, but included shaping the living environment of French citizens as well. Postwar reconstruction only melded into new construction in the mid-1950s, and a French public eager for both commodities and new homes in which to put them flocked to the Exposition on Habitation that the ministry of reconstruction (later construction) exhibited at the *Salon* each year.[86] Just as the annual event was a convenient locale for creating citizen consumers, it also provided a means for the state to shape the French public's ideas about solutions to the housing deficit and for soliciting public opinion on housing. The need to house millions of families following the war and the great excitement created by the *Salon* made this a good space for women and the reconstruction authorities to share ideas about homes. Women's magazines also contributed their own (sometimes quite radical) ideas for new home construction, including projects like *Elle's* "Plastic House" in 1956. The house was made of interlocking prefabricated plastic and was round at the center, similar in form to a snail.[87] At the *Salon*, the MRU sought to channel women's demands for modern housing in a direction that they felt was rational and practical, but the event also became a space for women, acting as citizen consumers and experts on the home, to shape the housing the state was building as well as to define what they

---

[85] Ibid.

[86] For information on postwar rebuilding, see Peggy Phillips, *Modern France*; Danièle Voldman, *La reconstruction des villes*; Rosemarie Wakeman, *Modernizing the French Provincial City*. For more on the activities of the ministry of construction at the *Salon des arts ménagers*, See W. Brian Newsome, "The Struggle for a Voice in the City."

[87] Anne-Marie Raimond, "La maison de ELLE, tout en plastique, unique au monde," *Elle* 530 (1956): 48–9, 671. *Maison en plastique*. CAC 19850024 article 49.

felt was necessary for the modern French family. Though manufacturers and state officials created their own image of modernity at the *Salon*, the active participation of women in audiences and planning committees meant that the flow of information was not entirely unidirectional.

As we have seen, the formula the MRU had chosen to house the greatest number of families as quickly and rationally as possible was that of the *grands ensembles*, the huge, modern, housing complexes that mushroomed around Paris and other French cities in the postwar years. Complaints about the *grands ensembles* registered at the MRU even while this type of housing remained central to reconstruction strategies. The kinds of exhibits mounted by the ministry of construction in the 1960s indicate the role of managed demand in shaping policy. At the 1962 *Salon*, the ministry's exhibit centered on the theme of "Collective Services in Housing Units." The exhibit grew out of the conviction that "the question is not whether we can avoid the *grands ensembles*, which are necessary for making up for the lag in housing construction between 1920 and 1940, for satisfying the needs of new population growth, and for reducing construction costs, it is essentially a matter of organizing these buildings around the services which are necessary to them."[88] The ministry of construction compiled information on services essential to the *grands ensembles*, including childcare, medical services, spaces for adults to socialize, and facilities for sports.[89]

Although women appreciated the new standards of comfort in the *grands ensembles*, inhabitants of the complexes also had multiple complaints, and the ministry of construction was eventually forced to take note of repeated criticisms. Women frequently lamented the noise in the buildings, the lack of storage space, and the fact that kitchens were often too small to eat in.[90] They also complained that men designed the interior of the apartments, and they did not seem to understand the needs of the homemaker. One very popular response to this problem was an exhibit at the 1959 *Salon des arts ménagers* called the "Apartment Referendum of the French Family."

The exhibit was part of the ministry of construction's theme for the year, "The Functional House and the Functional Neighborhood," which was an effort both to exhibit apartments planned to facilitate the work of the

---

[88] L'équipement social, culturel, et sportif des grands ensembles. CAC 19790660 article 9.
[89] Ibid.
[90] Chombart de Lauwe et al found that most families ate their meals in the kitchen despite the fact that architects had purposefully made the kitchen small in order to force families to eat dinner in the *salle de séjour*. Chombart de Lauwe, *Famille et habitation II*, 80–81.

housewife and to showcase new housing placed in an environment with easy access to schools and commerce.[91] Jeanne Picard, a representative of the UNAF at the *Conseil économique* and a future president of the UFC, described for journalist Merry Bromberger how architects had completed a plan for a *grand ensemble* of 5,000 units, meant to house 20,000 people. "At the last moment," she explained, "They discovered that they were building the two supermarkets of the development directly across from each other. If a woman had been authorized to look at those plans, she would have bothered to find out where the markets were going to go!"[92] Not a single woman had been consulted throughout the planning, despite their unique knowledge of family needs. Bromberger explained how Pierre Sudreau, commissioner of construction in the Paris region declared, "Find me a woman." He wanted, "An authentic housewife who knows how to read the plan for an apartment, a mother capable of critiquing a sink, choosing a water heater, and writing an administrative report. A woman who washes her own dishes and can confer with a prefect, who can hold her head amongst a pack of urban planners. A woman who has time, good sense, and practicality ... Oh! I forget: the obstinacy of a bulldozer as well."[93] Sudreau found Picard, who was, presumably, an "authentic" woman because along with being a bureaucrat, she was the mother of four daughters and had spent eight years constantly moving in search of an appropriate apartment for her family.[94]

Picard noted, "M. Sudreau, Minister of Construction, has wanted to know the opinions of women in matters of housing since his arrival at the Quai de Passy, saying frequently, 'It's men who build apartments, but it's women who live in them'."[95] Picard headed a group of thirty-four women's and family associations, groups representing a combined membership of more than three million, in designing an apartment according to women's needs.[96] The women spent six months visiting hundreds of apartments and interviewing their inhabitants in order to find out "everything that is not working" in current housing.[97]

[91] Relations avec ministre de la reconstruction. Exposition de l'Habitat. CAC 19850023 article 119.

[92] Merry Bromberger, "Enfin des femmes commandent dans la reconstruction," *Constellation* 126 (1958): 143.

[93] Ibid., 141.

[94] Ibid., 143.

[95] Jeanne Picard, "L'appartement referendum de la famille française 1959," *Arts Ménagers* 11 (1959): 105.

[96] Membership information from Rosie Delprat, "Appartement-referendum," *La femme dans la vie sociale* 295 (1959): 2.

[97] Picard, "L'appartement referendum," 105.

The group made observations about each part of the apartment they found important for women's tasks and family life. They noted that the entryway was indispensable in protecting the private space of the family, and that very often it did not exist. In the kitchens, the windows were often placed too high for a woman to be able to look through them, there was often no place for a refrigerator, and the sink was too close to the wall for a woman to be able to place clean dishes on one side of the sink, and dirty dishes on the other. In addition, the garbage chute was usually not in the kitchen. There was often no room for a washing machine in the bathroom and often no means of getting fresh air into the room. The women also disapproved of the general appearance of the bathrooms, one stating, "I saw one bathroom so horrible that you could have convinced me I was in the WC at a rail-station." The appearance of the HLMs in general was spotty. The women noted, "Certain HLMs have a nice exterior of solid construction, others are future slums."[98]

There was often no central lighting in the living room and when apartments had a balcony, it was usually only accessible through a small door. The bedrooms were often too small to place two single beds in the children's room, and too small to place a double bed in the parents' room. Chombart de Lauwe's urban ethnological work concurred with this observation. Women that he interviewed expressed frustration that they could not place a double bed in the room without having two sides against the walls, which made it difficult to make the bed.[99] To save money, there were usually no interior doors in the apartments, and when there were doors, they often did not match one another. The floors were frequently very difficult to clean, forcing families to re-cover them with carpet or linoleum at their own expense, and the windows were too close to the ceiling to hang curtains. There were often no closets in the apartment and no place to put a baby carriage.[100] Picard noted, "In the plans of the HLMs, I would like to know if they ever thought about closets. In certain 'termite houses' where there is no room for an armoire, they did not put closets. Clothes hang from the ceiling. And when the ceiling is two meters thirty, pants and dresses hang in the dust."[101]

The stairways were open and had gaps wide enough for a child to fall through. The paint on the stairs was ivory and, as Picard noted, "Kids

[98] Observations from Constatations faites au cours de visites d'HLM – SCIC – OCIL-Cités de transit, etc... CAC 19850023 article 120.
[99] Chombart de Lauwe et al, *Famille et habitation II*, 84.
[100] Chombart de Lauwe also noted that in the Maison Radieuse the apartments had no closets. Ibid., 85.
[101] Bromberger, "Enfin des femmes," 144.

climb up and down those stairs six or eight times a day. In a month, the light-colored paint has become leprous. And the budget for upkeep only allows their repainting every ten years."[102] The gardens around the HLMs were often pretty, but they did not have sandboxes and small children were not allowed to walk on the grass, forcing mothers to walk to public parks up to twenty-five minutes from their homes. Women often had to walk thirty to thirty-five minutes to a grocery store as well.[103]

The things that inhabitants did appreciate about their apartments, when these features existed, were eat-in kitchens, balconies, elevators, and storage space for baby carriages. Women wanted their apartments to have doors to each room, bigger rooms, insulation from noise, closets, room for a refrigerator, and more. Their demands for local service were, in order of importance, schools, transportation, stores with basic necessities, and social services like childcare. The women recommended working on providing these services. They also recommended that architects stop building extremely long bands of apartment complexes and provided examples of HLMs that they recommended never be repeated.[104]

After identifying the problems with the apartments, the women's groups designed an apartment to be presented at the *Salon des arts ménagers*. Marcel Roux served as architect, and afterwards used the design for an apartment complex at Thiais.[105] The apartment was to be comfortable, but not luxurious. It was to be practical and affordable for families, and was to use the norms established for an HLM in the region of Paris. The women designed the apartment to be for a family of six, including parents, two daughters aged fourteen and sixteen, and two sons aged six and eight. They noted that the noise in HLMs caused nervousness and prevented intimacy – something they believed to be of great importance in the modern home. Therefore, the apartment had good doors on every room. It included an entryway, bathroom with closet for drying clothes, a separate WC, living room, one bedroom for the parents, and two bedrooms for children.[106] There was a second sink in the hallway outside of the bathroom for extra washing facilities at busy times. Since

---

[102] Ibid.
[103] Constations faites au cours de visites.
[104] Ibid. Among the examples were Orly, Porte d'Ivry, and Bagneux.
[105] See W. Brian Newsome. "The Struggle for a Voice." Newsome sees the Apartment Referendum as the beginning of what he calls "participatory architecture" on the part of the ministry of construction.
[106] Chombart de Lauwe et al had noted that the state built too many apartments with only two bedrooms, causing problems for families with several children and forcing some families to turn the *salle de séjour* into a third bedroom. *Famille et habitation II*, 71.

the women placed great emphasis on the need for storage in each room, there were closets throughout, including in the entryway. The kitchen was big enough for family meals, and the large living room allowed the family to relax together and entertain, if desired. Importantly, the apartment was designed by and created for rational consumers. The imagined family had a budget of 11,620 francs a month including family allocations, and the women furnished the apartment, but placed different colored tags on the items to indicate when they would be bought.[107] All items could be purchased within the span of five years, but had to be acquired gradually to stay within the family budget.[108] In all, 330,000 francs were required for outfitting the apartment, and the organizers felt that the family could spend 8,000 francs a month to buy the furnishings, which would also include a washing machine and a refrigerator. These furnishings signified "neither luxury nor excess but the comfort indispensable to the normal fulfillment and happiness of a family."[109] Thus, the women defined what they saw as "essential" and "necessary" at the end of the 1950s.

Visitors to the apartment referendum could fill out a questionnaire with their thoughts on the design, which were presumably to be taken into account by the ministry of construction. The magazine *Arts Ménagers* also published the questionnaire so that women could fill it out and send it in. The exhibition was extremely popular, most women's journals and many national newspapers including articles on that particular exhibit along with other information on the *Salon des arts ménagers*.[110] However, at least one architect wrote to the ministry complaining that the women in the group were not experts in home design and that these matters should be left to professionals.[111] The women were undaunted, and the next year presented a model single family home to the public, again taking into account the budget of the French family and designing a home that could

[107] In 1959, the average salary of a father of two living in Paris was 58,805 francs a month. The average for a worker was 50,045 francs and for a professional 64,645 francs (all new francs). INSEE, *Annuaire statistique de la France* (Paris: Presses Universitaires de France, 1961): 259.

[108] Jeanne Picard, "L'appartement referendum," 276–278.

[109] Anne-Marie Pajot, "Avec *Arts Ménagers*, visitez l'appartement referendum," *Arts Ménagers* 112 (1959), 85.

[110] Interestingly, although the Communist *Heures claires* included an article on the *Salon*, it did not include an article on the Apartment Referendum. This seems to indicate that the UFF was not among the women's organizations included in the project, something that would not be surprising considering that the UFF was not part of the UNAF, the association of which Picard was a representative at the *Conseil économique*.

[111] Letter from Ionel Schien to Paul Breton, 1958. CAC 19850023 article 120.

be bought for less than 30,000 francs.[112] Along with their notions on the design of the home itself, the women's groups commented on procedures for buying homes, and in particular the difficulty of current practices. They recommended that the process be simplified so that a home could be purchased like any other consumer durable, stating that, "A house should be able to be bought or sold as easily as an automobile."[113] The *Maison Familiale* did not include a public referendum, but did attract attention, as did the Apartment Referendum, for its emphasis both on the needs of French families and for the novelty of being designed by women.

The Apartment Referendum of the French family was an attempt by the ministry of construction to answer women's and families' complaints about the *grands ensembles*, the projects preferred by the French government for the cheap, fast, and rational solution they ostensibly provided for the housing shortage. The fact that the ministry was forced to listen to other voices indicates the importance of both the role of demand on the part of women and families, and the management of it by the French state, in the changes that occurred in postwar France. Displaying the tensions inherent in both empowering and rationalizing consumers, the state gave the women's organizations the authority to design an apartment, but one that fit their prescribed norms. The Apartment Referendum was an attempt to gather information about the desires of the public at the same time as shaping French tastes in home design in appropriate, modern ways.

In the *Salon des arts ménagers*, many of the characteristics of the French path to postwar modernization and mass consumer society came together. As a government sponsored event that directed crowds of consumers to consumer durables and manufacturers, the *Salon* exemplified the importance of cooperation between state and industry in postwar economic planning. Here, too, consumer representatives worked with representatives of industry and distribution to create the "market community" that would rationalize the economy and drive healthy economic expansion. This required creating citizen consumers aware of their importance in the national economy and disciplined to make the right consumer decisions, and the *Salon* provided the perfect venue in which to do that. Events like the Fairy Homemaker contest increasingly emphasized the importance of consumer skills. The contest also reinforced the notion that homemaking

---

[112] "Arts ménagers 60: Dix femmes construisent une maison," *Aurore* (Paris), February 9, 1960. These are new francs.

[113] Vœu des associations féminines et familiales, 1960. CAC 19790660 article 9.

was a profession with a well-defined skill set that in turn reinforced the notion that the role of citizen consumer and domestic manager could balance women's emancipation with the need for normalcy and domestic stability after the war. The *Salon* was also a way for the centralized drive to create modernity and mass consumer society that began in Paris to reach out to the provinces. The Plan emphasized regional development by the early 1960s, but the *Salon* began reaching out even earlier through subsidized trains, the Fairy Homemaker Contest, and exhibits on rural modernization.

The *Salon* was in its heyday in the 1950s and early 1960s. By the mid-1960s, public attendance began to fall off and the event became more focused on those involved in the appliance trade. This change in audience reflected the fact that the French public had finally become experienced consumers who no longer needed the educative influence of the *Salon*. Paul Breton continued as *commissaire* until 1976 and the event itself continued until 1983. By the late 1960s, however, it seemed incongruous in a France swept by new feminist movements and a student population that openly rejected consumer society. By the time it closed in 1983, only a small section of the *Salon* was open to the public. France had become a mass consumer society and the French public no longer needed the festival of consumption that attracted so much attention in the postwar years.[114]

[114] For history of the *Salon* up to its demise in 1983, see Martine Segalen, "The Salon des Arts Ménagers," and Jacques Rouaud, *60 ans d'art ménagers*.

Epilogue

As I was completing the research for this project in the dossier collection at the *Sciences Po* library in Paris, I wondered at the irony of reading newspaper articles from the 1950s advocating consumer credit as the means for expanding the French economy and achieving American levels of economic growth, while at the same time the contemporary news media were reporting on the credit crisis and overindebtedness in the United States. As columnist David Brooks opined in *The New York Times* in the fall of 2009, what the United States now needs is a new kind of culture war, one not pitting religious conservatives against secular liberals, but a "movement to restore economic values" whose goal would be to "make the U.S. again a producer economy, not a consumer economy" and to "champion a return to financial self-restraint, large and small."[1] This book emerges at a time when Western governments and peoples are questioning the wisdom of unrestrained consumer spending. Suddenly, the argument that credit could be a kind of "future savings" seems suspect, and the pessimism of those who warned that excessive consumer credit could exacerbate a financial crisis seems prescient. The consumer-driven economy in which all people enjoy a comfortable standard of living is currently associated less with social justice than with excess.

The American and French economies and peoples are linked more closely than ever and facing much more similar economic challenges than they did in the immediate postwar decades, when the United States was an economic powerhouse that France strived to emulate. Despite present commonalities, differences remain. As we have seen, the French

[1] David Brooks, "The Next Culture War," *The New York Times*, September 28, 2009.

embraced increased spending and methods like consumer credit in the postwar years, but even in 2005, household debt as a share of disposable income was 64 percent in France, as compared to 135 percent in the United States.[2] At the end of 2004, there were 9.1 million credit cards in France for its 62.5 million people, compared to 1.5 billion cards in the United States in 1999, an average of ten cards per American.[3] Perhaps optimistically, Christian Noyer, governor of the *Banque de France* suggested in 2008 that the relatively low level of debt per household in France should mean a less disruptive economic crisis than that in the United States.[4] The lower level of consumer debt in France is in part a result of tighter regulation of the credit industry, but the reasoning behind economic policy offers insight into social and cultural norms as much as economic conditions. Gunnar Trumbull's comparison of consumer protection in the United Kingdom and France reveals that while in Britain, access to consumer credit is regarded as a means of incorporating the less fortunate into society by allowing them to achieve a higher standard of living, in France, credit is viewed as a tool for economic expansion, but also a potential danger to individuals and the economy. The unrestrained use of credit can too easily disenfranchise the poor further, by saddling them with overly burdensome debt. Behind current government regulation in France, one can discern the continued existence of the impulses that led regulators of the 1950s and 1960s to limit the time periods for loans, emphasize the fitness of credit for only durable goods, and require a hefty down payment for big purchases.[5]

Despite these cultural, social, and economic specificities, the French, like other Western Europeans, did spend an unprecedented amount of money on housing and consumer durables in the postwar decades, embracing new notions of necessity that dictated that all families deserved access to a certain standard of living, and proving themselves willing to use spending methods like credit. Economic expansion and rampant

[2] Gunnar Trumbull, "Consumer Protection in French and British Credit Markets," Unpublished paper from the Joint Center for Housing Studies, Harvard University (February 2008), 4. Copyright Gunnar Trumbull.

[3] De Blic and Lazarus, *Sociologie de l'argent*, 60.

[4] Christian Noyer, "Conducting monetary policy in times of financial stress – Speech of Mr. Christian Noyer, Governor of the Banque de France – European Banking and Financial Forum – Prague, April 1, 2008," Banque de France, www.banque-france.fr/gb/instit/telechar/discours/disco80401.pdf.

[5] Trumbull, "Consumer Protection." The *Conseil national du crédit* stopped regulating the length of loans and requiring a mandatory down payment in 1979. Alain Chatriot, "Protéger le consommateur," 105.

consumer spending lasted beyond the period of this study, into the early
1970s. Jean Fourastié has called the period between 1946 and 1975 the
"trente glorieuses" or "thirty glorious years" because of the continued
growth of French productivity and the changes to social and economic
conditions that accompanied it. The glorious period ended in 1975, in
large part due to the international oil crisis, but Fourastié asserted that he
had predicted the end as early as 1968 or 1970. The productivity of one
hour of work had increased an average of 5 percent per year since 1951,
and could not increase indefinitely, especially with the relative scarcity
of oil, other fuels, and raw materials.[6] As Daniel Cohen writes in the
preface to a recent edition of *Les trente glorieuses*, later economists have
placed more emphasis on the importance of the mid-1970s as the point at
which the gap between French and American living standards narrowed.
"Growth founded on the imitation of a *leader* cannot continue indefinitely," Cohen asserts, pointing out that by 1973 the French standard of
living was at about 80 percent of the American.[7]

FAILED PROMISES OF EQUALITY

By the end of the 1960s, the consumption of durables and the lifestyles
we associate with mass consumer society were widespread, as was the
notion that all families deserved a decent standard of living, a belief that
has only intensified since the late 1960s. The French have embraced the
changes that were necessary to become a mass consumer society. This
has even meant accepting changes that were unpopular in the postwar
period, such as eating more commercially prepared foods. The cost of
food in the French family's budget is now about half what it was in 1960,
and in 2006, 41 percent of French meals included packaged meat, fish,
or vegetable dishes.[8] Purchases of these items were likely made in large
supermarkets, as were 70 percent of French food purchases in 2006.[9] The
fact that the state records such statistics reveals the continuing importance in France of understanding consumer demand when formulating
economic policy.

[6] Jean Fourastié, *Les trente glorieuses, ou, la révolution invisible* (Paris: Librairie Arthème
Fayard, 1979), 254–55.
[7] Daniel Cohen, "Préface" of Fourastié, iv. Emphasis in original.
[8] Besson, Danièle, "Le repas depuis 45 ans: Moins de produits frais, plus de plats préparés,"
Insee Première 1208 (2008), 1, 3.
[9] Vanessa Bellamy and Laurent Léveillé, "Consommation des ménages. Quels lieux d'achat
pour quels produits?" *Insee Première* 1165 (2007), 1.

Sociologists point to the fact that consumption in France is no longer determined by class status, but by revenue, a similar situation to what Pierre Laroque identified as the structure of the American class system in the 1960s – evidence that the bourgeois regime of consumption has been discarded.[10] Studies of consumption continue to use socioprofessional classifications, as they did in the 1950s and 1960s, but only because they affect revenue; "if a *cadre* and a worker have different structures of consumption, it is more because of a gap in revenue than because of their professions."[11] This does not mean, of course, that social distinctions have disappeared. The category of "domestic service" no longer appears on budget analyses, but in addition to spending more money on "luxury goods," wealthy families spend much more on things such as childcare, since they can afford to hire a nanny for young children.[12] Educational achievement and other factors continue to divide the population. Sociologists Jeanne Lazarus and Damien de Blic argue, in fact, that socioeconomic status means less in France than in the United States and that social power depends more on Pierre Bourdieu's categories of social capital (relationships), cultural capital, and symbolic capital (the ability to mobilize these various kinds of capital).[13]

Since the late 1960s, economic and social changes in France have made ever more apparent the fact that mass consumer society is not necessarily egalitarian, even if the class formations important in the 1950s and 1960s have changed in the intervening period. The women of the Communist UFF and the working family movement saw no class barriers to consumption, but they identified strongly as workers and saw gaining consumer durables as a question of social justice. This is very different from what French sociologists see today when they analyze class and consumption. Agnès Villechaise's study of a *grand ensemble* community in Bordeaux examines the new kinds of inequalities that have arisen in France in the past decades. Villechaise conducted interviews at the *Hauts Garonne* estate in the early and mid-1990s and concluded that there was no longer a working-class identity among the estate's residents. The influx

[10] Pierre Laroque, *Les classes sociales*, 83.
[11] A. Bayet, C. Chambaz, Y. Guegano, and J.-M. Houriez, "Les choix de consommation des ménages; Une question de revenu avant tout," *Économie et Statistique* 248 (1991): 21.
[12] Ibid., 24. This study included domestic service in a larger category of "luxury expenses" including expenses for a second home, insurance, and taxi fares. Ibid., 26.
[13] De Blic and Lazarus, *Sociologie de l'argent*, 96. See Pierre Bourdieu, "What Makes a Social Class? On the Theoretical and Practical Existence of Groups," *Berkeley Journal of Sociology* 32 (1987): 1–18.

of new workers, including women and immigrants, without a grounding in French working-class traditions, the multiplication of positions and statuses within working-class professions, the diffusion of credit, and social mobility all meant that the workers that she spoke with no longer identified with a "working class," either politically or socially.[14]

Sociologists Thomas Amosé and Olivier Chardon have also examined class identity recently, hoping to begin the kind of discussion and debate that thrived in the 1960s as sociologists questioned whether class identity disappeared with the spread of mass consumer society. They argue that class identity declines as one descends the social ladder; a *cadre* is likely to identify by class, but among unskilled workers and employees, no such identity exists.[15] Amosé and Chardon point out the similarity in status of unskilled workers and employees, who traditionally would not have been lumped together in terms of occupational class, but share many of the same problems, including low revenue, underemployment, and precarious positions. A cashier in a supermarket, while considered an employee, also performs repetitive actions like one might do on an assembly line. Many of the least favored positions in these groups are held by older women, who identify more with their geographic location and family than a class, and immigrants, who tend to identify most strongly with people of the same background, a fact that manifests itself in choice of friends and, sometimes, religious community.[16]

The estate that Villechaise studied had a multitude of different groups with different standards of living, and she concluded that the one commonality across its residents was that they had the aspiration to live and consume like the middle classes. As members of what she identifies as the new "impoverished middle classes," they had assimilated culturally by accepting the norms of the middle class, but were excluded from that class socially and economically, leading to great frustration and anger. These people sought tranquility in the home, a desire amplified by their sense that the neighborhood was dangerous and degraded, but their

[14] Agnès Villechaise, "La banlieue sans qualités. Absence d'identité collective dans les grands ensembles," *Revue française de sociologie* 38 (1997): 351–374.
[15] Note that the French use of the term "employee" differs from the American. By "employées non qualifies," or unskilled employees, Amosé and Chardon are primarily referring to unskilled positions in service and retail, as opposed to industrial positions. Thomas Amosé and Olivier Chardon, "Les travailleurs non qualifies: Une nouvelle classe sociale?" *Économie et Statistique* 393–394 (2006): 203–229.
[16] Ibid., Amosé and Chardon also point out that it is difficult to identify, as sociologists would in the past, a "working-class family" because oftentimes employees are married to workers.

income was not sufficient to provide the comforts of a middle-class home. Furthermore, whereas the tranquil nature of the middle-class home is strengthened through its opposition to the world of work, unemployment made even this oppositional value unreachable for many families.[17] Without productive time outside, time spent in relaxing at home was devalued. Villechaise's work exhibits both how successfully the bourgeois regime of consumption has been obliterated in France and how salient is the notion that all families need and deserve the lifestyles associated with mass consumer society. Despite the fact that these people were living in conditions unreachable to working families in the wake of the Second World War, mass consumer society and modern apartments had not led to social equality.

MAY 1968 AND THE REJECTION OF LIBERATION THROUGH CONSUMPTION

The disillusionment with the promises of mass consumer society, already apparent in the late 1960s, was most forcefully expressed in the events of 1968. In May 1968, Paris erupted with student demonstrations that began at the Nanterre campus of the University of Paris and spread to the Sorbonne, eventually leading to what Kristen Ross has called "the largest mass movement in French history, the biggest strike in the history of the French labor movement, and the only 'general' insurrection the overdeveloped world has known since World War II."[18] The events began with groups advocating third worldism, a political position that grew out of opposition to the war in Algeria, then turned to a critique of American involvement in Vietnam. But the students were also unleashing a general critique of French society, which included rejection of the technocratic state and capitalism.[19]

Among the students' broad criticisms of the French system was the charge that mass consumer society was alienating and dehumanizing.[20]

---

[17] Agnès Villechaise, "La banlieue sans qualités." Villechaise uses the term *classes moyennes paupérisées*, which I have translated as "impoverished middle classes."

[18] Kristin Ross, "The French Declaration of Independence," in *Anti-Americanism*, edited by Andrew Ross and Kristin Ross (New York: New York University Press, 2004), 146.

[19] Michael Seidman, *The Imaginary Revolution: Parisian Students and Workers in 1968* (New York: Berghahn Books, 2004), 1–8. Kristin Ross emphasizes the political importance of May of 1968 in *May '68 and its Afterlives* (Chicago: University of Chicago Press, 2002).

[20] See Alain Schnapp and Pierre Vidal-Naquet, *The French Student Uprising, November 1967-June 1968: An Analytical Record* (Boston: Beacon Press, 1971).

The merits of mass consumer society and the accompanying changes that had occurred since the war were thus at the center of a cleavage in French society, one that broke, in many ways, along generational lines. In 1968, the children of the postwar baby boom were coming of age. Almost 34 percent of the French population was under the age of twenty, and there were about eight million people between the ages of sixteen and twenty-four.[21] One source of frustration in France was the inability of the university system to accommodate these young people. The Nanterre campus, where the events began, had been opened in 1964 to provide education to the baby boomers. Between its opening and 1968 it expanded from 2,300 to almost 15,000 students, and still had no library and few amenities for students.[22] The great number of students in France was a result of the demographic boom, but also of the benefits and demands of postwar economic change. School reforms in the late 1950s and 1960s helped to democratize education, but so, too, did the fact that more families were comfortable enough to forego the income that an eighteen-year old could contribute to the family economy, and were aware that job prospects were in technical and managerial positions, rather than the industrial sector.[23] It was these same technical and managerial positions, and the technocratic society that they created and represented, that the students of 1968 rejected. As Edgar Morin wrote at the time, it was not the difficulty of finding careers, but "contempt for the careers as *cadres*-technicians that await them" that motivated the students.[24] The university system was complicit as, in the words of Danny Cohn-Bendit, it was "a sausage machine, which turns people out without any real culture and incapable of thinking for themselves, but trained to fit into the economic system of a highly industrialized society."[25] Sociologist Alain Touraine, too, labeled the university system "an instrument of dependent participation" for turning out specialists unable to critique the society

[21] Jean-François Sirinelli, *Les baby-boomers: Une génération, 1945–1969* (Paris: Fayard, 2003), 9.

[22] Arthur Marwick, *The Sixties: Cultural Revolution in Britain, France, Italy, and the United States, 1958–1974* (Oxford: Oxford University Press, 1998), 556.

[23] On educational reforms and their limits, see Mendras, *Social Change in Modern France*, 99–103.

[24] Edgar Morin, "La commune étudiante" in *Mai 68: La brèche suivi de Vingt ans après*, by Edgar Morin, Claude Lefort, and Cornelius Castoriadis (Paris: Éditions Complexe, 1988), 14.

[25] Quoted in Claire Duchen, *Feminism in France: From May '68 to Mitterrand* (London: Routledge, 1986), 5.

that employed them.[26] The attack on technocratic consumer society was made precisely by the generation that had benefitted from the postwar economic transformation and was now being trained to be its "expert managers and administrators."[27]

These young people had not experienced the perils of war, occupation, and postwar penury, but had grown up along with mass consumer society. The rapid transformation of French society, both economic and demographic, made the contrast between generations especially shocking. As historian Tony Judt has noted of Europe in general, "The gap separating a large, prosperous, pampered, self-confident and culturally autonomous generation from the unusually small, insecure, Depression-scarred and war-ravaged generation of its parents was greater than the conventional distance between age groups."[28] The fact that relatively affluent young people were destroying private property and fomenting revolution led sociologist Ronald Inglehart to argue for a transition in political motivations that seemed to portend long-term political change. Inglehart maintained that everyone has a hierarchy of motivations in which the most important need is the one left unsatisfied. He distinguished between materialist or acquisitive values like economic needs and security, and nonmaterialist needs such as those of self-expression and autonomy. The young people that participated in May 1968, and other similar events in Europe and the United States, grew up in conditions of affluence in which economic problems seemed to be under control. Therefore, they had turned their attention to the postmaterialist or postbourgeois needs of participation and self-realization. Inglehart argued that this would have long-term consequences because rather than being an age-related condition that would change as these young people grew older, this was the result of socialization under affluence, and young people would retain these values throughout their lifetimes. Furthermore, as more of society grew affluent, there would be a decline in the attraction of right-wing parties, as they tended to be associated with the search for security.[29]

[26] Alain Touraine, *The Post-Industrial Society. Tomorrow's Social History: Classes, Conflicts and Culture in the Programmed Society* (New York: Random House, 1971), 12–13.

[27] Julian Bourg, *From Revolution to Ethics: May 1968 and Contemporary French Thought* (Montreal: McGill-Queen's University Press, 2007), 25.

[28] Judt, *Postwar*, 394.

[29] See Ronald Inglehart, "The Silent Revolution in Europe: Intergenerational Change in Post-Industrial Societies," *The American Political Science Review* 65 (1971): 991–1017 and "Révolutionnarisme post-bourgeois en France, en Allemagne, et aux États-Unis," *Il Politico* 36 (1971): 209–238. In 2007, Inglehart wrote an article confirming that

Another consequence of the postmaterialist turn, in Inglehart's esti-
mation, was that it subverted the association of the working class with
left-wing politics and the affluent middle class with right-wing politics.
In 1968, it was those who had the most to lose, presumably, who were
demanding radical change. When national elections were held shortly
after the crisis, it was the young middle class that supported the *Parti
socialiste unifié* (Unified Socialist Party, PSU), the only party that encouraged the demonstrations, whereas Gaullists gained votes from every other
population group, including the working class.[30] The most important sin-
gularity of the French events, which happened in a year of international
agitation, was the cooperation of students and workers, leading to the
mass strike. This cooperation fell apart, however, over access to mass consumer society. The Gaullist government was able to quell worker unrest
by agreeing to traditional workplace demands, including wage increases.
While the students attacked the structure of mass consumer society,
workers, many of whom had bought durables on credit and needed their
income to continue payments, asserted their right to return to work.[31] As
Inglehart explained, Cohn-Bendit had proclaimed, "We refuse a world
where the risk of dying of hunger has been conquered by the risk of dying
of boredom," but "for striking workers, in particular the oldest among
them, it was not so evident or certain that the risk of dying of hunger had
been forever eliminated."[32] Furthermore, the sight of students setting fire
to automobiles, an item many workers had only recently acquired, "was
shocking and looked like vandalism" to those workers.[33] Their desire to
enjoy the benefits of mass consumer society produced a break with the
students, many of whom were middle class, had been born after the war,
and had no recollection of the poverty and lack of basic necessities of the
late 1940s.

Historians have analyzed the ways in which the events of 1968
reflect continuities in French society from the early 1960s, and even
earlier. Kristin Ross sees them as the expression of "the problems and

this postmaterialist shift had happened, as evidenced by the fact that politics today are
more concerned with "lifestyle" issues than class-based demands. He did not address
his contention that right-wing parties would decline as more people grew affluent. See
Ronald Inglehart, "Changing Values Among Western Publics from 1970 to 2006," *West
European Politics* 31 (2008): 130–146.

[30] Inglehart, "Révolutionnarisme post-bourgeois," 225–226.

[31] See Seidman for discussion of the role of credit in prompting workers to return to work.
Seidman, 232–233.

[32] Inglehart, "Révolutionnarisme post-bourgeois," 232.

[33] Ibid., 232.

dissatisfactions surrounding the French lurch into modernization" over
the course of the 1950s, whereas Henri Mendras asserts that they were,
the "symbolic expression of a profound transformation that had been
taking place for three years" (and thus, since 1965).[34] Some historians
have decried the extent to which the political demands of students have
been overlooked in the characterization of events as dominated by cultural and sexual libertinism. Despite this, most agree that May 1968
was critical for leading to great social and cultural change in the 1970s.
Historian Janine Mossuz-Lavau argues that the hedonism of male students who demanded that they be able to visit women in their dorms
was a rejection of old rules and a harbinger of increased sexual freedom
among young people. She asserts, like many others, that the rejection
of hierarchies and traditions was an element that fed into the creation
of the women's movement in the early 1970s.[35] French women activists
who participated in the events of 1968 were excited by these rejections,
but frustrated by the discrepancy between the revolutionary rhetoric of
their male comrades and their unwillingness to treat women as equals.[36]
Dissatisfaction with the notion of women's liberation through the role
of the consumer for the nation and domestic manager was already clear
in the early 1960s, but the events of 1968 helped prompt the creation of
the *Mouvement de libération des femmes* (MLF) in 1970, which led to
a more assertive rejection of emancipation through consumption.[37] The
notion of fulfillment through domesticity and home comfort prominent
in women's magazines had never been without critics, and even in the
mid-1950s women wrote letters to the editors that expressed dissatisfaction with their role as full-time homemaker, only to be sternly instructed
not to turn to outside employment as a solution to their dilemma. During
the mid-1960s, however, women's magazines began to lose their appeal.
In the decade after 1966, subscriptions to women's titles dropped by 30
percent and editors sought new formats and ideas to attract women.[38]

[34] Kristin Ross, *Fast Cars, Clean Bodies*, 3 and Mendras, *Social Change in Modern France*, 9.
On the sixties more broadly, Arthur Marwick has proposed the category of the "long sixties," beginning around 1958 and lasting until Europeans and Americans felt the effects
of the oil crisis of 1973–1977. See Marwick, *The Sixties*.

[35] Janine Mossuz-Lavau, "Politics and Sexuality in France, 1950–1991," *Economic and
Political Weekly* 28 (1993): WS63–WS66.

[36] See Duchen, *Feminism in France*, 6–8.

[37] On the fact that while gender equality was voiced in the demonstrations in 1968, there
was little public discussion of the question, see Michelle Zancarini-Fournel, "Genre et
politique," 133–143.

[38] Bonvoisin and Maignien, *La presse féminine*, 29.

Articles about the home and full-time homemakers dominated in the 1950s. In the 1960s, fashion grew more prominent and articles on marital infidelity, the pill, and the female body began to appear in women's journals.[39] The MLF took on this notion of liberation, even staging a demonstration at the *Salon des arts ménagers* in 1975. Shouting "No, Moulinex does not liberate women!" and "No to household gadgets, yes to collective services!" the women offered a different version of liberation, in which outside services would provide domestic help, freeing women to work outside of the home without bearing a double burden.[40]

Since the late 1960s, women have entered the workforce *en masse*, but the belief that women are still primarily responsible for consuming for and managing the home has not changed. In 1960, there were 6.5 million women in the workforce. By the end of the century, that number was 11.5 million. Just between 1968 and 1975, one million women entered the workforce. Their entry has resulted in changes to the allocation system, including elimination in 1978 of the allocation for families with a single breadwinner. Despite these changes, one target of the feminist movement in the 1970s, the unequal sharing of domestic work, remained constant. Feminists asked why economists did not notice that much of the work being done in France was unpaid, since it was in the home.[41] Their claims revealed the blind spot of the postwar productivity enthusiasts who stressed the important impact of women's labor on the economy, but did not ask whether it should be remunerated. In many ways, their demands recalled the claims of women in the *Union féminine civique et sociale* (UFCS) and domestic science education, who hoped to professionalize women's work in the home and suggested that it should be recognized by bigger allocations and retirement benefits. But their goal, to valorize this work so as to recognize that women were professionals without entering the workforce, was very different from that of second-wave feminists who wanted to make it easier for women to work outside of the home by distributing the burden of housework to men, and in some cases, collective services. This demand was linked to criticism of the notion that women's class status was dependent on their husbands as heads of the family. Christine Delphy expressed frustration both at women's lack of status and their domestic servitude, asserting, "It is about as just to say

---

[39] I have seen these changes in my own reading of *Marie-France, Marie-Claire*, and *Elle*. See also Benoît, "La nouvelle féminité," 39–86.
[40] Rouad, *60 ans d'arts ménagers*, 162.
[41] Christine Bard, *Les femmes*, 215, 216, 226.

that the wives of the bourgeois are bourgeois themselves as to say that the slave of a planter is himself a planter."[42] Feminists overturned the post-war claim that women's important, but complementary, role in the family was a sign of equality by pointing out that in home, family, and marriage women were decidedly unequal.

Despite the strong critique voiced by feminists, in the early twenty-first century, women, even while employed outside of the home in large numbers, are still responsible for the tasks associated with emancipation through consumption in the postwar decades. At the beginning of the new millennium, women still performed about 70 percent of the domestic work in France, a figure that is roughly equivalent to the sexual division of household labor in the United States, Germany, and Great Britain, as well.[43] The unequal division of domestic work, especially that involving the care of young children, may be one of the reasons that in 2002 French women earned, on average, 25.3 percent less each month than men, a gap that had narrowed hardly one percentage point since 1990. The reasons given for this are often structural, namely that women, though equal to or even surpassing men in average educational achievements, are more likely to go into health related or social service fields, which pay much less than scientific and technical fields. Women are also more likely to be in positions where they work fewer hours, and therefore make up the overwhelming bulk of the part-time workforce in France, which is likely often an attempt on their part to balance work with domestic responsibilities.[44] The association of women and men with specific kinds of professions and schedules begins early, and a study of young people in French high schools in the early 1990s found that 72 percent of girls said that the need for free time was important in choosing a career, compared to 11 percent of boys.[45] The continued belief that domestic tasks are

[42] From Christine Delphy, *L'ennemi principal*, 1970. Quoted in Bard, *Les femmes*, 226.

[43] Dominique Anxo, Lennart Flood, and Yusuf Kocoglu, "Offre de travail et répartition des activités domestiques et parentales au sein du couple: Une comparaison entre la France et la Suède," *Économie et Statistique* 352–353 (2002): 128.

[44] Dominique Meurs and Sophie Ponthieux, "L'écart des salaires entre les femmes et les hommes peut-il encore baisser?" *Économie et Statistique* 398–399 (2006): 99, 111–112. In 2000, women made up only 24 percent of students in engineering schools, whereas men were only 19 percent of students in social and paramedical schools (111). In 2002, 87 percent of part-time employees were women (114). On the traditional aversion to part-time work in France, see Sîan Reynolds, "Who wanted the crèches?" On more recent efforts to balance family and work responsibilities, see Anne Revillard, "Stating Family Values and Women's Rights: Familialism and Feminism within the French Republic," *French Politics* 5 (2007): 210–228.

[45] Bard, *Les femmes*, 227.

women's work has, therefore, ramifications for professional employment, and women are not likely to make up the difference in salaries without men making up for the difference in household responsibilities.

END OF THE MARKET COMMUNITY AND THE ROLE
OF CONSUMER FOR THE NATION

Domestic consumption is still women's work, but the rhetoric of the citizen consumer remains tied to the postwar decades. Women still spend much of the money that circulates in France, continuing to make most of household purchases, and the importance of consumption for the national economy has only continued to grow since the period of this study, but the gendered citizenship of the consumer for the nation and her specific role in the "market community" of purchasers, distributers, and consumers has changed. The "market community" and this particular formulation of the citizen consumer were closely tied to the postwar period of faith in national planning and the spirit of cooperation and consultation that planning required and inspired. As journalist John Ardagh explained, there was a "certain mystique" and even an element of "faith healing" associated with planning, even if, by the 1960s, the even greater resurgence of the German economy led economists to question the importance of planning in economic terms.[46] By the 1960s, consumer organizations were growing impatient with their role in the planning process. Planning itself also changed as the increase in imports and exports, in part due to the lowering of tariff barriers that came with the Common Market, left the economy more open to international economic factors that could not be planned for internally. French planners could not, for example, predict the 1973 oil crisis. They could not, for that matter, predict the internal crisis of May 1968, which may have also hurt the prestige of planning. The growing strength of French industry also made the Plan less necessary, and it was further weakened by a lack of ideological commitment to planning on the part of leaders of the Fifth Republic. Immediately following the war, the French government held much of the capital in France, in large part because of Marshall Plan funds. As French industries grew more financially independent, they also grew more distant from the Plan. An INSEE survey from 1967 found that 51 percent of large firms said the Plan had a "significant effect on their investment decisions." By 1979,

[46] John Ardagh, *The New French Revolution* (New York: Harper and Row, 1969), 21.

80 percent of enterprises reported that they had not taken the Plan into account when defining their own objectives.[47]

The UFC had been born in the productivity drives characteristic of the early years of national enthusiasm for the Plan, but it and other consumer organizations were taking on different roles by the mid-1960s, which led to even greater changes in the 1970s. The UFC had been started at the initiative of the state, under the direction of André Romieu, who was at the time head of the Group for Distribution and Consumption at the *Commissariat à la productivité*. By the late 1960s, however, the UFC saw association with the state as something that hindered its appearance of objectivity when giving advice. By 1972, the UFC had abandoned the direction of the INC, the organization created by the CNC to assist consumers, and worked to distance itself from the state.[48] The UFC grew rapidly in the 1970s, in part by incorporating local consumer groups. From 1974 to 1980, the number of its local groups grew from twenty-eight to one-hundred and seventy, with an increase of individual members from five thousand to fifty thousand. *Que choisir?*, the journal of the UFC, reached a circulation of 320,000 in 1974.[49] It is difficult to say what influence the anticonsumerist messages of 1968, with their rejection of statist technocracy and celebration of participatory democracy, had on the growth of consumer organization, but it is clear that the actions of the 1970s had a much more grassroots feel than the cooperation between state, industry, and consumers that the UFC had worked to achieve in the postwar decades. The local consumer groups of the UFC took to the streets doing price surveys, product boycotts, and protests.[50] These kinds of direct actions echo the women's protests of the immediate postwar period much more than they do the later incorporation of the citizen consumer into the state productivity drive and the "market community." Gunnar Trumbull has emphasized the fact that while the state increased the funding of consumer organizations in this period, it also stepped

---

[47] Saul Estrin and Peter Holmes, "Recent Developments in French Economic Planning," *Economics of Planning* 18 (1982), 2. Estrin and Holmes point out that Valéry Giscard d'Estaing, who was ideologically opposed to planning, was either finance minister or president for much of the 1960s and 1970s.

[48] Michel Wieviorka, *L'état, le patronat, et les consommateurs. Étude des mouvements de consommateurs* (Paris: Presses Universitaires de France, 1977), 179–180.

[49] Gunnar Trumbull, "The Surprise of Collective Action: Consumer Mobilization in France, 1970–1985," in *Affluence and Activism: Organized Consumers in the Postwar Era*, eds. Iselin Theien and Even Lange (Oslo: Unipub forlag, 2004), 61–62, 67.

[50] Ibid., 61.

back, encouraging consumer representatives to negotiate directly with producers. The contrast with the "market community" is clear in that while interacting with producers, in this type of negotiation consumers were clearly in the stance of opposition. The state wanted to support and develop a "consumer counter-force" to industry, which is a very different goal from encouraging citizen consumers to inform producers of their needs so that they could answer them more efficiently, eliminating waste and creating the economic expansion that would benefit everyone.[51] The changing relationship of the UFC with the *Salon des arts ménagers* in the 1970s also shows the shift in focus of the organization and the disintegration of the notion of the "market community." In 1976, the UFC stand at the *Salon* caused a commotion requiring police intervention when representatives passed out a publication warning consumers against buying at the event. After running the "Days of the Consumer" in the postwar decades, in 1977, the UFC did not participate at the *Salon*. Another sign of the changing status of domestic consumption in French society was the fact that during the same year, the *Salon* reduced its public program from twelve to six days.[52]

The confrontational consumer-producer interaction that the state supported in the 1970s highlights the historical specificity of the postwar French citizen consumer. The kind of cooperation inherent in the "market community," in which consumer, producers, and distributers all cooperated with the state in raising productivity and creating a new standard of living in France was a hallmark of a period of intense faith in national planning, of the belief that higher productivity would be good for everyone, and the acceptance of the fact that France must modernize, or it would decline. This was a period in which the United States represented the ultimate achievement in national prosperity and widespread comfort.

By the late 1960s, the students who took to the streets initially in protest of American involvement in Vietnam were critiquing the United States not so much as the creator of mass consumer society, but as an imperialist nation. They had a different relationship with mass consumer society from that of their parents. Dominique Veillon points out that the arrival of the television set in family homes meant the inclusion of children in parents' evening entertainment, where they increasingly became the targets of advertising and, thereby, consumers in their own right. By

---

[51] For discussion of the consumer counter-force and state support, see Ibid., 72–73.
[52] Rouaud, *60 ans d'arts ménagers*, 163.

about 1964, brand-name fashion became important even for pre-teens.[53]
Sociologist Evelyn Sullerot has argued that the sheer force of numbers of
the baby-boom children forced society to change for them. She writes,
"This generation is what I call the star generation. What I mean to say
is that the discourse of French society is always centered on them or carried by them, all because of the number of them and the newness of the
problems they create."[54] Susan Weiner suggests that the postwar mass
media created "youth" as a category that defied gender and class distinctions and was much more comfortable with consumer culture than the
older generation.[55] And Sullerot recalls seeing this change in her own
children, describing a family trip in 1964: "We passed a young shepherd
who had his radio next to him while he watched his sheep. My son said
to me, "Stop! It's *copain*!" In fact, the young shepherd was listening to
the radio broadcast *Salut les copains*..." The generation gap between her
son and herself contrasted with the ability of these young people of very
different social backgrounds to identify with one another. As she notes,
"Between this son of Parisian intellectuals and this young shepherd, there
was complicity because they listened to the same radio program created
for people their age."[56]

By the end of the postwar decades, France had made such progress
in catching up to American modernity that, rather than easily conflating
Americanization and modernization, critics saw "all men in industrial
societies suffering common problems."[57] America was still a global power,
which was one of the reasons involvement in Vietnam sparked international anger, but as historian Richard Kuisel has argued, Charles de
Gaulle's efforts at promoting French *grandeur* and national independence
in the 1960s had helped attenuate French feelings of dependence on the
United States and went far toward "exorcising the American demon."[58]
At the same time, Kristin Ross has pointed out that the United States has
so successfully appropriated notions of modernity and progress that it
was no surprise when, during the debate over the Iraq War, European
leaders who disagreed with American objectives were labeled "unmod-
ern" and "outmoded."[59]

[53] Dominique Veillon, *Nous les enfants*, 10–11.
[54] Sullerot, "La démographie en France," 81.
[55] Susan Weiner, *Enfants Terribles*.
[56] Sullerot, "La démographie en France," 81–82.
[57] Paul Gagnon, "La Vie Future: Some French Responses to the Technological Society,"
Journal of European Studies 6 (1976): 175.
[58] Richard Kuisel, *Seducing the French*, 152.
[59] Kristin Ross, "The French Declaration," 144.

Immediately following the Second World War, France had been in an entirely different situation, and it seemed that the only options were, in the words of Jean Monnet, "modernization" or "decadence." The sense of national emergency inspired projects such as the productivity drive, which created a very particular role for the citizen consumer. This was a role that solved another apparent problem of the postwar decade: that women had become equal to men, but were still needed in the domestic sphere because the French people craved normalcy and needed population growth. Thus was born the notion of liberation through consumer citizenship and management of the modern household. In the role of consumer citizen and domestic manager, women could find a kind of emancipation in the home. Their consumer acts and domestic work were of vital importance to the national economy, but would not prevent them from devoting themselves to home and family.

The celebration of domesticity, home, and family in postwar French culture was very similar to that found across the United States and Western Europe, where many nations experienced baby booms and the growth of what British historian Claire Langhamer calls a "home-centered" lifestyle.[60] The retreat to the domestic sphere was considered intensely private, despite the fact that it was supported by expanding public welfare systems, was shaped by public policy, and was essential to visions of the American "way of life" that were propagated in the context of the Cold War.[61] The retreat to the private sphere was in some places, including France, a retreat from the politicization of the family and reproduction during the war.[62] Paolo Scrivano argues that in Italy, the postwar shift in social life from the public to the private was also tied to a rejection of fascism's populist myth of the masses. And though women's consumer activism in France was incorporated into a particular kind of state planning, the call for women to monitor prices, end inflation, and enforce rationing was important in Great Britain and Germany, as well.[63] Other kinds of consumer activism,

---

[60] Claire Langhamer, "The Meanings of Home." For the United States, see Elaine Tyler May, *Homeward Bound*. See Paolo Scrivano, "Signs of Americanization in Italian Domestic Life: Italy's Postwar Conversion to Consumerism," *Journal of Contemporary History* 20 (2005): 317–340.

[61] For analysis of the politics of the American kitchen in a variety of Western and Eastern European contexts, see Oldenziel and Zachman, *The Cold War Kitchen*. Elizabeth Heineman stresses the role of public policy in prompting the "retreat to domesticity" in her work on Germany. See Heineman, *What Different Does a Husband Make?*

[62] See Pollard, *Reign of Virtue* for the Vichy government's concern with gender and the domestic sphere.

[63] See Scrivano, "Signs of Americanization"; Carter, *How German is She?*; Pence, "Shopping for an 'Economic Miracle'"; Zweiniger-Bargielowska, *Austerity in Britain*.

including product evaluation and myriad attempts to educate and form consumers based on expert opinion, were also widespread in Europe and the United States.[64] And, of course, conflation of the categories of citizen and consumer was not exclusive to France, being of particular importance in Great Britain and the United States even before the Second World War and the postwar period of affluence.[65]

The aspect of the French postwar transformation and the creation of the citizen consumer identity that is unique is the way in which it was tied to the postwar situation of national emergency, in which modernization seemed essential and was nearly uncontested. The incorporation of the citizen consumer, her purchases, and even the work she did in her own home into the state driven, centralized productivity and modernization drives is an important hallmark of the French transition. This relationship between consumer and state is singular to this moment in French history. By the early 1960s, consumer organizations were growing frustrated with their role in state planning and the "market community." Perhaps even more apparent was women's frustration with the notion that emancipation could be found in the responsibilities of the citizen consumer and domestic manager. At the end of the war, the desire for normalcy was widespread, and fear for the French birthrate still lingered. Prewar France had been Malthusian both in its economic performance and its demographic characteristics. This, too, added to the atmosphere of national emergency, making women's concentration on the domestic sphere all the more important, despite the fact that they had finally been enfranchised and their right to work was inscribed in the constitution. The demographic fears were quickly overcome by the baby boom, but the celebration of children and families that this produced only intensified the association of women with the home and domesticity.

Along with assuaging fears about the French population, new families helped drive modernization and the creation of mass consumer society through their abundant consumer needs. Although consumption continued to increase after the period of this study, it was in the immediate postwar decades that the cultural and social changes making mass consumer

[64] Mathew Hilton shows the importance of this kind of organization, and middle-class women consumers in particular, in Britain, for example. See Hilton, *Consumerism in Twentieth-Century Britain*. Hilton has also pointed out that though this kind of organization, tied to postwar affluence, is usually seen as apolitical and individualistic, consumer groups have also been successful in working for social justice, in particular on an international level. Hilton, "Models of Consumer-Political Action in the Twentieth Century: Rights, Duties, and Justice," in *Affluence and Activism*, 21–39.

[65] See Cohen, *A Consumer's Republic* and Trentmann, ed., *The Making of the Consumer*.

society possible happened. Young families, and the social commentators who produced volumes of pages about them, redefined what was necessary for the modern French family. More than ever, those necessities included modern consumer durables and modern homes. The expansion of families meant an expanding consumer base, and once their demands for housing were met, young couples needed to equip their new domestic spaces. During these years, young families, many of them part of the expanding middle class, spent unprecedented sums on their homes, often expressing their faith in good jobs in an expanding economy by making those purchases on credit. Their attitudes and purchases helped to break down ideas about class and consumption at the same time that they drove the mass consumer economy.

The couples that married and had children in the late 1940s and the early 1950s created new definitions of necessity and notions of domesticity after the hardship of war and occupation. Their children grew up along with, but had a different relationship to, mass consumer society. In 1968, young people would unleash a new critique of consumer society and create new definitions of need – prioritizing not the consumer needs of their parents' generation, but the need for a re-evaluation of what they saw as the restrictions of the technocratic state and the inequalities and authoritarian nature of the capitalist system both in France and in the rest of the world. Theirs was also a discussion about consumption and emancipation, but one very different from that begun in the wake of war and with the imperatives of reconstruction and modernization at the center of national discourse.

Bibliography

Archival Sources

Archives nationales (AN)

Ministère de l'intérieur: Administration générale (F1)

Service Central des Commissariats de la République (1945–1947)
F1a 4020. Documentation générale: personnel administratif, élections, comités de Libération (CDL), etc. Rapports et correspondance du commissaire de la République à Bordeaux. 1945 (janvier)-1946 (mars).
F1a 4027–4029. Bulletins sur la situation dans les régions et départements.
Rapports des préfets
F1c III 1210. Rapports des préfets depuis la Libération. 1944–1946. Belfort et Bouches-du-Rhône.

Secrétariat générale du gouvernement et services du Premier ministre (F60)

F60 507. Maintien d'ordre public, manifestations publiques, 1935–1947.
F60 674. Rapports des préfets concernant l'application du décret du 2 janvier 1947 portant baisse générale de 5% sur les prix.
F60 1424. Santé publique et population.

Centre des archives contemporaines de Fontainebleau (CAC)

Archives de l'équipement

19790660 articles 7–9. Service de l'information et de la communication (MRU).
19771078 articles 1 and 6. Études de construction.

Archives du Salon des arts ménagers

19850023 article 9. Rapports du délégué du gouvernement.
19850023 article 10. Rapports du commissaire général du Salon des arts ménagers.
19850023 article 16. Statistiques et enquêtes.

19850023 article 18. Statistiques diverses – visiteurs et exposants.

19850023 article 20. Enquêtes auprès des visiteurs.

19850023 article 63. Fédération des familles de France, Société pour développement de l'électricité, Union fédérale de la consommation.

19850023 65–66. Catalogues de salons.

19850023 article 118. Manifestations diverses.

19850023 article 119. Relations avec ministre de la construction.

19850023 article 120. Manifestations – thèmes.

19850023 article 121. Documents sur l'habitation.

19850023 article 122. Le foyer d'aujourd'hui, Concours de la meilleure ménager.

19850023 article 123. Concours national d'enseignement ménager, organismes d'enseignement ménagers.

19850023 article 127. Statistiques sur garderie d'enfants, conférences au grand public.

19850023 article 152. Presse.

19850023 articles 1–130. Photographes, 1927–1982.

The CAC has dossiers of press clippings on the *Salon des arts ménagers* in 19850023. I consulted the following dossiers:

Articles 567, 569, 577, 578, 579, 584, 586, 587, 588, 589, 590, 591, 596, 611, 620, 626, and 637.

Centre des archives économiques et financières (CAEF)

B 55366. Rapport sur les obstacles à l'expansion économique, présenté par le comité institué par le décret n. 59–1284 du 13 Novembre 1959. Paris, 1960.

B 55872. Comité national de la consommation: réunions de travail, informations, consommateurs et le Plan.

B 55873. Institut national de la consommation: Organisation et fonctionnement.

B 55875. Labels.

B 55896. Politique générale des prix, 1948–1969, stabilité des prix, etc.

B 55897. Salaires, pouvoir d'achat.

B 55898. Travaux du comité national des prix. Composition, correspondance.

B 55898–55912. Procès verbaux des séances.

B 57613. Direction générale des prix. Demandes fixation où haussent des prix.

B 57619. Coopératives de production et consommation.

Ex. B 17663. Antoine Pinay, 1959–1964.

H 2011. Fonds statistiques, études économiques et prévision. Études et notes d'organismes travaillant pour le Plan. CREDOC, 1964.

H 1951. Situation économique au mois de septembre 1955. INSEE.

4 A 2577. Suites données au Rapport sur les obstacles à l'expansion économique, présenté par le comité institué par le décret n. 59–1284 du 13 novembre 1959. Juin 1968.

Other Government Sources

Allègre, Marius. "Étude du crédit à la consommation. Rapport présenté au nom du Conseil économique, par M. Marius Allègre." *Conseil économique* (March 4, 1954): 267–79.

"Avis et rapports du Conseil économique et social. Session de 1963. Séance du 7 Mai 1963. Étude des statistiques de la consommation. Rapport présenté au nom du Conseil économique et social, par. M. Pierre Laguionie." *Journal officiel de la république française* année 1963, no. 10 (1963): 381–394.

Conseil économique. *Le problème du logement*. Paris: Presses Universitaires de France, 1953.

Major Newspapers and Journals

These include only journals and newspapers I read extensively; all others are cited in the footnotes.

Arts Ménagers
Bulletin d'information de l'Institut français d'opinion publique
Les cahiers de l'Union des femmes françaises
Echo de la Mode (Le Petit Echo de la Mode until 1955*)*
Elle
L'Express
La femme
La femme dans la vie sociale (Notre journal: La femme dans la vie sociale until 1952*)*
Femme françaises (absorbed by Heures claires des femmes française in 1957*)*
La femme nouvelle
Heures claires des femmes françaises
L'Humanité
Informations Sociales
La maison française
Marie-Claire
Marie-France
Le Monde
Monde Ouvrier
Population
Productivité française
La vie de l'Union des femmes françaises
Rapports France-États-Unis
Sondages
Union fédérale de la consommation: Bulletin d'information
Vente et Publicité

Bibliothèque de Sciences Po

The library at Sciences Po has an extremely useful collection of dossiers of press clippings. I consulted the following series:
France 582: La consommation en France
France 582/6: Crédit à la consommation
France 408: Politique familiale

Published Primary and Secondary Sources

Accampo, Elinor A. "The Gendered Nature of Contraception in France: Neo-Malthusianism, 1900–1920." *Journal of Interdisciplinary History* 34 (2003): 235–262.

Accampo, Elinor A., Rachel G. Fuchs, and Mary Lynn Stewart. *Gender and the Politics of Social Reform in France 1870–1914*. Baltimore: The Johns Hopkins University Press, 1995.

Acquier, J. "Le matériel ménager dans les foyers français (parc et achats)." *Consommation: Annales du Centre de recherches et de documentation sur la consommation* 4 (1959): 65–82.

Adams, William James. *Restructuring the French Economy: Government and the Rise of Market Competition since World War II*. Washington, D.C.: The Brookings Institution, 1989.

Adler, Karen H. *Jews and Gender in Liberation France*. Cambridge: Cambridge University Press, 2003.

Alary, Éric and Dominique Veillon. "L'après-guerre des femmes: 1947, un tournant?" In *L'année 1947*, edited by Serge Berstein and Pierre Milza, 487–511. Paris: Presses de la Fondation nationale des sciences politiques, 2000.

Albert, Pierre. *Histoire de la presse*. Paris: Presses Universitaires de France, 1970.

Ambler, John S. *The French Welfare State: Surviving Social and Ideological Change*. New York: New York University Press, 1991.

Amosé, Thomas and Olivier Chardon. "Les travailleurs non qualifiés: Une nouvelle classe sociale?" *Économie et Statistique* 393–394 (2006): 203–229.

Anxo, Dominique, Lennart Flood, and Yusuf Kocoglu. "Offre de travail et répartition des activités domestiques et parentales au sein du couple: Une comparaison entre la France et la Suède." *Économie et Statistique* 352–353 (2002): 127–150.

Appaduri, Arjun, ed. *The Social Life of Things*. Cambridge: Cambridge University Press, 1986.

Ardagh, John. *The New French Revolution*. New York: Harper and Row, 1969.

Aron, Raymond. "Electeurs, partis, et élus." *Revue française de science politique* 5 (1955): 245–266.

Atkin, Nicholas. "Catholics and the Long Liberation: the Progressive Moment." In *The Uncertain Foundation: France at the Liberation, 1944–47*, edited by Andrew Knapp, 121–138. New York: Palgrave Macmillan, 2007.

Aubourg, R. "Deux problèmes de la consommation: L'évolution des besoins et le crédit." *Coopération* 31 (1961): 17–21.

Auslander, Leora. *Taste and Power: Furnishing Modern France*. Berkeley: University of California Press, 1996.

Avakoumovitch, Yvan. "Les manifestations des femmes 1940–1944." *Cahiers d'histoire de l'Institut de recherches marxistes* 45 (1991): 5–53.

Bachelier, Christian. "De la pénurie à la vie chère, l'opinion publique à travers les premiers sondages 1944–1949." In *Le temps des restrictions en France (1939–1949)*, edited by Dominique Veillon and Jean-Marie Flonneau, 479–500. Paris: Institut de l'histoire du temps présent, 1996.

Balaguy, Hubert. *Le crédit à la consommation en France*. Paris: Presses Universitaires de France, 1996.

Bard, Christine. *Les femmes dans la société française au 20e siècle*. Paris: Armand Colin, 2003.

Barjot, Dominique. *Catching Up With America: Productivity Missions and the Diffusion of American Economic and Technological Influence after the Second World War*. Paris: Presses de l'Université de Paris-Sorbonne, 2002.

Barjot, Dominique, Rémi Baudouï, and Danièle Voldman. *Les reconstructions en Europe, 1945–1949*. Bruxelles: Éditions Complexe, 1997.

Barthes, Roland. *Mythologies*. New York: Hill and Wang, 1972.

Bayet, A., C. Chambaz, Y. Guegano, J. M. Houriez. "Les choix de consommation des ménages; Une question de revenu avant tout." *Économie et Statistique* 248 (1991): 21–31.

Baudrillard, Jean. *The Consumer Society: Myths and Structures*. London: Sage Publications, 1998.

Beale, Marjorie A. *The Modernist Enterprise: French Elites and the Threat of Modernity, 1900–1940*. Stanford: Stanford University Press, 1999.

Bellamy, Vanessa and Laurent Léveillé. "Consommation des ménages. Quels lieux d'achat pour quels produits?" *Insee Première* 1165 (2007): 1–4.

Beltran, Alain and Patrice A. Carré. *La fée et la servante. La société française face à l'électricité: XIXe-XXe siècle*. Paris: Belin, 1991.

Benoît, Nicole, Edgar Morin, and Bernard Paillard. *La femme majeure: nouvelle féminité, nouvelle féminisme*. Paris: Éditions du Seuil, 1973.

Bernot, Lucien and René Blancard. *Nouville: Un village français*. Paris: Institut d'ethnologie, 1953.

Berstein, Serge and Pierre Milza eds. *L'année 1947*. Paris: Presses de Sciences Po, 2000.

Bess, Michael. *The Light Green Society: Ecology and Technological Modernity in France, 1960–2000*. Chicago: University of Chicago Press, 2003.

Bessel, Richard and Dirk Schumann eds. *Life after Death: Approaches to a Cultural and Social History of Europe during the 1940s and 1950s*. Cambridge: Cambridge University Press, 2003.

Besson, Danièle. "Le repas depuis 45 ans: Moins de produits frais, plus de plats préparés." *Insee Première* 1208 (2008): 1–4.

Bihl, Luc. *Une histoire du mouvement consommateur*. Paris: Éditions Aubier Montaigne, 1984.

Bindas, Kenneth J. *Remembering the Great Depression in the Rural South*. Gainesville: University Press of Florida, 2007.

Black, Naomi. *Social Feminism*. Ithaca: Cornell University Press, 1989.

Bocock, Robert. *Consumption*. New York: Routledge, 1993.

Boltanski, Luc. *The Making of a Class: Cadres in French Society*. Cambridge: Cambridge University Press, 1987.

Bonvoisin, Samra-Martine and Michèle Maignien. *La presse féminine*. Paris: Presses Universitaires de France, 1986.

Bossuat, Gérard. *La France, l'aide américaine et la construction européenne 1944–1954*. Paris: Comité pour l'histoire économique et financière de la France, 1997.

Boudet, Robert. "La famille bourgeoise." In *Sociologie comparée de la famille contemporaine*, 141–151. Paris: Centre national de la recherche scientifique, 1955.

Boulat, Régis. "Jean Fourastié et la naissance de la société de la consommation en France." In *Au nom du consommateur: Consommation et politique en France et aux États-Unis au XXe siècle*, edited by Alain Chatriot, Marie-Emmanuelle Chessel, and Matthew Hilton, 98–114. Paris: La Découverte, 2004.

Bourdieu, Pierre. *The Bachelors' Ball: The Crisis of Peasant Society in Bearn.* Chicago: University of Chicago Press, 2008.

"Célibat et conditions paysannes." *Études Rurales* 5/6 (1962): 32–135.

Distinction: A Social Critique of the Judgment of Taste. Cambridge: Harvard University Press, 1984.

"What makes a social class? On the Theoretical and Practical Existence of Groups." *Berkeley Journal of Sociology* 32 (1987): 1–18.

Bourdieu, Pierre and Jean-Claude Passeron. "Sociology and Philosophy in France since 1945: Death and Resurrection of a Philosophy without Subject." *Social Research* 34 (1967): 162–212.

Bourg, Julian. *From Revolution to Ethics: May 1968 and Contemporary French Thought.* Montreal: McGill-Queen's University Press, 2007.

Bourgeois, Jean. "La situation démographique." *Population* 1 (1946): 117–142.

Bowden, Sue and Avner Offer. "The Technological Revolution That Never Was: Gender, Class, and the Diffusion of Household Appliances in Interwar England." In *The Sex of Things: Gender and Consumption in Historical Perspective*, edited by Victoria De Grazia with Ellen Furlough, 244–274. Berkeley: University of California Press, 1996.

Brive, Marie-France. "L'image des femmes à la Libération." In *La Libération dans le Midi de la France*, edited by Rolande Trempé, 390–398. Toulouse: Eché Éditions, 1986.

Calder, Lendol. *Financing the American Dream: A Cultural History of Consumer Credit.* Princeton: Princeton University Press, 1999.

Canning, Kathleen and Sonya O. Rose. *Gender, Citizenships and Subjectivities.* Oxford: Blackwell Publishing, 2002.

Capdevila, Luc. "The Quest for Masculinity in a Defeated France, 1940–1945." *Contemporary European History* 10 (2001): 423–445.

Carter, Erica. "Deviant Pleasures? Women, Melodrama, and Consumer Nationalism in West Germany." In *The Sex of Things: Gender and Consumption in Historical Perspective*, edited by Victoria De Grazia with Ellen Furlough, 359–380. Berkeley: University of California Press, 1996.

How German Is She? Postwar West German Reconstruction and the Consuming Woman. Ann Arbor: University of Michigan Press, 1991.

Ceccaldi, Dominique. "The Family in France." *Marriage and Family Living* 16 (1954): 326–330.

Centre d'études du commerce. *Commerce et consommation aux États-Unis.* Paris: Centre d'études du commerce, 1952.

Chaperon, Sylvie. *Les années Beauvoir, 1945–1970.* Paris: Fayard, 2000.

"'Feminism Is Dead. Long Live Feminism!' The Women's Movement in France at the Liberation, 1944–1946." In *When the War Was Over*, edited by Claire Duchen and Irene Bandhauer-Schöffmann, 146–160. London: Leicester University Press, 2000.

Chaplin, Tamara. *Turning on the Mind: French Philosophers on Television.* Chicago: University of Chicago Press, 2007.

Chapman, Herrick. "France's Liberation Era, 1944–47: A Social and Economic Settlement?" In *The Uncertain Foundation: France at the Liberation, 1944–47*, edited by Andrew Knapp, 103–120. New York: Palgrave Macmillan, 2007.

"Modernity and National Identity in Postwar France." *French Historical Studies* 22 (1999): 291–314.

Chatriot, Alain. "Consumers' Associations and the State: Protection and Defence of the Consumer in France, 1950–2000." In *The Expert Consumer: Associations and Professionals in Consumer Society*, edited by Alain Chatriot, Marie-Emmanuelle Chessel, and Matthew Hilton, 123–136. Aldershot: Ashgate, 2006.

"Protéger le consommateur contre lui-même: La régulation du crédit à la consommation." *Vingtième Siècle* 91 (2006): 95–109.

"Qui défend le consommateur? Associations, institutions et politiques publiques en France (1972–2003)." In *Au nom du consommateur: Consommation et politique en Europe et aux États-Unis au XXe siècle*, edited by Alain Chatriot, Marie-Emmanuelle Chessel, and Matthew Hilton, 165–181. Paris: La Découverte, 2004.

Chatriot, Alain, Marie-Emmanuelle Chessel, and Matthew Hilton, eds. *Au nom du consommateur: Consommation et politique en Europe et aux États-Unis au XXe siècle*. Paris: La Découverte, 2004.

Chauvière, Michel and Bruno Duriez. *De l'Action catholique au mouvement ouvrier: La déconfessionnalisation du Mouvement populaire des familles, 1941–1950*. Forest sur Marque: Groupement pour la recherche des mouvements familiaux, 1983.

Chélini, Michel-Pierre. *Inflation, état et opinion en France de 1944 à 1952*. Paris: Comite pour l'histoire économique et financière de la France, 1998.

Chenut, Helen. *The Fabric of Gender: Working-Class Culture in Third Republic France*. University Park: The Pennsylvania State University Press, 2005.

Chessel, Marie-Emmanuelle. "Consommation, action sociale et engagement public fin de siècle des États-Unis à la France." In *Au nom du consommateur: Consommation et politique en Europe et aux États-Unis au XXe siècle*, edited by Alain Chatriot, Marie-Emmanuelle Chessel, and Matthew Hilton, 247–261. Paris: La Découverte, 2004.

"Women and the Ethics of Consumption in France at the Turn of the Century." In *The Making of the Consumer: Knowledge, Power, and Identity in the Modern World*, edited by Frank Trentmann, 81–98. Oxford: Berg, 2006.

Childers, Kristen Stromberg. *Fathers, Families, and the State in France, 1914–1945*. Ithaca: Cornell University Press, 2003.

Chombart de Lauwe, Paul-Henry. *La vie quotidienne des familles ouvrières*. Paris: Centre national de la recherche scientifique, 1956.

Chombart de Lauwe, Paul-Henry et al. *Famille et habitation I: Sciences humaines et conceptions de l'habitation*. Paris: Centre national de la recherche scientifique, 1959.

Famille et habitation II: Un essai d'observation expérimentale. Paris: Centre national de la recherche scientifique, 1960.

Chombart de Lauwe, Paul-Henry, and Marie-José. "L'évolution des besoins et la conception dynamique de la famille." *Revue française de sociologie* 1 (1960): 403–425.

Clark, Linda L. *Schooling the Daughters of Marianne: Textbooks and the Socialization of Girls in Modern French Primary Schools*. Albany: State University of New York Press, 1984.

Clarke, David B., Marcus A. Doel, and Kate M. L. Housiaux, eds. *The Consumption Reader*. New York: Routledge, 2003.

Clarke, Jackie. "France, America and the Metanarrative of Modernization: From Postwar Social Science to the New Culturalism." *Contemporary French and Francophone Studies* 8 (2004): 365–377.

——. "Homecomings: Paulette Bernège, Scientific Management and the Return to the Land in Vichy France." In *Vichy, Resistance, and Liberation: New Perspectives on Wartime France*, edited by Simon Kitson and Hanna Diamond, 171–182. Oxford: Berg, 2005.

——. "L'organisation ménagère comme pédagogie: Paulette Bernège et la formation d'une nouvelle classe moyenne dans les années 1930 et 1940." *Travail, genre, et sociétés* 13 (2005): 139–156.

Clément, Jean-Louis. "L'église catholique et l'opinion publique à la Libération." In *La Libération dans le Midi de la France*, edited by Rolande Trempé, 377–385. Toulouse: Eché Éditions, 1986.

Cochoy, Franck. "A Brief History of 'Customers,' or the Gradual Standardization of Markets and Organizations." *Sociologie du travail* 47 (2005): S36–S56.

Coffin, Judith. *The Politics of Women's Work: The Paris Garment Trades, 1750–1915*. Princeton: Princeton University Press, 1996.

——. "A 'Standard' of Living? European Perspectives on Class and Consumption in the Early Twentieth Century." *International Labor and Working-Class History* 55 (1999): 6–26.

Cogan, Charles and Andrew Knapp "Washington at the Liberation, 1944–47." In *The Uncertain Foundation: France at the Liberation, 1944–47*, edited by Andrew Knapp, 183–206. New York: Palgrave Macmillan, 2007.

Cohen, Lizabeth. *A Consumer's Republic: The Politics of Mass Consumption in Postwar America*. New York: Alfred A. Knopf, 2003.

Cohen, Stephen S. *Modern Capitalist Planning: The French Model*. Updated Edition. Berkeley: University of California Press, 1977.

Cole, Joshua. *The Power of Large Numbers: Population, Politics, and Gender in Nineteenth Century France*. Ithaca: Cornell University Press, 2000.

Colloques Internationaux du CNRS. *Sociologie comparée de la famille contemporaine*. Paris: Éditions du Centre national de la recherche scientifique, 1955.

Comité national de la consommation. "1945, Une prise de conscience." *Un monde en mouvement: Les organisations de consommateurs* (Paris: Ministère de l'économie et des finances et le Comité national de la consommation, 1975): 6–10.

Les conclusions du comité Armand-Rueff, texte de la conférence faite au 21e diner d'information du C.E.P.E.C. le 25 octobre 1960. Paris: Centre d'études politiques et civiques, 1960.

"La consommation dans l'économie française." *Consommation: Annales du Centre de recherches et de documentation sur la consommation* 2 (1958): 23–38.

Coquart, Elizabeth. *La France des GI's: Histoire d'un amour déçu*. Paris: Albin Michel, 2003.

Courthéoux, Jean-Paul. "Problèmes sociologiques d'une planification indicative." *Revue économique* 19 (1968): 785–818.

Cowan, Ruth Schwartz. *More Work for Mother: The Ironies of Household Technology from the Open Hearth to the Microwave.* New York: Basic Books, Inc., 1983.

Cowans, Jon. "French Public Opinion and the Founding of the Fourth Republic." *French Historical Studies* 17 (1991): 62–95.

Cross, Gary. *Time and Money: The Making of Consumer Culture.* London: Routledge, 1993.

"Time, Money, and Labor History's Encounter with Consumer Culture." *International Labor and Working-Class History* 43 (1993): 2–17.

Crowston, Clare. "Family Affairs: Wives, Credit, Consumption, and the Law in Old Regime France." In *Family, Gender, and Law in Early Modern France,* edited by Suzanne Desan and Jeffrey Merrick, 62–100. University Park: The Pennsylvania State University Press, 2009.

Dao Dang, T. Giao. *Monnaie et crédit: Le financement du développement des sociétés modernes.* Paris: Éditions S.T.H, 1991.

Daric, Jean. "La population féminine active en France et à l'étranger." *Population* 1 (1947): 61–66.

"Une enquête de l'Institut national d'études démographiques: Vieillissement démographique et prolongation de la vie active." *Population* 1 (1946): 69–78.

Darras. *Le partage des bénéfices, expansion et inégalités en France.* Paris: Les Éditions de Minuit, 1966.

Daujam, François. "Information et pouvoir des consommateurs: Le rôle de l'Union fédérale des consommateurs." Thèse, Université des Sciences Sociales de Toulouse, 1980.

Daunton, Martin and Matthew Hilton. *The Politics of Consumption: Material Culture and Citizenship in Europe and America.* Oxford: Berg, 2001.

Davidoff, Leonore and Catherine Hall. *Family Fortunes: Men and Women of the English Middle-Class, 1780–1850.* Chicago: University of Chicago Press, 1991.

Davis, Belinda. *Home Fires Burning: Food, Politics, and Everyday Life in World War I Berlin.* Chapel Hill: University of North Carolina Press, 2000.

"What's Left? Popular Political Participation in Postwar Europe." *The American Historical Review* 113 (2008): 363–390.

De Blic, Damien, and Jeanne Lazarus. *Sociologie de l'argent.* Paris: La Découverte, 2007.

De Grazia, Victoria. "Beyond Time and Money." *International Labor and Working-Class History* 43 (1993): 24–30.

"Changing Consumer Regimes in Europe, 1930–1970: Comparative Perspectives on the Distribution Problem," In *Getting and Spending: European and American Consumer Societies in the Twentieth Century,* edited by Susan Strasser, Charles McGovern, and Matthias Judt, 59–83. Cambridge: Cambridge University Press, 1998.

Irresistible Empire: America's Advance through Twentieth-Century Europe. Cambridge: Belknap Press of Harvard University Press, 2005.

"Mass Culture and Sovereignty: The American Challenge to European Cinemas, 1920–1960." *Journal of Modern History* 61 (1989): 53–87.

"Nationalizing Women: The Competition Between Fascist and Commercial Cultural Models in Mussolini's Italy." In *The Sex of Things: Gender and Consumption in Historical Perspective*, edited by Victoria De Grazia with Ellen Furlough, 337–358. Berkeley: University of California Press, 1996.

De Grazia, Victoria with Ellen Furlough. *The Sex of Things: Gender and Consumption in Historical Perspective*. Berkeley: University of California Press, 1996.

De Grazia, Victoria and Lizabeth Cohen. "Class and Consumption: Introduction." *International Labor and Working-Class History* 55 (1999): 1–5.

Defossez, Marie-Paule. *Le chrétien devant la presse féminine*. Paris: Centrale technique d'information catholique, 1959.

De la 4 CV à la vidéo, 1954–1983, ces trente années qui ont changé nôtre vie. Paris: Communica International, 1983.

Delaume, Georges René. "Marital Property and American-French Conflict of Laws." *American Journal of Comparative Law* 4 (1955): 35–59.

Delaunay, Quynh. *Histoire de la machine à laver: Un objet technique dans la société française*. Rennes: Presses Universitaires de Rennes, 1994.

Delbreil, Jean-Claude. "The French Catholic Left and the Political Parties." In *Left Catholicism, 1943–1955. Catholics and Society in Western Europe at the Point of Liberation*, edited by Gerd-Rainer Horn and Emmanuel Gerard, 45–63. Leuven: Leuven University Press, 2001.

Dermenjian, Geneviève and Dominique Loiseau. "La maternité sociale et le Mouvement populaire des familles durant les Trente Glorieuses." *CLIO, Histoire, Femmes et Sociétés* 21 (2005): 91–106.

Dermenjian, Geneviève, ed. *Femmes, famille et action ouvrière: Pratiques et responsabilités féminines dans les mouvements familiaux populaires (1935–1958)*. Villeneuve d'Ascq: Groupement pour la recherche sur les mouvements familiaux, 1991.

Desplanques, Léon. "La consommation en 1957." *Consommation: Annales du Centre de recherches et de documentation sur la consommation* 1 (1958): 55–69.

Diamond, Hanna. "Gaining the Vote: A Liberating Experience?" *Modern and Contemporary France* 3 (1995): 129–139.

Women and the Second World War in France, 1939–1948: Choices and Constraints. London: Longman, 1999.

Dogan, Mattei and Jacques Narbonne. *Les françaises face à la politique*. Paris: Cahiers de la Fondation nationale des sciences politiques, 1955.

Doneaud, Thérèse and Christian Guérin, eds. *Les femmes agissent, le monde change. Histoire inédite de l'Union féminine civique et sociale*. Paris: Éditions du Cerf, 2005.

Doublet, Jacques. "Parents et enfants dans la famille ouvrière." In *Sociologie comparée de la famille contemporaine*, 157–168. Paris: Centre national de la recherche scientifique, 1954.

Downs, Laura Lee. *Childhood in the Promised Land: Working-Class Movements and the Colonies de Vacances in France, 1880–1960*. Durham: Duke University Press, 2002.

Drouard, Alain. "Réflexions sur une chronologie: Le développement des sciences sociales en France de 1945 à la fin des années soixante." *Revue française de sociologie* 23 (1982): 55–85.

Dubesset, Mathilde. "Les figures du féminine à travers deux revues féminines, l'une catholique, l'autre protestante, *La femme dans la vie sociale* et *Jeunes femmes*, dans les années 1950–1960." *Le Mouvement Social* 198 (2002): 9–34.

Duchen, Claire. "Occupation Housewife: the Domestic Ideal in 1950s France." *French Cultural Studies* 2 (1991): 1–11.

Feminism in France: From May '68 to Mitterrand. London: Routledge, 1986.

"Une femme nouvelle pour une France nouvelle." *CLIO, Histoire, Femmes et Sociétés* 1 (1995): 151–164.

Women's Rights and Women's Lives in France, 1944–1968. London: Routledge, 1994.

Duriez, Bruno. "Left-Wing Catholicism in France. From Catholic Action to the Political Left: The *Mouvement populaire des familles*." In *Left Catholicism, 1943–1955. Catholics and Society in Western Europe at the Point of Liberation*, edited by Gerd-Rainer Horn and Emmanuel Gerard, 64–90. Leuven: Leuven University Press, 2001.

Duriez, Bruno, et al. *Chrétiens et ouvriers en France, 1937–1970*. Paris: Les Éditions de l'Atelier, 2001.

Dutton, Paul V. *Origins of the French Welfare State: The Struggle for Social Reform in France 1914–1947*. Cambridge: Cambridge University Press, 2002.

Duverger, Maurice. "Public Opinion and Political Parties in France." *The American Political Science Review* 46 (1952): 1069–1078.

Edwards, Nancy Jocelyn. "The Science of Domesticity: Women, Education, and National Identity in Third Republic France, 1880–1914." PhD diss., University of California, Berkeley, 1997.

Eley, Geoff and Keith Nield. "Farewell to the Working Class?" *International Labor and Working-Class History* 57 (2000): 1–30.

Endy, Christopher. *Cold War Holidays: American Tourism in France*. Chapel Hill: University of North Carolina Press, 2004.

Enquête sur les tendances de la consommation des salariés urbains. Vous gagnez 20% de plus qu'en faites-vous? Paris: Commission des Industries de transformation, 1955.

Estrin, Saul and Peter Holmes. "Recent Developments in French Economic Planning." *Economics of Planning* 18 (1982): 1–10.

Farmer, Sarah. *Martyred Village: Commemorating the 1944 Massacre at Oradour-sur-Glane*. Berkeley: University of California Press, 1999.

Fayolle, Sandra. "L'Union des femmes françaises: Une organisation féminine de masse du parti communiste français, 1945–1965." Thèse de doctorat, Université Paris I, 2005.

Fishman, Sarah. *The Battle for Children: World War II, Youth Crime, and Juvenile Justice in Twentieth-Century France*. Cambridge: Harvard University Press, 2002.

We Will Wait: Wives of French Prisoners of War, 1940–1945. New Haven: Yale University Press, 1991.

Fogg, Shannon L. *The Politics of Everyday Life in Vichy France: Foreigners, Undesirables, and Strangers*. Cambridge: Cambridge University Press, 2009.

Footitt, Hilary and John Simmonds. *France, 1943–1945*. New York: Holmes and Meier, 1988.

Fourastié, Jean. *Les trente glorieuses, ou, la révolution invisible*. Paris: Librairie Arthème Fayard, 1979.

Fourastié, Jean and Françoise Fourastié. *Histoire du confort*. Second Edition. Paris: Presses Universitaires de France, 1962.

Frader, Laura Levine. *Breadwinners and Citizens: Gender in the Making of the French Social Model*. Durham: Duke University Press, 2008.

"Engendering Work and Wages: The French Labor Movement and the Family Wage." In *Gender and Class in Modern Europe*, edited by Laura L. Frader and Sonya O. Rose, 142–164. Ithaca: Cornell University Press, 1996.

Frost, Robert L. *Alternating Currents: Nationalized Power in France, 1946–1970*. Ithaca: Cornell University Press, 1991.

"The Flood of "Progress": Technocrats and Peasants at Tignes (Savoy), 1946–1952." *French Historical Studies* 14 (1985): 117–140.

"Machine Liberation: Inventing Housewives and Home Appliances in Interwar France." *French Historical Studies* 18 (1993): 109–130.

Fuchs, Rachel G. "France in a Comparative Perspective." In *Gender and the Politics of Social Reform in France 1870–1914*, edited by Elinor A. Accampo, Rachel G. Fuchs, and Mary Lynn Stewart, 157–187. Baltimore: Johns Hopkins University Press, 1995.

Furlough, Ellen. *Consumer Cooperation in France: The Politics of Consumption, 1834–1930*. Ithaca: Cornell University Press, 1991.

"Making Mass Vacations: Tourism and Consumer Culture in France, 1930s to 1970s." *Comparative Studies in Society and History* 40 (1998): 247–286.

"Selling the American Way in Interwar France: *Prix Uniques* and the *Salons des arts ménagers*." *Journal of Social History* 26 (1993): 491–519.

"French Consumer Cooperation, 1885–1930: From the 'Third Pillar' of Socialism to 'A Movement for all Consumers'." In *Consumers Against Capitalism? Consumer Cooperation in Europe, North America, and Japan, 1840–1990*, edited by Ellen Furlough and Carl Strikwerda, 173–190. Oxford: Rowman and Littlefield Publishers, Inc., 1999.

Furlough, Ellen and Carl Strikwerda, eds. *Consumers Against Capitalism? Consumer Cooperation in Europe, North America, and Japan, 1840–1990*. Oxford: Rowman and Littlefield Publishers, Inc., 1999.

Furlough, Ellen and Rosemary Wakeman. "La Grande Motte: Regional Development, Tourism, and the State." In *Being Elsewhere: Tourism, Consumer Culture, and Identity in Modern Europe and North America*, edited by Shelley Baranowski and Ellen Furlough, 348–372. Ann Arbor: University of Michigan Press, 2001.

Gagnon, Paul A. "La Vie Future: Some French Responses to the Technological Society." *Journal of European Studies* 6 (1976): 172–189.

Gardner, Roy. "The Marshall Plan Fifty Years Later: Three What-Ifs and a When." In *The Marshall Plan Fifty Years After*, edited by Martin A. Schain, 119–129. New York: Palgrave Macmillan, 2001.

Gelpi, Rosa-Maria and François Julien-Labruyère. *Histoire du crédit à la consommation: Doctrines et pratiques*. Paris: Éditions de la Découverte, 1994.

Géraud, Jean and Gérard Spitzer. "Le moral des agriculteurs." *Revue française de sociologie* 6 (1965): 2–15.

Gienow-Hecht, Jessica C. E. "Shame on US? Academics, Cultural Transfer, and the Cold War – a Critical Review." *Diplomatic History* 24 (2000): 465–494.

Gildea, Robert. *France Since 1945*. Oxford: Oxford University Press, 1996.

Giles, Frank. *The Locust Years: The Story of the Fourth French Republic, 1946–1958*. London: Secker and Warburg, 1991.

Gilles, Catherine and François Fauvin. "Du blocage des prix vers la déréglementation: 50 ans de prix à la consommation." *Insee Première* 483 (1996): 1–4.

Girard, Alain. "Le budget-temps de la femme mariée dans les agglomérations urbaines." *Population* 13 (1958): 591–618.

"Une enquête sur les besoins des familles." *Population* 5 (1950): 713–732.

"Situation de la famille française contemporaine." *Économie et Humanisme* 103 (1957): 3–48.

Giroud, Françoise with Claude Glayman. *Si je mens… conversations avec Claude Glayman*. Paris: Société Express-Union et Éditions Stock, 1972.

Golsan, Richard J. "From French Anti-Americanism and Americanization to the 'American Enemy'?" *The Americanization of Europe: Culture, Diplomacy, and Anti-Americanism after 1945*. Edited by Alexander Stephan, 44–68. New York: Berghahn Books, 2006.

Goubert, J.-P., ed. *Du luxe au confort*. Paris: Éditions Belin, 1988.

Green, Nancy L. *Ready-to-Wear and Ready-to-Work: A Century of Industry and Immigrants in Paris and New York*. Durham: Duke University Press, 1997.

Gruson, Claude. "Planification économique et recherches sociologiques." *Revue française de sociologie* 5 (1964): 435–446.

Guéraiche, William, ed. "Documents: Le débat du 24 mars 1944 à l'Assemblée Consultative d'Alger: 'Les femmes seront électrices et éligibles dans les mêmes conditions que les hommes'." *CLIO, Histoire, Femmes et Sociétés* 1 (1995): 263–271.

Guéraiche, William. *Les femmes et la république: Essai sur la répartition du pouvoir de 1943 à 1979*. Paris: Les Éditions de l'Atelier, 1999.

"Les femmes politiques de 1944 à 1947: Quelle libération?" *CLIO, Histoire, Femmes et Sociétés* 1 (1995): 165–186.

"La question "femmes" dans les partis (1946–1962)." *Historiens et Géographes* 358 (1997): 235–248.

Guglielmi, J.-L. and M. Perrot. *Salaires et revendications sociales en France, 1944–1952*. Paris: Librairie Armand Colin, 1953.

Hackett, John and Anne-Marie Hackett. *Economic Planning in France*. Cambridge: Harvard University Press, 1965.

Haddow, Robert. *Pavilions of Plenty: Exhibiting American Culture Abroad in the 1950s*. Washington: Smithsonian Institution Press, 1997.

Hamilton, Richard F. *Affluence and the French Worker in the Fourth Republic*. Princeton: Princeton University Press, 1967.

Harp, Stephen L. *Marketing Michelin: Advertising and Cultural Identity in Twentieth-Century France*. Baltimore: Johns Hopkins University Press, 2001.

Haumont, Nicole. "Habitat et modèles culturels." *Revue française de sociologie* 9 (1968): 180–190.

Heineman, Elizabeth. *What Difference Does a Husband Make? Women and Marital Status in Nazi and Postwar Germany.* Berkeley: University of California Press, 1999.

Henry, Odile. "The Acquisition of Symbolic Capital by Consultants: The French Case." *Management Consulting: Emergence and Dynamics of a Knowledge Industry*, edited by Matthias Kipping and Lars Engwall, 19–35. Oxford: Oxford University Press, 2002.

Higonnet, Margaret Randolph, Jane Jenson, Sonya Michel, and Margaret Collins Weitz, eds. *Behind the Lines: Gender and the Two World Wars.* New Haven: Yale University Press, 1987.

Hillel, Marc. *Vie et mœurs des GI's en Europe, 1942–1947.* Paris: Balland, 1981.

Hilton, Matthew. *Consumerism in Twentieth-Century Britain.* Cambridge: Cambridge University Press, 2003.

  "Models of Consumer-Political Action in the Twentieth Century: Rights, Duties, and Justice." In *Affluence and Activism: Organized Consumers in the Postwar Era*, edited by Iselin Theien and Even Lange, 21–39. Oslo: Unipub Forlag, 2004.

Hitchcock, William I. *France Restored: Cold War Diplomacy and the Quest for Leadership in Europe, 1944–1954.* Chapel Hill: University of North Carolina Press, 1998.

Hixson, Walter. *Parting the Curtain: Propaganda, Culture, and the Cold War, 1945–1961.* New York: St. Martin's Press, 1997.

Hoffmann, Stanley. "The Effects of World War II on French Society and Politics." *French Historical Studies* 2 (1961): 28–63.

Hoffmann, Stanley et al. *France: Change and Tradition.* London: Victor Gollancz Ltd., 1963.

Horn, Gerd-Rainer. *The Spirit of '68: Rebellion in Western Europe and North America, 1956–1976.* Oxford: Oxford University Press, 2007.

  Western European Liberation Theology: The First Wave (1924–1959). Oxford: Oxford University Press, 2008.

Horowitz, Roger and Arwen Mohun, eds. *His and Hers: Gender, Consumption, and Technology.* Charlottesville: The University Press of Virginia, 1998.

Houdeville, Louis. *Pour une civilisation de l'habitat.* Paris: Les Éditions Ouvrières, 1969.

Hufton, Olwen. *Women and the Limits of Citizenship in the French Revolution.* Toronto: University of Toronto Press, 1999.

Hunt, Karen. "Negotiating the Boundaries of the Domestic: British Socialist Women and the Politics of Consumption." *Women's History Review* 9 (2000): 389–410.

"Informations: Sociologie rurale." *Revue française de sociologie* 5 (1964): 193–203.

Inglehart, Ronald. "Révolutionnarisme post-bourgeois en France, en Allemagne, et aux États-Unis." *Il Politico* 36 (1971): 209–238.

  "The Silent Revolution in Europe: Intergenerational Change in Post-Industrial Societies." *The American Political Science Review* 65 (1971): 991–1017.

"Changing Values Among Western Publics from 1970 to 2006." *West European Politics* 31 (2008): 130–146.

INSEE. *Annuaire statistique de la France*. Paris: Presses Universitaires de France, 1961.

Annuaire statistique de la France. Résumé rétrospectif. 72nd Volume. New Series 14. Paris: INSEE, 1966.

Institut français de presse. *Cahiers de l'Institut français de presse*. Paris: Institut français de presse et des sciences de l'information, 1989.

Jamet, Michel. *La presse périodique en France*. Paris: Armand Colin, 1983.

Jenson, Jane. "The Liberation and New Rights for French Women." In *Behind the Lines: Gender and the Two World Wars*, edited by Margaret Randolph Higgonet, Jane Jenson, Sonya Michel, and Margaret Collins Weitz, 272–284. New Haven: Yale University Press, 1987.

Jobs, Richard Ivan. *Riding the New Wave: Youth and the Rejuvenation of France after the Second World War*. Stanford: Stanford University Press, 2007.

Judt, Tony. *Postwar: A History of Europe Since 1945*. New York: The Penguin Press, 2005.

Kelly, Michael. "Catholicism and the Left in Twentieth-Century France." In *Catholicism, Politics, and Society in Twentieth-Century France*, edited by Kay Chadwick, 142–174. Liverpool: Liverpool University Press, 2000.

Koreman, Megan. *The Expectation of Justice: France, 1944–1946*. Durham: Duke University Press, 1999.

Kroen, Sheryl. "Negotiations with the American Way: The Consumer and the Social Contract in Post-war Europe." In *Consuming Cultures, Global Perspectives: Historical Trajectories, Transnational Exchanges*, edited by John Brewer and Frank Trentmann, 251–277.Oxford: Berg, 2006.

Kroes, Rob. "World Wars and Watersheds: The Problem of Continuity in the Process of Americanization." *Diplomatic History* 23 (1999): 71–77.

Kuisel, Richard. "Americanization for Historians." *Diplomatic History* 24 (2000): 509–515.

Capitalism and the State in Modern France: Renovation and Economic Management in the Twentieth Century. Cambridge: Cambridge University Press, 1981.

"Coca-Cola and the Cold War: The French Face Americanization, 1948–1953." *French Historical Studies* 17 (1991): 96–116.

"The Gallic Rooster Crows Again: The Paradox of French Anti-Americanism." *French Politics, Culture, and Society* 19 (2001): 1–16.

Seducing the French: The Dilemma of Americanization. Berkeley: University of California Press, 1993.

Landes, David. "French Business and the Businessman: A Social and Cultural Analysis." In *Modern France*, edited by Edward Meade Earl, 334–353. Princeton: Princeton University Press, 1951.

Landes, Joan. *Women and the Public Sphere in the Age of the French Revolution*. Ithaca: Cornell University Press, 1988.

Lane, Jeremy F. *Pierre Bourdieu: A Critical Introduction*. London: Pluto Press, 2000.

Langhamer, Claire. "The Meanings of Home in Postwar Britain." *Journal of Contemporary History* 40 (2005): 341–362.

Langlois, Simon. *Consommer en France: Cinquante ans de travaux scientifiques au Crédoc*. Paris: Éditions de l'Aube, 2005.

Laroque, Pierre. *Les classes sociales*. Paris: Presses Universitaires de France, 1962.

Laroque, Pierre, director. *La politique familiale en France depuis 1945*. Paris: Documentation française, 1985.

Lazarus, Jeanne. "Les pauvres et la consommation." *Vingtième Siècle* 91 (2006): 137–152.

Lebrigand, Yvette. "Les archives du Salon des arts ménagers." *Bulletin de l'Institut d'histoire du temps présent* 26 (1986): 9–13.

Lecaillon, Jacques. "Le revenu des cadres," *Revue économique* 3 (1952): 206–245.

Lefebvre, Henri. *The Urban Revolution*. Minneapolis: University of Minnesota Press, 2003.

Lenoir, Rémi. "Family Policy in France since 1938." In *The French Welfare State: Surviving Social and Ideological Change*, edited by John S. Ambler, 144–186. New York: New York University Press, 1991.

Les associations féminines et familiales. *L'appartement référendum de la famille française*. Paris, 1959.

Lewis, Edward. "The Operation of the French Economic Council." *The American Political Science Review* 49 (1955): 161–172.

Leymonerie, Claire. "Le Salon des arts ménagers dans les années 1950: Théâtre d'une conversion à la consommation de masse." *Vingtième Siècle* 91 (2006): 43–56.

Loeb, Lori Ann. *Consuming Angels: Advertising and Victorian Women*. Oxford: Oxford University Press, 1994.

Loehlin, Jennifer A. *From Rugs to Riches: Housework, Consumption and Modernity in Germany*. Oxford: Berg, 1999.

Lynch, Frances M. B. "Resolving the Paradox of the Monnet Plan: National and International Planning in French Reconstruction." *The Economic History Review* New Series, 37 (1984): 229–243.

Lyons, Amelia H. "Invisible Immigrants: Algerian Families and the French Welfare State in the Era of Decolonization (1947–1974)." PhD. diss., University of California, Irvine, 2004.

Mangan, Sherry. "French Worker." *Fortune* (1948): 102–107, 202–207.

Maquenne, Paul. "Un fait économique nouveau: Les consommateurs s'organisent." *L'Actualité Fiduciaire* 261 (1954): 114–119.

Marchal, Jean and Jacques Lecaillon. "Is the Income of the 'Cadres' a Special Class of Wages? (A Study in the Light of French Experience)." *The Quarterly Journal of Economics* 72 (1958): 166–182.

Marcus-Jeisler, Simone. "Réponse à l'enquête sur les effets psychologiques de la guerre sur les enfants et jeunes gens en France." *Sauvegarde: Revue des associations régionales pour la sauvegarde de l'enfance et d'adolescence* 9 (1947): 3–18.

Marcus-Steiff, Joachim. "Eléments d'une psycho-sociologie de la consommation." *Revue française de sociologie* 3 (1962): 55–62.

Margairaz, Michel. "La reconstruction matérielle: crise, infléchissement, ou ajustement." In *L'année 1947*, edited by Pierre Berstein and Serge Milza, 17–44. Paris: Presses de Sciences Po, 2000.

Martin, Martine. "Ménagère: Une profession? Les dilemmes de l'entre-deux-guerres." *Le Mouvement Social* 140 (1987): 89–106.

Marwick, Arthur. *The Sixties: Cultural Revolution in Britain, France, Italy, and the United States, 1958–1974*. Oxford: Oxford University Press, 1998.

Maspétiol, Roland. "Sociologie de la famille rurale de type traditionnel en France." In *Sociologie comparée de la famille contemporaine*, 129–137. Paris: Centre national de la recherche scientifique, 1954.

Matthews, Glenna. *"Just a Housewife": The Rise and Fall of Domesticity in America*. Oxford: Oxford University Press, 1987.

May, Elaine Tyler. *Homeward Bound: American Families in the Cold War Era*. New York: Basic Books, Inc., 1988.

McGovern, Charles F. *Sold American: Consumption and Citizenship, 1890–1945*. Chapel Hill: North Carolina University Press, 2006.

McKenzie, Brian Angus. *Remaking France: Americanization, Public Diplomacy, and the Marshall Plan*. New York: Berghahn Books, 2005.

McLaren, Angus. *Sexuality and the Social Order: The Debate over the Fertility of Women and Workers in France, 1770–1920*. New York: Holmes and Meier Publishers, Inc., 1983.

Mendras, Henri. "L'étude comparée du changement dans les sociétés rurales françaises." *Revue française de sociologie* 6 (1965): 16–32.

"The Invention of the Peasantry: A Moment in the History of Post-World War II French Sociology." *Revue française de sociologie* 43 (2002): 157–171.

The Vanishing Peasant: Innovation and Change in French Agriculture. Cambridge: MIT Press, 1970.

Mendras, Henri with Alistair Cole. *Social Change in Modern France: Towards a Cultural Anthropology of the Fifth Republic*. Cambridge: Cambridge University Press, 1991.

Meynaud, Jean. *Les consommateurs et le pouvoir*. Paris: Études de Sciences Politiques, 1964.

Meynaud, Jean and Alan Lancelot. "Groupes de pression et politique du logement. Essai d'analyse monographique." *Revue française de science politique* 8 (1958): 821–860.

Meurs, Dominique and Sophie Ponthieux. "L'écart des salaires entre les femmes et les hommes peut-il encore baisser?" *Économie et Statistique* 398–399 (2006): 99–129.

Michel, Andrée. "Comparative Data Concerning the Interaction in French and American Families." *Journal of Marriage and Family* 29 (1967): 337–344.

Famille, industrialisation, logement. Paris: Centre national de la recherche scientifique, 1959.

Les femmes dans la société marchande. Paris: Presses Universitaires de France, 1978.

"Interaction and Family Planning in the French Urban Family." *Demography* 4 (1967): 615–625.

Sociologie de la famille et du mariage. Paris: Presses Universitaires de France, 1972.

"Statut professionnel féminin et interaction dans le couple en France et aux États-Unis." In *Sociologie de la famille*, edited by Andrée Michel, 281–291. Paris: École Pratique des Hautes Études and Mouton, 1970.

Michel, Andrée and Geneviève Texier. *La condition de la française d'aujourd'hui*. Paris: Éditions Gonthier, 1964.

Michot, Albert. "Les conditions d'existence des familles: Comparaison des revenus et des besoins des familles modestes au 1er octobre 1947 suivant le nombre d'enfants." *Population* 4 (1947): 691–703.

Miller, Michael. *The Bon Marché: Bourgeois Culture and the Department Store, 1869–1920*. Princeton: Princeton University Press, 1981.

Morin, Edgar. *Commune en France: La métamorphose de Plodémet*. Paris: Fayard, 1967.

The Red and the White: Report from a French Village. New York: Pantheon Books, 1970.

Morin, Edgar, Claude Lefort, and Cornelius Castoriadis. *Mai 68: La brèche suivi de Vingt ans après*. Paris: Éditions Complexe, 1988.

Morot de Pazzis, H. and Jean Ilovici. *L'éducation des ménagères dans le monde. Recherches et informations*. Paris: Les éditions sociales françaises, 1956.

Morsel, Henri. *Histoire de l'électricité en France. Tome troisième 1946–1987*. Paris: Fayard, 1996.

Moscovici, Marie. "Le changement social en milieu rural et le rôle des femmes." *Revue française de sociologie* 1 (1960): 314–322.

Mossuz-Lavau, Janine. "Politics and Sexuality in France, 1950–1991." *Economic and Political Weekly* 28 (1993): WS63–WS66.

"Les électrices françaises de 1945 à 1993." *Vingtième Siècle* 42 (1994): 67–75.

Muel-Dreyfus, Francine. *Vichy and the Eternal Feminine: A Contribution to a Political Sociology of Gender*. Durham: Duke University Press, 2001.

Nettelbeck, Colin W. "The Eldest Daughter and the *Trente Glorieuses*: Catholicism and National Identity in Postwar France." *Modern and Contemporary France* 6 (1998): 445–462.

Neulander, Joelle. *Programming National Identity: The Culture of Radio in 1930s France*. (Baton Rouge: Louisiana State University Press, 2009).

Newsome, W. Brian. "The Apartment Referendum of 1959: Toward Participatory Architectural and Urban Planning in Postwar France." *French Historical Studies* 28 (2005): 329–358.

"The Rise of the *Grands Ensembles*: Government, Business, and Housing in Postwar France." *The Historian* 66 (2004): 793–817.

"Paul-Henry Chombart de Lauwe: Catholicism, Social Science, and Democratic Planning." *French Politics, Culture, and Society* 26 (2008): 61–91.

"The Struggle for a Voice in the City: The Development of Participatory Architectural and Urban Planning in France, 1940–1960." PhD diss., University of South Carolina, 2002.

Niaudet, Jacqueline. "L'évolution de la consommation des ménages de 1959 à 1968." *Consommation: Annales du Centre de recherches et de documentation sur la consommation* 16 (1970): 7–76.

Nolan, Mary. "Consuming America, Producing Gender." *The American Century in Europe*, edited by R. Laurence Moore and Maurizio Vaudagna, 243–261. Ithaca: Cornell University Press, 2003.

Nord, Philip. *France's New Deal: From the Thirties to the Postwar Era.* Princeton: Princeton University Press, 2010.

Nouveau Larousse Ménager. Paris: Libraire Larousse, 1955.

O'Brien, Patricia. "The Kleptomania Diagnosis: Bourgeois Women and Theft in Late Nineteenth-Century France." *Journal of Social History* 17 (1983): 65–77.

Offen, Karen. "Depopulation, Nationalism, and Feminism in Fin-de-siècle France." *The American Historical Review* 89 (1984): 648–676.

Oldenzeil, Ruth and Karin Zachmann, eds. *Cold War Kitchen: Americanization, Technology, and European Users*. Boston: MIT Press, 2009.

Oraison, Marc. *Union in Marital Love: Its Physical and Spiritual Foundations.* New York: The Macmillan Company, 1958.

Orlow, Dietrich. *Common Destiny: A Comparative History of the Dutch, French, and German Social Democratic Parties, 1945–1969*. New York: Berghahn Books, 2000.

Parr, Joy. *Domestic Goods: The Material, the Moral, and the Economic in the Postwar Years*. Toronto: University of Toronto Press, 1999.

Pascaud, Fernand. "La consommation des ménages de 1959 a 1972." *Les collections de L'INSEE*. Série M. No. 134 de Collections. 35 (1974): 1–173.

Patrick, Stewart. "Embedded Liberalism in France? American Hegemony, the Monnet Plan, and Postwar Multilateralism." In *The Marshall Plan: Fifty Years After*, edited by Martin A. Schain, 205–245. New York: Palgrave Macmillan, 2001.

Pedersen, Susan. *Family, Dependence, and the Origins of the Welfare State: Britain and France, 1914–1945*. Cambridge: Cambridge University Press, 1993.

Pells, Richard. *Not Like Us: How Europeans Have Loved, Hated, and Transformed American Culture Since World War II*. New York: Basic Books, 1997.

"Who's Afraid of Steven Spielberg?" *Diplomatic History* 24 (2000): 495–502.

Pence, Katherine. "Shopping for an 'Economic Miracle': Gendered Politics of Consumer Citizenship in Divided Germany." In *The Expert Consumer: Associations and Professionals in Consumer Society*, edited by Alain Chatriot, Marie-Emmanuelle Chessel, and Matthew Hilton, 105–120. Aldershot: Ashgate, 2006.

"From Rations to Fashions: The Gendered Politics of East and West German Consumption, 1945–1961." PhD diss., University of Michigan, 1999.

Perec, Georges. *Les choses: Une histoire des années soixante*. Paris: René Juilliard, 1965.

Perrot, Marguerite. *Le mode de vie des familles bourgeoises, 1873–1953*. Paris: Librairie Armand Colin, 1961.

Petit guide de la ménagère. Pour tout faire bien... et vite. Paris: Les éditions sociales françaises, 1956.

Phillips, Peggy A. *Modern France: Theories and Realities of Urban Planning.* Lanham: University Press of America, Inc., 1987.

Pinto, Louis. "Le consommateur: Agent économique et acteur politique." *Revue française de sociologie* 31 (1990): 179–198.

Pitts, Jesse R. "Continuity and Change in Bourgeois France." In *France: Change and Tradition*, edited by Stanley Hoffmann, 235–304. London: Victor Gollancz Ltd., 1963.

Poiger, Uta G. "Beyond 'Modernization' and 'Colonization'." *Diplomatic History* 23 (1999): 45–56.

Jazz, Rock, and Rebels: Cold War Politics and American Culture in a Divided Germany. Berkeley: University of California Press, 2000.

"Rock 'n' Roll, Female Sexuality, and the Cold War Battle over German Identities." In *West Germany under Construction: Politics, Society, and Culture in the Adenauer Era*, edited by Robert G. Moeller, 373–410. Ann Arbor: University of Michigan Press.

Pollard, Miranda. *Reign of Virtue: Mobilizing Gender in Vichy France*. Chicago: University of Chicago Press, 1998.

Porter, Roy and John Brewer, eds. *Consumption and the World of Goods*. London: Routledge, 1993.

"Premier congrés de l'Union nationale des professeurs et monitrices d'enseignement ménager familial." *Cahiers d'enseignement* 11 (1957): 5–48.

Prigent, Robert. "Notion modern du couple humain uni par le mariage." In *Renouveau des idées sur la famille*, edited by Robert Prigent, 304–318. Paris: Presses Universitaires de France, 1954.

Prigent, Robert, ed. *Renouveau des idées sur la famille*. Paris: Presses Universitaires de France, 1954.

Prost, Antoine. "Public and Private Spheres in France." In *A History of Private Life: Riddles of Identity in Modern Times*, by Antoine Prost and Gérard Vincent, 1–143. Vol. 5. Cambridge: Harvard University Press, 1991.

"L'évolution de la politique familiale en France de 1938 à 1981." *Le Mouvement Social* 129 (1984): 7–28.

Pulju, Rebecca J. "The Woman's Paradise: The American Fantasy, Home Appliances, and Consumer Demand in Liberation France, 1944–1947." In *Material Women: Consuming Desires and Collecting Objects, 1770–1950*, edited by Beth Tobin and Maureen Goggin, 111–124. Aldershot: Ashgate Publishing, 2009.

"Consumers for the Nation: Women, Politics and Consumer Organization in France, 1944–1965," *Journal of Women's History* 18 (2006): 68–90.

"Changing Homes, Changing Lives: Material Conditions, Women's Demands, and Consumer Society in Post-World War II France." 2003 *Proceedings of the Western Society for French History* 31 (2003): 290–307.

Raffy, G. "Le fief de la femme: La cuisine." *Electro Magazine* 65 (1957): 36–39.

Rappaport, Erika Diane. *Shopping for Pleasure: Women in the Making of London's West End*. Princeton: Princeton University Press, 2000.

Revillard, Anne. "Stating Family Values and Women's Rights: Familialism and Feminism within the French Republic." *French Politics* 5 (2007): 210–228.

Reynolds, Sîan. "Who Wanted the Crèches? Working Mothers and the Birth-Rate in France 1900–1950." *Continuity and Change* 5 (1990): 173–197.

Rioux, Jean-Pierre. *The Fourth Republic, 1944–1958*. Cambridge: Cambridge University Press, 1987.

Roberts, Mary Louise. *Civilization without Sexes: Reconstructing Gender in Postwar France, 1917–1927*. Chicago: University of Chicago Press, 1994.

"Gender, Consumption, and Commodity Culture." *The American Historical Review* 103 (1998): 817–844.

"Samson and Delilah Revisited: The Politics of Women's Fashion in 1920s France." *The American Historical Review* 98 (1993): 657–684.

"The Silver Foxhole: The GIs and Prostitution in Paris, 1944–1945." *French Historical Studies* 33 (2010): 99–128.

Rochefort, Christiane. *Les petits enfants du siècle*. Paris: Éditions Bernard Grasset, 1961.

Rochefort, Robert. *La société des consommateurs*. Paris: Odile Jacob, 1995.

Roger, Philippe. *The American Enemy: The History of French Anti-Americanism*. Chicago: University of Chicago Press, 2005.

Rêves et cauchemars américains: Les États-Unis au miroir de l'opinion publique française (1943–1953). Villeneuve d'Ascq: Presses Universitaires du Septentrion, 1996.

Rogers, Susan Carol. *Shaping Modern Times in Rural France: The Transformation and Reproduction of an Aveyronnais Community*. Princeton: Princeton University Press, 1991.

Ronsin, Francis. "Guerre et nuptialité: Réflexions sur l'influence de la Seconde Guerre Mondiale, et de deux autres, sur la nuptialité des français." *Population* 50 (1995): 119–148.

Rosenberg, Emily. "Consuming Women: Images of Americanization in the American Century." *Diplomatic History* 23 (1999): 479–497.

Spreading the American Dream: American Economic and Cultural Expansion, 1890–1945. New York: Hill and Wang, 1982.

Ross, Kristin. *Fast Cars, Clean Bodies: Decolonization and the Reordering of French Culture*. Boston: MIT Press, 1996.

"The French Declaration of Independence." In *Anti-Americanism*, edited by Andrew Ross and Kristin Ross, 144–157. New York: New York University Press, 2004.

May '68 and its Afterlives. Chicago: University of Chicago Press, 2002.

Rottier, Georges. "Nourriture, logement ou télévision." *Esprit* (December 1957): 737–746.

Rottier, Georges and Elisabeth Salembien. "Les budgets familiaux en 1956." *Consommation: Annales du Centre de recherches et de documentation sur la consommation* 1 (1958): 29–53.

Rouaud, Jacques. *60 ans d'Arts ménagers. Tome 1: 1923–1939, Le confort*. Paris: Syros Alternatives, 1989.

60 ans d'Arts ménagers. Tome 2: 1948–1983, La consommation. Paris: Syros Alternatives, 1993.

Rudolph, Nicole. "At Home in Postwar France, the Design and Construction of Domestic Space, 1945–1975." PhD diss., New York University, 2005.

"Domestic Politics: the *Cité Expérimentale* at Noisy-le-Sec in Greater Paris." *Modern and Contemporary France* 12 (2004): 483–495.

"Who should be the author of a dwelling? Architects versus Housewives in 1950s France." *Gender and History* 29 (2009): 541–559.

Ryan, Donna F. "Ordinary Acts and Resistance: Women in Street Demonstrations and Food Riots in Vichy France." *Proceedings of the Annual Meeting of the Western Society for French History* 16 (1989): 400–407.

Sauvy, Alfred. "Les conditions d'existence des familles." *Population* 2 (1947): 243–266.

"Évaluation des besoins de l'immigration française." *Population* 1 (1946): 91–98.

"Faits et problèmes du jour." *Population* 2 (1947): 415–420.

Scanlon, Jennifer. *Inarticulate Longings: The Ladies' Home Journal, Gender, and the Promises of Consumer Culture*. New York: Routledge, 1995.

Schain, Martin A., ed. *The Marshall Plan: Fifty Years After*. New York: Palgrave Macmillan, 2001.

Schnapp, Alain and Pierre Vidal-Naquet. *The French Student Uprising, November 1967-June 1968: An Analytical Record*. Boston: Beacon Press, 1971.

Schwartz, Paula. "The Politics of Food and Gender in Occupied Paris." *Modern and Contemporary France* 7 (1999): 35–45.

"Redefining Resistance: Women's Activism in Wartime France." In *Behind the Lines: Gender and the Two World Wars*, edited by Margaret Randolph Higonnet, Jane Jenson, Sonya Michel, and Margaret Collins Weitz, 143–153. New Haven: Yale University Press, 1987.

Schwartz, Vanessa. *It's So French: Hollywood, Paris, and the Making of Cosmopolitan Film Culture*. Chicago: University of Chicago Press, 2007.

Spectacular Realities: Early Mass Culture in Fin-de-siècle Paris. Berkeley: University of California Press, 1998.

Scott, Joan W. "Gender: A Useful Category of Historical Analysis." *Oxford Readings in Feminism: Feminism and History*, 152–180. Oxford: Oxford University Press, 1996.

Scrivano, Paolo. "Signs of Americanization in Italian Domestic Life: Italy's Postwar Conversion to Consumerism." *Journal of Contemporary History* 20 (2005): 317–340.

Segalen, Martine. "The Salon des Arts Ménagers, 1923–1983: A French Effort to Instill the Virtues of Home and the Norms of Good Taste." *Journal of Design History* 7 (1994): 267–275.

Sociologie de la famille. Paris: Armand Colin, 1981.

Seidman, Michael. *The Imaginary Revolution: Parisian Students and Workers in 1968*. New York: Berghahn Books, 2004.

Sewell, William. *Logics of History: Social Theory and Social Transformation*. Chicago: University of Chicago Press, 2005.

Sèze, Claudette. "La Modification." In *Confort moderne: Une nouvelle culture du bien-être*, directed by Claudette Sèze, 110–124. Paris: Éditions Autrement, 1994.

Shennan, Andrew. *Rethinking France: Plans for Renewal 1940–1946*. Oxford: Oxford Clarendon Press, 1989.

Shepard, Todd. *The Invention of Decolonization: The Algerian War and the Remaking of France*. Ithaca: Cornell University Press, 2006.

Singer-Kerel, Jeanne. *Le cout de la vie à Paris de 1840 à 1954*. Paris: Librairie Armand Colin, 1961.

Sirinelli, Jean-François. *Les baby-boomers: Une génération, 1945–1969.* Paris: Fayard, 2003.

Stanley, Adam C. *Modernizing Tradition: Gender and Consumerism in Interwar France and Germany.* Baton Rouge: Louisiana State University Press, 2008.

Stearns, Peter N. "Stages of Consumerism: Recent Work on the Issues of Periodization." *Journal of Modern History* 69 (1997): 102–117.

M. P. Steck, "L'évolution des prestations familiales de 1945 à 1983." In *La politique familiale en France depuis 1945*, directed by Pierre Laroque, 187–289. (Paris: Documentation française, 1985).

Steigerwald, David. "All Hail the Republic of Choice: Consumer History As Contemporary Thought." *The Journal of American History* 93 (2006): 385–403.

Stetson, Dorothy McBride. *Women's Rights in France.* New York: Greenwood Press, 1987.

Stoetzel, Jean. "Les changements dans les fonctions familiales." In *Renouveau des idées sur la famille*, edited by Robert Prigent, 343–369. Paris: Presses Universitaires de France, 1954.

"Une étude du budget-temps de la femme dans les agglomérations urbaines." *Population* 3 (1948): 47–62.

Stohl, Helene. "Inside and Outside the Home: How Our Lives Have Changed Through Domestic Automation." *Women and the State: The Shifting Boundaries of Public and Private*, edited by Anne Showstack Sassoon, 279–301. London: Hutchinson Education, 1987.

Strasser, Susan. *Never Done: A History of American Housework.* New York: Pantheon Books, 1982.

Strasser, Susan, Charles McGovern, and Matthias Judt eds. *Getting and Spending: European and American Consumer Societies in the Twentieth Century.* Cambridge: Cambridge University Press, 1998.

Sullerot, Evelyne. "La démographie en France," "Mariage et famille," and "Les femmes et le travail." In *Société et culture de la France contemporaine*, edited by Georges Santoni, 64–123. Albany: State University of New York, 1981.

La presse féminine. Paris: Armand Colin, 1963.

Tamburini, Georges, ed. *Une politique de l'agir: Stratégie et pédagogie du Mouvement populaire des familles.* Villeneuve d'Ascq: Groupement pour la recherche sur les mouvements familiaux, 1997.

Tartakowsky, Danielle. "Manifester pour le pain, novembre 1940-octobre 1947." In *Le temps des restrictions en France (1939–1949)*, edited by Dominique Veillon and Jean-Marie Flonneau, 465–478 (Paris: Institut d'histoire du temps présent, 1996).

Taylor, Lynne. *Between Resistance and Collaboration: Popular Protest in Northern France, 1940–1945.* New York: St. Martin's Press, 2000.

"Food Riots Revisited." *Journal of Social History* 30 (1996): 483–496.

Thibaud, Paul and Benigno Caceres. *Regard neufs sur les budgets familiaux: Initiation aux mécanismes économiques.* Paris: Éditions du Seuil, 1958.

Thébaud, Françoise. *A History of Women: Toward a Cultural Identity in the Twentieth Century.* Cambridge: Harvard University Press, 1996.

Tiersten, Lisa. *Marianne in the Market: Envisioning Consumer Society in Fin-de-siècle France*. Berkeley: University of California Press, 2001.

"Redefining Consumer Culture: Recent Literature on Consumption and the Bourgeoisie in Western Europe." *Radical History Review* 57 (1993): 116–159.

Tilly, Louise and Joan Scott. *Women, Work, and Family*. New edition. New York: Routledge, 1987.

Touraine, Alain. *The Post-Industrial Society. Tomorrow's Social History: Classes, Conflicts and Culture in the Programmed Society*. New York: Random House, 1971.

Trentmann, Frank. *Free Trade Nation: Commerce, Consumption, and Civil Society in Modern Britain*. Oxford: Oxford University Press, 2009.

Trentmann, Frank. ed. *The Making of the Consumer: Knowledge, Power, and Identity in the Modern World*. Oxford: Berg, 2006.

Triolet, Elsa. *Roses à crédit*. Paris: Éditions Gallimard, 1959.

Trumbull, Gunnar. "Consumer Protection in French and British Credit Markets." Harvard University Joint Center for Housing Studies, 2008. Unpublished paper, copyright Gunnar Trumbull.

"Strategies of Consumer-Group Mobilization: France and Germany in the 1970s." In *The Politics of Consumption: Material Culture and Citizenship in Europe and America*, edited by Martin Daunton and Matthew Hilton, 261–282. (Oxford: Berg Publishers, 2001).

"The Surprise of Collective Action: Consumer Mobilization in France, 1970–1985." In *Affluence and Activism: Organized Consumers in the Postwar Era*, edited by Iselin Theien and Even Lange. Oslo: Unipub Forlag, 2004.

Turnaturi, Gabriella. "Between Public and Private: The Birth of the Professional Housewife and the Female Consumer." In *Women and the State: The Shifting Boundaries of Public and Private*, edited by Anne Showstack Sassoon, 255–278. London: Hutchinson Education, 1987.

UNIMAREL. *La "démocratisation" de l'équipement ménager*. Paris: UNIMAREL, 1959.

Évolution des applications domestiques de l'électricité en France et dans quelques pays d'Europe. Paris: UNIMAREL, 1961.

Expérience d'Orléans: Les effets de l'action commerciale sur le marché domestique de l'électricité. Paris: UNIMAREL, 1960.

Expérience d'Orléans: Éléments pour l'orientation de la campagne commerciale. Paris: UNIMAREL, 1958.

Le marché électrodomestique en 1958, perspectives pour 1959. Paris: UNIMAREL, 1959.

Le marché de la machine à laver domestique. Paris: UNIMAREL, 1955.

La prospection du marché rural de l'électricité: Cadre psychologique. Paris: UNIMAREL, 1959.

Qui possède les appareils électrodomestiques et les téléviseurs? Analyse socio-professionnelle et géographique des clientèles, 1957–1961. Paris: UNIMAREL, 1962.

Union des femmes françaises. *Programme d'action de l'Union des femmes françaises adopté au 1er Congrès national*. Paris, 1945.

Vangrevelinghe, Gabriel. "Les niveaux de vie en France, 1956 et 1965." *Économie et Statistique* 1 (1969): 7–21.

Veillon, Dominique. *Nous les enfants: 1950–1970*. Paris: Hachette Littératures, 2003.

—— *Vivre et survivre en France, 1939–1947*. Paris: Éditions Payot et Rivages, 1995.

Veillon, Dominique and Jean-Marie Flonneau, eds. *Le temps des restrictions en France (1939–1949)*. Paris: Institut d'histoire du temps présent, 1996.

Villechaise, Agnès. "La banlieue sans qualités. Absence d'identité collective dans les grands ensembles." *Revue française de sociologie* 38 (1997): 351–374.

Vinen, Richard. *Bourgeois Politics in France: 1945–1951*. Cambridge: Cambridge University Press, 1995.

Virgili, Fabrice. *La France "virile": Des femmes tondues à la Libération*. Paris: Éditions Payot et Rivages, 2000.

Voldman, Danièle. *La reconstruction des villes françaises de 1940 à 1954: Histoire d'une politique*. Paris: Éditions l'Harmattan, 1997.

Vouillod-Mounier, Anne. "Étude sur la demande en logement des ménages." *Consommation: Annales du Centre de recherches et documentation sur la consommation* 15 (1969): 83–89.

Wacquant, Loïc. "Following Pierre Bourdieu into the Field." *Ethnography* 5 (2004): 387–414.

Wakeman, Rosemary. *The Heroic City: Paris, 1945–1958*. Chicago: University of Chicago Press, 2009.

—— *Modernizing the Provincial City: Toulouse, 1945–1975*. Cambridge: Harvard University Press, 1997.

Wall, Irwin. *The United States and the Making of Postwar France, 1945–1954*. Cambridge: Cambridge University Press, 1991.

Walton, Whitney. *France at the Crystal Palace: Bourgeois Taste and Artisan Manufacture in the Nineteenth Century*. Berkeley: University of California Press, 1992.

—— *Internationalism, National Identities, and Study Abroad: France and the United States, 1890–1970*. Stanford: Stanford University Press, 2010.

Warner, Carolyn. *Confessions of an Interest Group: The Catholic Church and Political Parties in Europe*. Princeton: Princeton University Press, 2000.

Weiner, Susan. "The *Consommatrice* of the 1950s in Elsa Triolet's *Roses à crédit*." *French Cultural Studies* 6 (1995): 123–144.

—— *Enfants Terribles: Youth and Femininity in the Mass Media in France, 1945–1968*. Baltimore: The Johns Hopkins University Press, 2001.

—— "Two Modernities: From *Elle* to *Mademoiselle*. Women's Magazines in Postwar France." *Contemporary European History* 8 (1999): 395–409.

Wieviorka, Michel. *L'état, le patronat, et les consommateurs. Étude des mouvements de consommateurs*. Paris: Presses Universitaires de France, 1977.

Wildt, Michel. "Continuities and Discontinuities of Consumer Mentality in West Germany in the 1950s." In *Life after Death: Approaches to a Cultural and Social History of Europe during the 1940s and 1950s*, edited by Richard Bessel and Dirk Schumann, 211–229. Cambridge: Cambridge University Press, 2003.

Williams, Philip. *Politics in Postwar France: Parties and the Constitution in the Fourth Republic.* London: Longmans, 1954.

Williams, Rosalind. *Dream Worlds: Mass Consumption in Late Nineteenth-Century France.* Berkeley: University of California Press, 1982.

Willoughby, Gertrude. "The Family: Two French Studies." *The British Journal of Sociology* 6 (1955): 364–369.

Winock, Michel. *Chroniques des années soixante.* Paris: Éditions du Seuil, 1987.

Wylie, Laurence. *Village in the Vaucluse: An Account of Life in a French Village.* Second edition. New York: Colophon Books, 1964.

Xe Congres International de l'Enseignement Ménager. "Bulletin d'information: Service de presse." *L'Esprit de l'enseignement ménager moderne.* Paris, 1963.

Zancarini-Fournel, Michelle. "Genre et politique: Les années 1968." *Vingtième Siècle* 75 (2002): 133–143.

Zweiniger-Bargielowska, Ina. *Austerity in Britain: Rationing, Controls, and Consumption, 1939–1955.* Oxford: Oxford University Press, 2000.

Index